To Martin —
all best wishes,

Lord Zac Willis

28 - x - 21

Evening All

Evening All

Fifty Years Over a Hot Typewriter

Ted Willis

MACMILLAN
LONDON

First published 1991 by
MACMILLAN LONDON LIMITED
Cavaye Place, London SW10 9PG
and Basingstoke

Associated companies in Auckland, Delhi, Dublin, Gaborone,
Hamburg, Harare, Hong Kong, Johannesburg, Kuala Lumpur,
Lagos, Manzini, Melbourne, Mexico City, Nairobi, New York,
Singapore and Tokyo

A CIP catalogue record for this book is available from the British Library.

ISBN 0-333-54686-5

Typeset by Macmillan Production Limited

Printed by Billing and Sons Limited, Worcester

*For Harvey Unna, Charles and
Elsie Warren, Rhoda Fynes and
Pam Henson who were around
most of the time*

Other works by Ted Willis

Films include:

Holiday Camp
The Undefeated
The Blue Lamp
Trouble in Store
The Huggetts Abroad
Good Time Girl
The Wallet
Top of the Form
Burnt Evidence
Up to his Neck
It's Great to be Young
Woman in a Dressing Gown

The Young and the Guilty
No Trees in the Street
The Horsemasters
Flame in the Streets
Bitter Harvest
Last Bus to Banjo Creek
The Long Road to Sheba
Mrs Harris, MP
Mrs Harris Goes to New York
Mrs Harris Goes to Moscow
Mrs Harris Goes to Monte Carlo
Mrs Harris Goes to Cyprus

Stageplays produced:

Buster
God Bless the Guv'nor
The Yellow Star
All Change Here
No Trees in the Street
The Magnificent Moodies
What Happens to Love?
Doctor in the House
The Lady Purrs
The Blue Lamp
Brothers-in-Law
The History of Mr Polly
  (Musical)
Stardust

Hot Summer Night
The Eyes of Youth
Doctor at Sea
A Slow Roll of Drums
Mother
Woman in a Dressing Gown
Duel at Wapping Creek
A Murder of Crows
Queenie (Musical)
Dead on Saturday
Old Soldiers
Doctor on the Boil
Tommy Boy
Intent to Kill

Television plays:

The Ballad of Queenie Swann
Dream of a Summer Night
What Happens to Love?
Woman in a Dressing Gown
The Young and the Guilty
Look in any Window
Strictly for the Sparrows
Street Party

Hot Summer Night
Scent of Fear
The Sad Smile of the Mona Lisa
Knock On Any Door
Little Gold Mine
The Four Seasons of Rosie Carr
Old Soldiers

Original television series created by Ted Willis include:

The Pattern of Marriage (BBC)
Dixon of Dock Green (BBC)
Big City (ITV)
Dial 999 (ITV)
Lifeline (ITV)
Virgin of the Secret Service (ITV)
Days of Vengeance (BBC)
Flower of Evil (BBC)
A Place for Animals (Phoenix
  Film, Berlin)
Vincent Vincent (Phoenix Film,
  Berlin)
Outbreak of Murder (BBC)

Sergeant Cork (ITV)
The Sullavan Brothers (ITV)
Mrs Thursday (ITV)
Taxi (BBC)
Crime of Passion (ITV)
Hunter's Walk (ITV)
Black Beauty (ITV)
Rivals of the Racecourse
  (Phoenix Film, Berlin)
Minna, Anna & Luzie
  (Phoenix Film, Berlin)
Bess, Grandpa & Ruby
  (Phoenix Film, Berlin)

Publications:

Woman in a Dressing Gown and Other Plays
Whatever Happened to Tom Mix?
Death May Surprise Us
The Left-Handed Sleeper
Man Eater
The Churchill Commando
The Buckingham Palace Connection
The Lions of Judah
The Naked Sun
The Most Beautiful Girl in the World
Spring at the Winged Horse
The Green Leaves of Summer
Mother Christmas
The Bells of Autumn

Prologue

The scene is Cannes in the south of France, early in the 1950s. The city is in the middle of the annual Film Festival, a bizarre thrash which has attracted a swarming mass of cinema people of all ranks, shapes and sizes. I am there as a struggling young writer attached to the entourage of the late Jack Hylton, band-leader turned impresario. Jack has bought a popular Italian musical which he intends to put on in London and has asked me to write the English version. I am in Cannes at his invitation and expense to meet the Italian authors and talk through the various problems which have arisen.

On this particular afternoon I had made my way down to the packed beach opposite the Carlton Hotel and shoe-horned myself into a small space among the heaving bodies which all but obscured the sand. It was like lying in a sardine tin. The smell of sun-tan oil drifted on the air as bosomy young girls with bottoms like peaches and skins cooked to the colour of breakfast kippers, knelt over pigeon-plump producers, directors, and money-men and anointed their dough-white bellies with skilful, sensual fingers. I saw one such man who became so elevated by this treatment that he rose hastily, thrust a towel around his waist in a vain attempt to disguise his excitement, and hurried off to the hotel followed by his willing handmaiden.

Eventually I made myself enough room to stretch out and, in the warmth of the sun, I dozed off. A few minutes later I was aroused by a crunching pain as someone stumbled over my leg and followed this by putting a heavy foot down on one of mine.

I sat up sharply and looked up into the benign face of

1

Peter Ustinov. 'Sorry,' he muttered, 'so sorry.' He moved on a pace and then checked and turned, a smile of recognition on his face.

'Good God,' he said, 'it's Ted Willis.'

'Hello, Peter,' I replied gruffly, massaging my aching foot.

'Two days ago,' he continued, 'I was having tea in New York with Noël Coward. Now I trip over you in Cannes. I feel as though I've run the whole gamut of British drama from A to Z.' He spoke, as always, without malice and then, having put me firmly in my league position, he stumbled on.

I tell this story simply to place what follows into a proper perspective.

Chapter One

1

I suppose I could claim, with some truth, that I became a professional writer way back in 1936 at the age of eighteen. Or, to put it more accurately, I discovered then that it was possible to earn money by putting words on paper in more or less the right order.

I had been out of work for some months, following an incident at the Chiswick Works of London Transport where I had been training as a coach-builder. After weeks of harassment by a particularly obnoxious foreman I exacted a sweet revenge by nailing him up in one of the lavatories. An inferior craftsman in most respects, I had just about managed to master the intricacies of the hammer and I closed him in to such good effect that it took his rescuers a good half-hour to cut him free. The crime was traced to me and, after a short spell in a so-called punishment job in the engineering works, I was dismissed.

Jobs were almost as rare as hot dinners in those depression days. I rose early each morning to go to the local library, where the Situations Vacant columns from the newspapers were pinned up on an outside board, and I signed on at what was mockingly called the Juvenile Labour Exchange but nothing in the shape of gainful employment came my way.

I talked the problem over with Joe, a young man who was in much the same situation as myself, and we decided that it was time to head towards the horizon and take a look at what lay beyond. Accordingly, we set forth one spring morning and for the next few months, in the role of young Gentlemen of the Road, we tramped around England, sleeping in fields, barns and the occasional spike (the tramp's name for workhouse),

3

doing odd jobs here and there to earn a crust and begging at
back doors when no such jobs were available.

The seasons were warm and kindly as I remember and,
apart from a day here and a couple of days there, I felt
no sense of hardship. Joe was a bold, self-taught, well-read
young fellow and we spent hours with his tattered copy of
Palgrave's *Golden Treasury*, reading, memorising and reciting
the poems in that stunning anthology.

One day in summer we found ourselves in the Yorkshire
Dales. I began to rhapsodise about the natural beauty which
lay all around us, going on at some length, until Joe, who
had been listening in what I hoped was appreciative silence,
suddenly interrupted my flow.

'Wait!' he commanded. 'That's good. That's very good.
I reckon if you wrote that down we could sell it.'

I was doubtful but Joe's confidence and enthusiasm swept
aside all but one of my objections. There remained one crucial
problem – we had no writing materials and no money.

'That's the least of our worries,' Joe said blithely, and strode
towards Shipley, the nearest town. On the outskirts he ran an
approving eye over a row of neat cottages. 'Just the job,' he
said, and knocked at the first door with all the confidence of
a man who is the bearer of good tidings.

A bright-eyed and well-favoured young woman opened
the door, her face darkening with suspicion as she looked
out upon two travel-stained and unlovely young men. Her
physical endowments were such that, for a few moments,
our thoughts were diverted into directions which had no
connection whatsoever with my proposed début as a writer.

Joe was the first to recover. With all the charm that
had served us so well on a hundred other doorsteps he
said, 'Excuse me, madam. I wonder if you can help us?'

'What do you want?' she asked warily.

'Could you possibly spare a few sheets of writing paper
and a pencil?'

Not surprisingly, astonishment chased the caution from
her face. I doubt if she had ever received, at her own front
door, such an unusual, not to say extraordinary, request. The
change of expression made her look even more beautiful.
Before she could recover, Joe added disarmingly, 'You see,
madam, we've been on the road looking for work for some

time. My friend here wants to write to his mother in London, to let her know that he is fit and well. She worries, you see. But we haven't any paper, not even a pencil.'

She turned luminous brown eyes on me in wonder. I did my best to look like a sensitive, mother-loving son, lowering my head modestly. I heard a soft feminine voice murmur, 'Hold on. I'll see what I can do.'

When I looked up she had gone, leaving behind a drift of body-scent which teased my senses. Joe glanced at me and lifted a thumb in a gesture of triumph. 'I think we've struck oil,' he whispered.

We had indeed. A minute or so passed and then the vision returned and pressed a brown paper bag into my hands. It was then that I noticed the wedding ring on her finger and felt a surge of envy for the lucky husband.

'There,' she said, with a glowing smile. 'Will that do you?'

I looked in the bag. It contained a brand-new school exercise book, two pencils and, as an unexpected bonus, two postage stamps and a few envelopes.

I restrained the urge to kiss her damask cheek and murmured my thanks. As we made our way along the lane she came to the gate and watched our progress. As we reached a corner she waved and we returned the gesture. Then, like a mirage, she was gone.

2

An hour later we were settled in the Reading Room of the local library. While I tried to remember the fine words I had spouted in the Dales and commit them to paper, Joe studied the racks of magazines to determine which of them should have the privilege of being the first to discover my extraordinary talent.

He came to the conclusion that the lucky one should be a publication called *Cycling*, which devoted two or three pages in each issue to pieces which described the beauties of the English countryside and illustrated them with pen and ink drawings. So when I had finished, and my work had received Joe's approval, we sealed the pages in one of the envelopes and, with fingers crossed, posted them to the editor.

We did have one small problem, which Joe solved with typical élan. Since we had no fixed abode but knew that we would be moving south, I asked the editor, in a covering letter, to address his reply to me care of the Bedford Workhouse and to mark it with the words, To Await Arrival.

I never discovered whether the editor actually liked the article which, I suspect, was florid to the point of pretension, or whether he was intrigued by the unusual request in my letter and decided to send me a charitable donation. At all events, when we arrived at the spike some three weeks later, an envelope was waiting. Addressed to E. Henry Willis, the name upon which I had decided to confer literary immortality, it contained a brief but generous note of acceptance and, wonder of wonders, a cheque for seven shillings and sixpence.

We passed it to each other at least a half-dozen times gazing at the figures with awe. Plans for what we should do with this great wealth surfaced in our minds. A long delicious soak at the Municipal Bath House, a haircut apiece and then a double meal of fish and chips. And there would be enough over to buy a bacon, egg and fried bread breakfast the next morning.

There was, of course, a snag. There always is. I had nothing in the way of papers that could identify me as the E. Henry Willis named on the cheque and my tramp-like appearance did not exactly inspire confidence. The only bit of evidence that I possessed was a well-worn copy of *Lady Chatterley's Lover* in which I had inscribed my name and this, apart from being flimsy in the extreme, was more likely to be taken as proof of degeneracy than anything else.

Still, we presented ourselves at the bank where a startled cashier took one look at the cheque and a longer look at us and went to consult a superior. He returned with the suggestion that we should leave the cheque with him and return the next day. The suspicion in his eyes led us to believe that his boss was already on the telephone to the police to report the presence of two suspicious characters.

We departed in some haste to try our luck elsewhere. But where? We tried, without success, to buy a packet of Park Drive cigarettes with the cheque and collect the balance in cash but the shopkeeper's hostility drove us back to the street.

A bartender simply sniffed and contemptuously ordered us out of his pub.

Later that evening, our expectations dashed and our stomachs knocking with hunger, we abandoned all hope and began to make our way back to the workhouse. A mile or so from our destination a police car drew up alongside and a stern voice ordered us to stop. A sergeant got out of the car and looked us up and down for a full half-minute, his nose twitching.

'Where do you think you are going?' he asked at last.

The thought that we were about to be arrested as vagabonds with no visible means of support gripped my mind. I was about to mumble a reply but Joe, dear Joe, beat me to it. In a voice which was a blend of respect and complete self-confidence he said, 'As a matter of fact, sir, we were looking for somewhere to cash a cheque.'

The sergeant was clearly shaken by this and it took him a little time to recover. Joe took advantage of this brief interlude to nudge me in the ribs. 'Show him the letter. Go on, show him.'

I produced the by now grubby envelope and handed it over. It was clear from the sergeant's expression that he had now reached the conclusion that he was dealing with a couple of con men, but he read the letter and studied the cheque nevertheless.

'It's on the level,' said Joe. 'He collected it from the workhouse this morning. You can check, if you like.'

'You wrote an article for this paper?' asked the sergeant, glaring at me.

'Yes, sir.'

'He's by way of being an author,' Joe explained. 'We are on the road, collecting background material for his new novel.' Careful, Joe, I thought, don't overdo it, don't gild the lily.

The sergeant plucked at his chin thoughtfully. He studied the letter again, then the cheque, and then me. He asked three or four further questions which I must have answered to his satisfaction for eventually he gave a deep sigh in the manner of a punter who is about to plunge his last pound on a doubtful horse and said, 'You want to cash the cheque?'

'Yes, please,' I said fervently, seeing a ray of hope at last.

'Here,' he said, taking out a pen, 'write what I tell you on the back.'

I laid the cheque on the bonnet of the police car and endorsed it as he instructed. *Pay to E. C. Collins – signed E. Henry Willis*. A young constable seated behind the wheel eyed these proceedings with a puckered brow.

The sergeant took the cheque, nodded, and sank a large hand into his trouser pocket. It came up with two half-crowns.

'Here,' he said. 'Five bob. A bargain?'

I was in no position to argue. 'A bargain,' I breathed and took the two coins. The transaction had cost me a half-crown in what might be loosely described as commission but, on the other hand, we still had more than enough for fish and chips and other delights.

I have often thought since that Sergeant Collins was in the wrong profession. He would have made a great literary agent.

3

For the next few years I set my literary ambitions firmly on the back burner and put all my energies into the political struggles of the late thirties, activities which, together with my growing-up years in North London, I have described elsewhere.*

The next nudge towards authorship came in the unlikely setting of an ABC tea-shop in Southampton Row in the early summer of 1941. ABC tea-shops, along with the fragrant young Nippies who waited on table at the tea-shops of Joe Lyons, the Kardomah coffee-houses and the workmen's cafés which advertised themselves as 'A Good Pull-Up for Car-Men' have long since vanished but, in their time, they were as conspicuous a part of the urban landscape – and a good deal more attractive – as the burger bars and fast-food joints of today.

It was at a table in this particular ABC, over a cup of tea and a sugar bun, that I talked with Vernon Beste, the secretary of Unity Theatre. Vernon had lost most of one arm

*Whatever Happened to Tom Mix, The Story of One of My Lives. (Cassell, 1970)

in a childhood accident, a circumstance which exempted him from military service. In later years when I briefly met that brilliant but larger-than-life actor, Donald Wolfit, I realised that Vernon had many of his better qualities. He was the poor man's actor-manager. A very good performer, with a deep musical voice which seemed to boom up from the pit of his stomach, he had unfailing energy allied to considerable organising ability plus a blazing passion for the theatre in general and for Unity in particular.

Germany had invaded the Soviet Union a few days before, giving a new and vital twist to the war situation. We discussed this development with enthusiasm, convinced that Hitler had made a fatal error, that this was a turning-point in the struggle. Doubts that had surfaced a couple of years before when Stalin and Hitler had signed a non-aggression pact were swept away. We were all in it together now and Russia was our ally.

Vernon was concerned that this new situation should be reflected in the plays presented at Unity. In particular, he was looking for material for his Outside Show Group, which performed in air-raid shelters, Underground stations, parks and on streetcorners, and he asked if I had any ideas.

That evening I sat down and wrote a one-act play called *Erna Kremer of Ebenstadt*. It was, I think, inspired by a news item which revealed that the Russians were trying to speak directly to the German people by means of powerful radio broadcasts.

In the play, a German woman, Erna Kremer accidentally picks up Moscow Radio on her set and hears her own name. The announcer tells her that her husband, Ludwig, has been killed in action. He continues,

> But we ask you, Erna Kremer, why was your husband on the Beresina? And what benefit are his crosses to your children? Is it right to go into other people's homes, to kill women and children? You want peace and we want peace but Hitler doesn't want it. He wants war. Why should women like you be made to suffer? Hasn't enough blood been spilt?

Erna, shattered by this news, is confronted by a Nazi official who threatens to report her for listening to an illegal broadcast. But Erna and her family defy him.

I hurried down to Unity Theatre in Camden Town and handed this offering to Vernon Beste. To my astonishment and delight he liked the piece and within a few weeks *Erna Kremer of Ebenstadt* was part of the regular repertoire of the Outside Show Group.

Looking back at the little play across the years, it seems naïve and didactic but, for me, the first performance, before an audience sheltering in a London Underground station, was touched with magic. Men, women and children, with tired, blanched faces listened in what the critic of *Our Time* described as an 'electric silence'. Some women wept. At the end, I lived through one of the longer twenty seconds of my life as the audience waited, tensed and hushed. Then, to my relief, the silent circle stirred as if waking from a dream and broke into passionate, echoing applause.

This was my first confrontation with an audience as a writer and it would be no exaggeration to say that it changed the direction of my life. From that evening on, I knew that I wanted, above all, to be a dramatist, an author.

I had written *Erna Kremer* under a pseudonym, stealing the name John Bishop from one of my close friends in the army. My next play, *Sabotage*, a full-length drama, was also credited in the same way. At the time, I was editor of *Challenge*, the weekly newspaper of the Young Communist League and I reasoned that I should keep my political life separate from my fledgling efforts at authorship.

Sabotage proved to be more topical than 1 could have imagined. It was a sort of wartime thriller in which a British commando squad raids a French coastal village to save members of the Resistance. The day before we opened there were news headlines reporting a similar event in real life – a British attack on a German radar installation near Le Havre. We gained some useful publicity from this and even more when, halfway through the run of the play, there was a major raid on St Nazaire.

The only other notable thing about *Sabotage* was that it was taken up and performed on several occasions by a group of amateurs in Devon, the Buckfast Players. The group was led by a titled lady whose name I have sadly forgotten. She wrote me several enthusiastic letters on notepaper that bore her crest in the top right-hand corner, letters that raised an ironic smile from the case-hardened, class-conscious proletarians of Unity.

By 1943, as the writing bug took stronger hold, I was beginning to slip out of mainstream political activity and felt confident enough to put my own name to my second full-length play. It was called *Buster*, it opened at Unity Theatre, and it starred a young Unity stalwart, an amateur actor named Alfie Bass.

There is a legend, which is perpetuated in Colin Chambers's excellent book, *The Story of Unity Theatre*, that the theatre's play department had to reshape and partly rewrite *Buster* to make it playable. This is simply not true. There were, of course, minor adjustments and rewrites during rehearsal, which I did myself, but otherwise the play was performed as first written. I have both the original manuscript and the version printed later as proof of this.

At any rate, thanks to a fine production by Eric Capon and a bravura performance by Alfie Bass, *Buster* was a whacking success, pulling in huge audiences. It ran for several weeks, was revived on many occasions and even transferred to the Arts Theatre in Leicester Square for a short run – my first taste of the West End.

The play drew favourable notices even from those who did not care for Unity's stern left-wing stance. Beverley Baxter, theatre critic of the London *Evening Standard* wrote,

> Buster reveals flashes of humour, a broad if untidy humanitarianism, a genuine gift for observing and creating character and a sense of irony. It is from such stuff that playwrights are made.

In his book, Colin Chambers comments that the play 'brought new life to Unity'. Whether this be true or not, it certainly brought the beginning of a new life to Alfie and to me, opening all kinds of doors. In my case, the first evidence of this was a letter from J. B. Priestley inviting me to call upon him in his rooms in the Albany, near Piccadilly.

It was, as they say, an offer I could not refuse.

Chapter Two

1

Going to the Albany was like crossing the tracks and entering another world. Set back from the bustle of Piccadilly, this peaceful enclave seemed to me to be the epitome of dignified luxury, light years away from the seedy, bustling streets of Camden Town.

Priestley, like his apartment, was large and comfortable emanating a warmth which, in his public life, he often tried to disguise under a mask of Yorkshire crustiness. It goes without saying that I was nervous, for J. B. was then at the height of his fame, a well-known and successful novelist and playwright who was also known to millions through his popular wartime broadcasts.

Some two or three years before, obsessed with the thought that I looked too boyish for my years I had taken to smoking a pipe, hoping that this would add a proper touch of serious maturity to my appearance. When Priestley pulled out a pipe I did the same. He looked a little surprised but then offered me the tobacco jar and we went into a brief discussion of the relative merits of such blends as Three Nuns and Gold Block.

He went on to make some favourable comments about *Buster* which he had seen a few days before and further flattered me by asking about my working methods. It was not something to which I had given much thought so I answered, truthfully, that I had none. I simply sat down and wrote, without any fixed plan and, so to speak, let the spirit move me. He nodded in what I took to be approval.

'I do much the same,' he said. 'I start with the germ of an idea and build on that, making it up as I go along. I can't make detailed notes of plot or characters – that would spoil everything for me. There would be no pleasure in the writing, no sense of discovery.' And then he changed direction abruptly and added sternly, 'What are you going to do with your life?'

When you are young this sort of question crops up at regular intervals and, equally, when you are young you seldom have an answer to it. I had this urge to become a writer but I had given little thought to the means of achieving it and, as is the way with most young people, I just took each day as it came. Which is roughly what I told Priestley in reply.

He shook his large head. 'Not the point. Not the point. You are caught up in politics, right? Up to your neck in them. Nothing wrong with that, nothing at all. But the fact is that politics and writing make a bad mix. You can't do both properly. You will have to make up your mind whether you want to be a full-time writer or a full-time politician.'

Of course, the same thought had occurred to me but I had always left it unresolved, thrusting it to the back of my mind. Priestley, with typical bluntness, had dragged it out in the open.

'I suppose – yes – I'd like to be a writer, a professional writer,' I replied hesitantly.

'Good!' he said directly. 'There are plenty of people who can do the political jobs. They are ten a penny. Decent writers are thin on the ground. How are you off for money? What do you live on?'

I told him that I was wholly dependent on the three pounds a week that I earned as editor of *Challenge*.

'Give it up,' he said. 'Give it up as soon as you can. And I will stake you for a year.' I remember staring at him in total disbelief, watching the smoke curl from his pipe.

'I mean it,' he continued. 'I will give you three hundred pounds. That is about six pounds a week spread over a year. You can probably make it last longer. There is only one condition – you must devote yourself to writing full-time.'

'But how could I ever pay you back?' I stammered.

'Who said anything about that?' he demanded. 'When you are successful, you can help a new writer to get started. That will be payment enough.'

It was at once a staggering and generous offer as well as a massive boost to my confidence. Three hundred pounds was a very large sum at that time and it seemed even larger to me since I had seldom had more than a fiver to my name. At six pounds a week, Priestley was offering to double my income at a stroke and, in addition, give me the freedom to write. To this day I don't know what prompted my negative response. Perhaps it was some streak of proletarian pride but I heard myself saying, 'Thank you, Mr Priestley. I really am grateful. But if I am to become a writer, I must make it on my own. Don't be offended. I hope you understand.'

He smiled. 'I understand and I'm not offended.' He held out a broad hand. 'Good luck, lad.'

2

An agent? It seemed too good to be true. But Alfie Bass assured me that he was not joking, and that a leading agent had seen *Buster* and been so impressed that she wished to represent us both. We were invited to join her for lunch at a West End restaurant the next day. I believe it was the Ivy, a venue much patronised by actors and producers.

It took me a good five minutes to adjust to Rita Cave. The descriptive word that comes to mind is loud. *Fortissimo* would be to understate her. She was also very blonde in a brassy way, aggressive and patronising. Not until later did I learn that she had been the mistress of Oscar Deutsch, the founder of the Odeon cinema chain.

When he died she discovered that Oscar had omitted to mention her in his will and faced with this setback she had decided to use her contacts in show business to launch the Rita Cave Agency – Personal Management for Artists and Authors. She did not tell us over lunch that Alfie and I were to be her first clients, three amateurs together!

She fed us well although she seemed a little surprised by the extent of our youthful appetites. We ate our way through the wartime menu while she harangued us in a voice that would have cut a plate-glass window at thirty paces. Under her expert guidance, a glittering professional career would be ours. Within a couple of years our names would be up in lights. Wealth and fame would go hand in hand with inevitable success.

I was puzzled at first as to why she interrupted this speech at intervals to look beyond me towards the door. Occasionally she would flash her gleaming teeth, in what I took to be a smile, or wave towards someone. Eventually I realised that she had come to the restaurant to be seen and that these irritating glances over my shoulder were a sign of her anxiety not to miss or be missed by any VIP who might enter. I had the impression that she would have abandoned us like a shot if someone more important had summoned her to his table.

Alfie was a small, puckish, mischievous young man with a face that was full of character and as flexible as Plasticine. He was to become a considerable and successful actor, finding popular fame in, among other things, the television series *The Army Game* and the leading role in *Fiddler on the Roof* in London. In many ways he was a delightful innocent with little respect for money or knowledge of how to handle it and, to the end of his life, he was regarded by a few unscrupulous so-called friends as a 'soft touch'.

All the same, he had a lovely knack of coming directly to a point. Words fell from his mind straight on to his tongue and came out without refinement or sophistry. On this occasion he fixed his impudent eyes on Rita Cave and said, 'What's in it for you?'

She was not the least bit disconcerted. This was clearly her kind of language. 'Ten per cent of all you earn, whether I do the deal or not. You sign an exclusive seven-year contract with my agency to that effect.' For the first time a hint of pleading showed in her voice as she continued, 'It's a great chance for you both. I have the contacts. I've already got a famous producer very interested in buying the film rights of *Buster*. He wants you, Alfie, to play the lead and Ted to write the screenplay.'

That clinched it for us. We went round to Rita's office after lunch and signed the contracts. The only amendment I was able to persuade her to accept was a clause which allowed us to escape after three years if she failed to deliver. She agreed to this sorrowfully, expressing regret that, at the very beginning of our association, I should show what appeared to be a cynical lack of faith.

I resigned from *Challenge* that afternoon, not without trepidation since I was giving up a certain income of three pounds

a week and replacing it with nothing except the promises of
Miss Rita Cave and a degree of hope.

3

To my surprise, Rita came through the next day to tell me
that the film of *Buster* was no longer just a possibility but a
near certainty. A well-known director, Brian Desmond Hurst,
wished to see Alfie and me to discuss the project and she had
arranged for us to go to his Chelsea apartment the following
afternoon.

'On no account talk money,' she ordered. 'Leave that to me.'
And for good measure she repeated, 'Don't discuss money. I'll
handle the contracts. Don't sign anything, you understand?'

The large drawing-room into which we were shown reminded me a little of a Hollywood film set. It had a central
staircase running up to a balcony which skirted the room on
three sides and gave access to the bedrooms. Expensive rugs
seemed to have been thrown carelessly on the polished floor,
there were some exquisite pieces of porcelain, two or three
modern paintings which I did not understand and, on a grand
piano, several photographs of the director with various people
most of whom were instantly recognisable as famous film stars.
But, for my raw taste, the room had little appeal; it seemed to
have as much warmth and homeliness as a display in a shop
window.

Alfie must have felt much the same for he took a startled
look round and whispered, 'Blimey, it's as camp as a row of
tents!'

Brian Desmond Hurst, however, was all courtesy and
kindness. A shrewd-eyed, slightly puffy man, he dispensed
tea from a silver teapot into bone-china cups, offered us the
kind of biscuits that we hadn't seen since before the war,
and talked to us as if we were equals, already established
in the profession. We felt flattered and at ease, although I
could not quite quench a certain curiosity as to why this
highly cultivated and, to my mind, upper-class man should be
interested in our little working-class play. What did he know
of the life of ordinary people like Buster and would he be able
to reflect that life truthfully on screen?

It turned out that the man behind the project was the legendary Gabriel Pascal. He was one of those flamboyant Middle Europeans who pop up in show business at regular intervals, set themselves up as producers, and perform the feat of turning an empty purse into a stacked wallet before you can say Metro Goldwyn Mayer. For years the great George Bernard Shaw had resisted all approaches from the cinema, steadfastly refusing permission for his plays to be translated to film. But Pascal went to see him and the citadel fell. Shaw gave him an option on all his plays. I was told that very little money changed hands at the time. It was a coup of enormous magnitude and it established Pascal as a considerable force in the film industry.

Brian Desmond Hurst told us that Pascal was about to produce a major film at one of the big British studios but that there had been a hiccup and the filming would have to be postponed for three months. The difficulty lay in that the studio would still have to be paid for that idle period so Pascal had come up with the idea that he would fill in the time by making a quickie, that is to say a relatively inexpensive second feature. He had read a review of *Buster* and, on an impulse, decided that this would be his choice. Hurst had seen the play at the Arts Theatre and agreed to direct.

'We haven't much time,' Hurst said. 'How long will it take you to write a draft screenplay?'

Since I had never seen a screenplay let alone written one I looked blank. 'Could you do it in three weeks?' he asked.

I had written the stage play in ten days and three weeks seemed to my inexperienced mind to be a more than reasonable amount of time so I nodded. At this moment the telephone rang in an adjoining room and Hurst went to answer it. Alfie took advantage of his absence to pocket a couple of the biscuits. He winked and said, 'For my mum.'

Hurst came back beaming. 'That was Mr Pascal. He is delighted that things are going so well. He would like to meet you both – tomorrow morning at eleven at Claridge's – to finalise matters.' Alfie and I looked at each other, our faces reflecting the same thought. Claridge's! We were moving in exalted circles indeed.

Our host then produced two five-pound notes. We stared at them with wide eyes. 'I daresay you've run into a bit of expense already. Getting here and so forth. And you have to get to the hotel tomorrow. I hope this will cover it.' He handed one note to Alfie and one to me without any condescension.

It was a decent gesture for, in truth, we were both so broke that we scarcely had the bus fare home between us. Hurst had been sensitive enough to realise this and my heart warmed to him.

The interview was ended abruptly by a petulant voice from the top of the stairs. 'Brian! Are you going to spend the whole afternoon with those boys?'

We looked up and saw a young blond RAF officer glaring at us. He was in a uniform that must have been especially tailored for the tunic shaped his girlish waist like a Victorian corset as he stood with hands on hips, his face the picture of petulance.

'We've almost finished, Freddie,' said Hurst apologetically.

'So I should hope!' squeaked Freddie.

A door slammed behind him and we hastily made our departure. It occurred to me later that Freddie might have been jealous but whether of Alfie or me I never managed to decide.

4

I had been inside Claridge's Hotel only once before, in the mid-thirties when I was a member of a group of unemployed which staged a sit-down protest in the lounge. Our purpose had been to draw attention to the contrast between the luxury life of the guests and the depressed poverty of most Londoners. We had alerted the press and were hoping that we could generate publicity by being forcibly ejected from the hotel.

The management out-manoeuvred us at every turn. Instead of threats, they treated us as if we were respected guests. We demanded tea and sandwiches and announced in advance our inability to pay. We sat there, defiantly militant, for about ten minutes glaring our class-consciousness at the startled guests until an elderly waiter appeared and announced that our tea and sandwiches were waiting in a private room, compliments of the management. Sheepishly we followed him to the feast and our little revolution was over.

My second visit, to meet Pascal, was of a different order. With the two fivers provided by Brian Desmond Hurst, Alfie and I had paid a visit to the Fifty Shilling Tailors and kitted ourselves out with new suits. In the local shoe shop, appropriately named Freeman, Hardy and Willis, we splashed out on new footwear. This still left us with almost two pounds each, so we did not go hungry.

Thus clothed with the respectability which we considered appropriate to our position in show business, we presented ourselves at the reception desk of the hotel and, after the clerk had made a call on the internal line, we were directed to Pascal's suite. The door was opened by a little balding man who wore the harassed look of a rabbit that had just had a brush with a ferret.

'Mr Pascal?' I asked, with a distinct feeling of disappointment. Could this colourless man really be the great producer whose exploits featured in the news with such frequency?

In a voice that might have been left over from a funeral the little man replied, 'Mr Pascal is expecting you. Come in.'

We waited like two nervous suitors in the centre of an enormous room as he crossed to a door and knocked respectfully. A distant voice growled, 'Vat is it?'

The little man opened the door and murmured, 'Mr Bass and Mr Willis are here, Mr Pascal.'

'So – send them in.'

We were beckoned towards the door and ushered into a bedroom. A figure, clad in a dressing-gown of such startling and varied hues that it might have made Joseph's coat of many colours look modest by comparison, lay at full-length on a bed which, to my overactive imagination, seemed to be half the size of a tennis-court. Seated on one side of the bed, a notebook perched on her knees, a pencil in her hand, was a girl with shining ebony-black hair, matching eyes and a high-cheeked oval face which had the sheen of Devonshire cream. For a moment I thought that I was looking at a double of Hedy Lamarr, one of Hollywood's screen goddesses. I met those eyes full-tilt and as her delicious face opened in an even more delicious smile I felt my heart quicken and my knees tremble.

As we were about to edge forward, the figure on the bed held up a large commanding hand and cried, 'Vait! Vait! Vich is the poet and vich is the Pagliacci?'

Alfie and I stared at each other in bewilderment, lost for an answer. Pascal stirred irritably and snapped, 'Come, please! Vich is the author and vich the actor?'

We were on firmer ground now and introduced ourselves. He nodded and sat up, resting his head on the back of the bed. It was a biggish head, with a broad Slav look about it, the eyes fox-sharp and the voice deep and guttural.

'I am Gabriel Pascal,' he announced unnecessarily. We knew that we were in the presence of the real thing, your actual Hollywood-style film magnate. Alfie told me later that the thought of genuflecting had occurred to him at this moment but he decided that this would be rather overdoing things.

It became clear in the next few minutes that Pascal had not read my play and had only the vaguest idea of what it was about. He demanded that I describe the plot and action. I did my best, a procedure which was made more difficult because the telephone interrupted me at regular intervals and Pascal went off into long conversations most of which, as far as I could gather, concerned money. During these interludes I became more and more conscious of the girl seated at the side of the bed and of the subtle perfume which drifted towards me.

At the end of each telephone call, Pascal would bang down the receiver, turn to me and, in an imperious voice, issue the command, 'Continue!' Again, I did my best but the doubtful look that seemed to have set on his broad face was not encouraging. This pessimistic impression was confirmed when, as I finished, his face creased in a puzzled frown and he said, 'And this is all?'

'That's all,' I replied.

'And this you call a play?'

'It's a bloody good play!' interjected the redoubtable Alfie.

This statement had the effect of deflecting Pascal's attention from me to my companion and for the next few minutes Alfie was sternly auditioned. He went through most of his key speeches in *Buster* with such gusto that even Pascal showed interest. It must have been difficult since they had a strong

Cockney flavour and Alfie made no concessions to his listener, to whom the Cockney accent must have sounded like yet another foreign language.

Alfie's performance was followed by a long pause, while Pascal gave the subject some thought. He did this by constantly shaking his head from side to side and pursing his lips, a gesture which suggested to me that we might as well kiss the whole project goodbye. But he came suddenly to life, clapped the bedside table and cried, 'I will do it! I will do it!'

He snapped his fingers at the black-haired girl and she rose on long, lovely legs and went to a table on which there was a brown attaché case. From this she produced four sheets of headed notepaper on which I could see some paragraphs of typing. She handed these to Pascal and smiled at me.

'You, Mr Willis, I will pay one thousand pounds. Five hundred for the rights of your play and five hundred for writing the screenplay. To you, Mr Bass, I will also pay one thousand pounds – two hundred pounds a week for five weeks of work. Sign here and I will give you each a cheque for half this amount before you leave. The rest will be paid when the screenplay has been approved or on the first day of shooting. Proper contracts will follow later.'

A thousand pounds! The words rang in my head like a bell. The only time in my life that I had seen such a sum was at a rally at the Empress Hall, Earls Court, during the Spanish civil war, where a collection had been taken up to buy food supplies for the Republican side. But this was different. One thousand pounds! I could not begin to imagine what I would do with such a staggering sum.

And then, like a shadow obscuring the sun, I remembered Rita Cave and her pointed admonition. We should not discuss money, we should leave all negotiations to her. I struggled against this depressing thought for a few moments, desperately trying to think of a way to satisfy Rita and still walk out of Claridge's with Pascal's cheque clutched in my hot little hand. It was no use. At last, I heard myself murmur, 'Excuse me, Mr Pascal. I think you should discuss the financial details with our agent.'

'Agent!' he bellowed. The look on his face suggested that agents were rated in his mind as only a cut above child molesters. At the same time I was conscious of a painful pressure on my foot as an angry Alfie tried to convey his displeasure at what he obviously thought was madness on my part. I could also hear him breathing heavily.

'Who is this agent?' Pascal demanded.

I tried to convey the impression that our relationship with Rita Cave was of long standing, that we always put negotiations in her hands and added that since she had arranged our meetings with Brian Desmond Hurst and Pascal we owed her an obligation.

I don't think this went down too well. Pascal shook his head and waved a hand in dismissal. 'OK. I will speak vith this voman. Please to inform her that she should call me.' And, as we headed for the door, he went on, 'Also please to tell her that I have made the final offer. You understand? Final, final.'

As I went out the girl looked at me with large, pitying eyes.

5

'You stupid sod,' said Alfie when we reached the street, 'you've blown it, you've blown it.'

I knew he was right ten minutes or so later as we sat in Rita's office and heard her negotiate, if that is the word, with Pascal by telephone. She began on a confident note but her voice was shrill even shrewish.

'This is a valuable property, Mr Pascal. Your offer is quite unacceptable. In fact, it is downright ridiculous.' A pause while she listened and my blood turned to ice, then she continued, 'We shall want two thousand pounds for the rights and fifteen hundred for the screenplay.' Another pause and then she spluttered, 'But Mr Pascal . . . '

We could hear the click as his telephone went down. 'What did he say?' I whispered.

In a stunned voice she replied, 'He said – no deal. Forget it.' We were to learn that Rita's powers of recovery were remarkable. In the next moment she was beaming at us. 'Don't worry. He will come back to us.'

But he never did. When she tried to ring him he refused to accept her calls. She made contact with Brian Desmond Hurst who confirmed that Pascal had lost interest in *Buster*.

A week or so later the producer Sydney Box made an offer of two hundred pounds for the film rights and a further two hundred for writing the screenplay. I begged Rita to accept it but she poured scorn on my weakness. She was certain that she could persuade Box to pay more.

He refused. Once again dear Rita had priced me out of the market. Sydney was to tell me some years later that it was not so much the money but her attitude. She had the unhappy knack of antagonising people, especially producers – a grievous fault in almost anyone, a fatal flaw in an agent.

That was more or less the end of the *Buster* saga. Other side benefits were to flow from the success of the play but it was never filmed. All I had to show for my first contact with a film producer were a new suit and a pair of shoes.

Chapter Three

1

Old habits die hard, bad habits take even longer. My years of experience in the youth movement had turned me into a pretty good organiser and administrator and it was, I suppose, inevitable that I should become increasingly involved in the running of Unity Theatre. I continued to write the plays and to try and scratch a living from other writing but, at the same time, I found myself serving on several committees and taking on increasing responsibility.

This was a mistake that I was to regret later. Like many left-wing organisations Unity was much given to internal debate. Political sectarianism is bad enough but in combination with the artistic temperament it can become a bitter mixture. The production of a play was always preceded by lengthy discussions as to whether the work was ideologically sound and these were often the occasions for polemical fireworks of such an intensity that they threatened to do more damage to the roof than Hitler's Blitz. Just after the war, for instance, there was heated opposition to a proposal to present Sean O'Casey's mighty classic *Juno and the Paycock* on the grounds that the play was politically unsound. And I remember a debate which reached the conclusion that Noël Coward, on the evidence of his plays, was a die-hard reactionary.

It was all stimulating, exciting and never dull but it was also a great drain on one's emotional energies.

There were, of course, compensations. The work was good and fulfilling, the comradeship marvellous, and there were some lovely lasses around. Vernon Beste and I had rented a flat in Belsize Park in which we regularly held what were loosely known as auditions for young actresses of promise.

24

To avoid complications we bought a doormat on one side of which was the word 'Welcome'. If, on returning home, I found the mat had been turned over hiding the 'Welcome', I knew that Vernon was entertaining a companion inside. In those circumstances I would let myself in quietly and slide straight into my bedroom to wait until he sounded the all clear. Of course, he did the same for me.

I did not really need the doormat signal when Vernon was entertaining. Kippers had a strange fascination for him, so much so that I came to believe that he used them as a sexual stimulant. He did not invite a girl back to see his etchings but to enjoy his kippers. As soon as I stepped into the hall of the house and smelled the pungent odour of grilled kippers drifting from our flat I knew that Vernon was in full flood.

One Belsize Park encounter almost ended in disaster. I had become greatly attached to a beautiful young Irish girl called Kitty, so attached that with Vernon's consent, though against his advice, she moved in. Before very long it became clear that I had taken a tigress by the tail. Kitty was violently possessive and jealous, so much so that if I arrived home late from an innocent committee meeting or rehearsal she would greet me in a passionate rage, hurling abuse and accusations in scenes that lasted well into the night.

On one occasion, I got to the front door to find that she had tossed all my clothes into the street. In another incident, after a breakfast row, I slammed out of the flat in despair and Kitty, throwing off her dressing-gown, chased me up the street to Belsize Park Underground station in the nude! The neighbours, ever conscious that they were English, politely looked the other way and I was able to coax her back to the flat with my jacket around her shoulders.

However, when she greeted me one evening with a bread knife in one hand and what looked like murderous intent in her lovely hazel eyes, I decided that the time had come to lower the curtain on the affair. Not without difficulty, she was persuaded to move on. She still haunted me from time to time, often turning up at the flat in remorseful tears, and for the sake of safety and peace of mind, I moved out and took a room in a friend's flat in Hampstead. Kitty gradually accepted the situation, developed interests elsewhere, and at last I was free.

My new landlord was Tom Russell, then the secretary of the London Philharmonic Orchestra which, under his leadership, was being run by its players as a co-operative enterprise. He was a man of extraordinary drive and wide-ranging tastes and it is thanks to his influence that I developed an interest in classical music, helping to fill one of the many gaps in my haphazard education.

Tom was having an affair with the military at the time in the comely shape of a girl called Jean, a private in the women's section of the army, the ATS. Whenever her duties permitted Jean would turn up at the flat, looking incredibly sexy in her khaki uniform, and turn our meagre wartime rations into a succession of delicious meals. Their relationship was firm and strong – they were married shortly after the war – and, subconsciously I suppose, I began to look for the same sort of stability in my own private life. After a while, sowing wild oats can become very boring.

2

From where I was standing, at the side of the stage, the spotlight illuminated only the lower half of the girl who was standing on a rostrum sweetly singing the sentimental old Victorian ballad, 'Don't go out Tonight, Dear Father'. Since rationing was in full force at the time, Unity had to make up its costumes with whatever material it could lay hands on, and this girl's long dress had been fashioned from some pretty flimsy stuff. The result was that I found myself staring in wonder at a pair of the most beautiful legs I had ever seen.

It did not take me long to discover that the top half of this vision was more than a match for the parts that had held me entranced. Long fair hair held in a blue ribbon band framed a face for which the word lovely would be grossly inadequate, and the figure was sublimely proportioned. A perfect English rose is an overworked description but I can think of nothing better.

Her name was Audrey Hale, she was nineteen years of age, and I at once laid siege to her. During the day she worked as a clerk in the Lisson Grove offices of the London and North Eastern Railway and I invited her to lunch the next day, lunch being a euphemism for fish and chips paid for with money borrowed from Tom Russell. I sent roses to her home in Enfield, also paid for by Tom, and caused her acute embarrassment by sending a telegram which read, 'RUTH, CHAPTER ONE, VERSES 16 AND 17, LOVE, TED.'

Her mother, fearful that the telegram might contain bad news, opened it in Audrey's absence. When the poor girl arrived home she found the whole family gathered round an open Bible, grinning like Cheshire cats. What Audrey read were those famous lines of Ruth, directed to Naomi,

Intreat me not to leave thee, or to return from following after thee: for whither thou goest I will go and where thou lodgest I will lodge: thy people shall be my people and thy God, my God:
Where thou diest, will I die, and there will I be buried: the Lord do so to me and more also if ought but death part thee and me.

This message had the effect of putting Mrs Hale on full alert. My exploits at Belsize Park were a matter of fairly common knowledge and she was, not unnaturally, suspicious of my intentions towards her young daughter. She did her best to discourage the association.

At the theatre there were others who considered it their responsibility to protect Audrey from my philandering. She had – and has still – a great friend called Elsie Chisnell who kept a wary eye on my manoeuvres and shadowed me like a sleuth hound.

At around this time a Unity Theatre Group in Bristol was putting on a production of my newest play *All Change Here*, a Living Newspaper documentary-type drama about bus workers, and I managed to persuade Audrey to come to see it with me. The producer, a woman whom I had not had the pleasure of meeting, kindly offered to put us up. It proved to be a traumatic weekend, for the producer turned out to be a lesbian who took an immediate fancy to my beautiful girlfriend. Nor was she slow to press her suit, a circumstance which proved a bonus for me.

After a hectic and exhausting evening Audrey fled to my room and took refuge in my bed, declaring with a certain optimism that she felt safer there than in her own room. I locked the door and we spent our first full blissful night together. The bed, as I remember, had green sheets.

On our return to London I went to H. Samuel's, the Jewellers in King's Cross, and paid over my last two pounds in exchange for a modest engagement ring. I made a formal proposal on the upstairs back seat of a 29 bus that evening and handed over the ring, still wrapped in the bit of tissue paper which the shop had so generously provided.

This decisive move on my part finally put an end to the opposition of her parents and the faithful Elsie, and on 12 August 1944 we were married at Tottenham Register Office. It cost me more than I had intended for I realised the day before the ceremony that I had forgotten to buy a marriage licence, priced in those days at seven shillings and sixpence. In a panic I forked out six times as much to buy the special licence which was needed to allow the marriage to go ahead.

After the ceremony Audrey's mother, intending no doubt to shed a little cheerful sunshine over the proceedings, shook her head and declared firmly, 'It will never last.'

It took her almost forty years to retract this statement.

3

The problem of where to go for our honeymoon and, more crucial, how to pay for it was solved by an extraordinary piece of luck. Out of the blue, a week or so before the wedding, I received a telephone call from a man named Basil Woon, inviting me to lunch. He wanted, he said, to discuss an exciting new film project. I accepted the invitation but, fearing a hoax, I asked Rita Cave to check on Mr Woon. She came back with the news that he was a producer who worked for the legendary Hollywood company Warner Brothers at Teddington Studios.

Rita warned me once again to leave all negotiations to her but I was wiser now and determined not to have a repeat performance of the Gabriel Pascal fiasco. I went to meet my host, determined to accept any reasonable offer on the spot.

Mr Woon was all affability. A sturdy, slightly balding

American who could have been anything between thirty-five and fifty, dressed in a suit that made my fifty-bob outfit look exactly that, he spent the first ten minutes telling me that, although he had not actually seen *Buster*, his spies had informed him that it was clearly the work of a brilliant writer. He went on about the need for the film industry to invest in new talent, suggesting modestly that his mission in life was to encourage young writers like myself.

He suspected, he said, that I was already inundated with offers and would be too busy to become involved with his project, but would I do him a great favour and listen to his idea? I told him that, as it happened, I had a certain amount of free time since a major film for which I was to do the screenplay had been postponed. He listened to this blatant lie without allowing a single facial muscle to twitch, and then outlined his proposal.

The film, to be set in Cornwall, was to be called *The Waves Roll On* and Ann Todd, then a big star, would play the lead. She would portray a wild, untamed girl from a fishing village who, I gathered, spent most of her time in a secret cove, leaping barefoot from rock to rock. She is loved by a handsome young member of the local lifeboat crew but moodily resists his shy advances. Then one night during a great storm, a ship is wrecked on the rocks and the crew is rescued by the lifeboat. Among these is a virile young seaman who takes one look at Ann Todd and determines that she shall be his. Poor Ann falls for this stranger like a ton of bricks and, of course, he betrays her. The young lifeboatman beats him up and rushes after Ann who has fled in despair to a convenient cliff-top. Too late. As he arrives, crying her name against the call of the sea-birds, she hurls herself on to the rocks below.

I think I have got it just about right but at this distance of time I may be a little confused. Indeed, as I remember, I was more than a little confused at the lunch. At any rate, Mr Woon related this preposterous melodrama in a tone of reverence, for all the world as if he were unveiling a masterpiece and I was a privileged spectator. I should, of course, have told him what to do with his story but poverty has ever been a threat to principle. I was broke, I was flat broke and, moreover, I was soon to be married. And, after all, he was from Warner Brothers, he was in the big time.

So I responded with as much spurious enthusiasm as I felt to be appropriate. He shook my hand, declared it to be a deal and that I had made him a very happy man. Had I an agent? Reluctantly I confessed to the existence of Rita Cave and he agreed to speak to her that afternoon. It was then that I had the sort of inspiration which comes only once or twice in a lifetime.

There was, I said, a problem. I was the kind of writer who liked to soak up the background to a story and I had never been to Cornwall. As far as I was concerned it was a foreign country. Before I could even contemplate writing the screenplay I would need to go there and do a reconnaissance in depth. And I would need to have my secretary with me to take note of my thoughts, to catch them on the wing, as it were.

'I like it,' he said. 'I like your approach. How long will you need for this research?'

'A week?' I suggested hopefully.

'OK,' he agreed. 'A week. Let me think. Fares, hotel accommodation, incidental expenses. Would three hundred pounds cover it?'

And that is how Audrey and I set out, the morning after our wedding, to travel to Cornwall and the Wellington Hotel in Boscastle for seven days of honeymooning courtesy of Mr Woon and Warner Brothers. Very little film research was done in that week.

4

The Wellington was, and still is, a splendid hotel but for the two newly wed youngsters from North London in 1944 it came as something of a cultural and gastronomic shock. We had become used to survival on a weekly wartime ration which consisted of a handful of dried egg powder, two ounces of meat, and similar minute quantities of sugar, margarine and other foods. If you were lucky enough to have a sympathetic butcher you could supplement this on occasion with a couple of sausages or a slice or two of liver.

But at the Wellington it was as if some fairy godmother had opened a long-locked pantry door. Plump chickens, ducks, pheasants, liver and bacon, steak and kidney pie, lamb chops, mackerel, cod, sole, crab and lobster were on offer at lunch or dinner on one day or another, served with a wide and mouth-watering selection of locally grown fresh vegetables. And there appeared to be no shortage of sugar for a range of succulent puddings.

As for breakfast, my favourite meal of the day, we had not seen the like, even in pre-war times. Not a spoonful of dried egg in sight. It took me a full twenty seconds to recover from the shock when, on the first morning, the waitress asked if I would like one egg or two with my gammon rashers and sausages!

The other guests were, to our eyes, a strange mixed lot, creatures from another world. About half of them were permanent residents, wealthy men and women who had retreated from the cities and the bombs to endure the horrors of war in Boscastle. The others were holidaymakers who, like us, were enjoying a brief respite from the rigours of rationing but, unlike us, came from what appeared to be solid, secure, middle-class backgrounds. For the most part they were kind and considerate towards the young honeymooners although, for the sake of peace, it was necessary to avoid political discussions since most of them were so staunchly right wing that the word socialist or Labour raised their blood pressure to dangerous levels.

Thankfully, the talk in the bar and on the terrace centred around the progress of the war. The Allies had taken Normandy and were closing in on Paris. Each morning at breakfast an elderly retired colonel marked the rapidly changing fronts on a large wall map with coloured pins and offered, at the same time, his expert views on how the Allied Command should handle the situation. I remember that in his opinion we were moving too quickly, exposing too many flanks. His solution was that the Allies should halt, shorten their lines, dig in and sit out the coming autumn and winter in the trenches in preparation for a renewed offensive in the spring. He was a much-respected military tactician among the residents.

He was also a gentleman as he proved one sunny afternoon. Audrey and I had found our way down to an isolated little cove where the only other living creature in view was a solitary seal swimming lazily offshore. It was a romantic setting and what with one thing and another we began to make love. The seal ignored our embraces, showing no sign of jealousy, but at some point we heard the crunch of footsteps. Covering ourselves as best we could, though not too successfully, we looked up to see the Colonel approaching. With perfect aplomb he smiled, raised his hat briefly, then strode on regardless. No mention was made of the incident later.

Two other men came to our attention. I was spending a few hours each day in our room working on notes for the film, leaving Audrey to her own devices. One of the guests, a tall man whom we dubbed Long John, took advantage of the situation to move in on this lovely young girl offering to escort her on various brief excursions. He was genial and quite good-looking, and Audrey was glad of the company, but it became obvious after a day or so that he was growing more and more attracted to her. He waited around corners for her, took her to tea, bought flowers, paid extravagant compliments.

She accepted all this in good part, more amused by his dog-like devotion than annoyed, while I took it all as evidence that he was a man of excellent taste. Moreover, I was quite happy to have him as a stand-in while I was working, knowing full well that Audrey would slap him down pretty smartly if he got too frisky. To be fair, he never put a foot or a hand wrong and when we left at the end of the week he stood at the entrance to the hotel looking after us with wide, wistful eyes.

Another guest, a chubby little solicitor from a town on the south coast, gave me something of a surprise on our last evening. During the week he had seemed to be showing an undue interest in our movements, an interest which I took to be directed towards Audrey. This sort of thing was not unusual. She frequently turned a few heads when she entered a room and I was getting used to the attention she attracted. Not a bit of it. The little solicitor's target was me. Fortunately it was not my body he was after but my mind.

He had some connection with spiritualism and his firm had actually represented a famous medium in a case which captured the headlines. He took me to one side and fixing me with eyes of such a pale blue that they were almost colourless, he said, 'I have been watching you all the week. In fact, I have been observing you closely. I apologise, but I could not help myself. I believe that you may have spiritual powers. Would you be prepared to undergo one or two simple tests to establish whether I am correct?'

He was so obviously serious that I did not have the heart to laugh. I asked him to explain exactly what he meant.

'You could possibly be a medium,' he said earnestly. 'One of the privileged few who are able to make contact with the other side. Would you consider it?'

I had no idea what he had seen in me to provoke this absurd notion but, not wishing to hurt his feelings, I promised to think it over and write to him. He gave me his card with the radiant smile of a man who has just seen the new Jerusalem. I am afraid that I did not keep the promise.

Those were idyllic days. What can be better than to be young, to have the sun on your face, and to be in love? The film of *The Waves Roll On* was never made, which is a blessed relief, but I shall be for ever thankful to Warner Brothers.

5

We came home to the flat which, greatly daring, we had rented in Delaware Road, Maida Vale. It had been offered to us at a reduced rent of two pounds a week, mainly because it was on the top floor of a large block and, with Hitler's buzz bombs, the V1 and V2 rockets, flying in at regular intervals there was a natural reluctance to take up the tenancy.

Two pounds a week seemed to be a massive amount at the time and we were understandably concerned about how we should keep up the payments. But I had saved a few pounds out of our honeymoon expenses and bits and pieces of free-lance work were coming my way, so we decided to take a chance.

It was a good decision. We were surrounded by a mixture of wonderful neighbours – Jews, German and Austrian refugees, a few black marketeers, a prostitute or two – all drawn together in that community spirit which was typical of the war years.

There was a cellar under the apartments which had been

adapted as an air-raid shelter but we did not use it. We had
agreed that, if the building was bombed, we would rather be
alone and together. So, whenever a flying bomb came in our
direction or the air-raid alert sounded, we used to put our arms
around each other and wait until the danger had passed. I was
often quite sorry to hear the All Clear siren.

Chapter Four

1

By the end of 1944 I had begun to earn a slight if barely adequate living from free-lance writing. I'd had the good fortune to meet a certain Jimmy Carr who, with backing from Sydney Box, had set up office in Soho Square as a documentary film producer. A measure of his ambition and enthusiasm was that he named the tiny one-room company World-Wide Pictures Ltd.

Jimmy was a quirky, totally honest, pint-sized dynamo. He was also one of the best film producers I have ever known, a man who could pick up the weak spots in a script or the rough cut of a film in less time than it took him to sink a pint of Guinness in the Dog and Duck.

I cannot say that I learned the craft of documentary screen-writing at Jimmy's knee because of his Hop-o'-My-Thumb lack of inches but learn it from him I did. It was often a painful process for he was not a man to wrap his words in cotton-wool. Contemplating one of my efforts one morning he fixed me with a pitying eye and said, 'This may not be the worst script I have ever read but it comes damn near it.' Then followed a process of dissection and suggestion, following which I went home and rewrote the whole thing. If he approved of the revised version of a script he would merely sniff and say, 'Well, it's an improvement.' That, from Jimmy, was the equivalent of an Oscar.

World-Wide specialised in making sponsored films, mainly for industry or specialist organisations. That is to say, the customer would put up the money, specify the sort of thing he required, and World-Wide would make the film. Among our clients at the time were the Ministry of Information, Shell, the

Royal National Lifeboat Institution, Unilever and some trade unions.

Jimmy never allowed any of his sponsors to believe that because they were paying the piper it was their privilege to call the tune. I remember a very fraught meeting at Unilever House after the war, a meeting which was crucial to the fortunes of World-Wide because Jimmy was having financial problems and badly needed to seal a contract with Unilever, the huge company which, among hundreds of other products, made Sunlight soap and Stork margarine. And, apart from World-Wide's problems, I desperately wanted to get the script job I'd been promised if the deal went through.

One uppity executive launched into a lengthy description of what the film should contain and how it should be made. During this, I glanced apprehensively at Jimmy. He sat with his head down, glowering at the table. Eventually, the executive finished his spiel and, passing a folder down to Jimmy, remarked, 'I have taken the opportunity to put my ideas down on paper in the form of a draft script. You'll find everything you need there, I believe, Mr Carr.'

Jimmy looked up. I held my breath. Very slowly he took the so-called draft from the folder holding it as if it were impregnated with smallpox. With equal deliberation, he tore it into four pieces. Then he growled, 'If you don't tell me how to make films I promise not to tell you how to make soap.'

At that moment, I kissed the contract goodbye and with it my fee as scriptwriter. To my relief, the chairman at the meeting had a sense of humour and he led the laughter at the expense of his hapless colleague. Jimmy got the job, I wrote the script and the final film, *A Story of Achievement*, won an award at the Edinburgh Film Festival. Not too bad for a film which took the romance of margarine as its central theme!

This epic, incidentally, provided me with my first experience of being drunk. I went to Holland to do some preliminary research and was met in Amsterdam on arrival by a man called Jan. Tall, bearded and rugged, he had the appearance of a sea-captain who had just stepped off the deck of a tall ship. He was, in fact, a manager in the public relations department but to this day I still think that he would have been more suited to a life at sea.

When I arrived, around noon, he had already decided

that it was far too late to begin any serious work and took me off to a seventeenth-century bar where I was introduced to the delights of apricot brandy. And plum brandy. And several other specialities of the house. One of the distinctive features of the place was that one had to drink the first brandy without lifting the glass or using one's hands in any way – if this was achieved successfully, the host immediately refilled the glass. I won Jan's praise for my skill and was rewarded accordingly.

One of the problems was that all the brandies tasted rather sweet to my palate and, in my innocence, I knocked them back like so many fruit juices. It was only when I got to my feet that I observed that Holland seemed to be moving unsteadily beneath my feet. The rest of the afternoon was a blur of bars and restaurants as we pub-crawled from Amsterdam to Rotterdam. Whenever I peered through the alcoholic mist I saw the smiling untroubled face of my friend Jan, a glass at his lips.

The next thing I remember was the sound of a corps of regimental drummers beating a tattoo in my head. I climbed painfully into consciousness to find that I was lying fully clothed and face down on the floor of my hotel room. The tattoo was a cheerful, exuberant Jan knocking on my door to tell me that it was 11 a.m. and that, since the best of the new day had gone, perhaps we should repair to the bar for an opening drink.

Ever since that time I have been wary of sweet-tasting drinks and hospitable Dutchmen.

2

Apart from World-Wide Pictures I was also able to supplement my frugal income by writing scripts for the theatre unit of the Army Bureau of Current Affairs (ABCA). As a result of the success of *Buster* I was approached by Major Michael Macowan, a successful and highly respected theatre director, and put to work in a small creative team with André van Gyseghem, Stephen Murray, Jack Lindsay, Miles Tomalin and Bridget Boland.

They were all experienced professionals and I was very

much the amateur. It would be true to say, I think, that in terms of the theatre, Unity and ABCA were my universities. The opportunity to work with writers and actors who knew their craft from top to bottom was a priceless bonus for me. What is more, we were writing mainly for the private soldier, the other ranks of the army, an audience which was not familiar with the theatre but which I knew well.

Our brief was at once simple yet complicated. We had to write short topical plays illustrating a war theme or problem which would then be presented by a company of professional actors, all of whom were serving soldiers. That was the simple bit. The difficulty was that the plays had to be taken to the troops wherever they might be and put on in the most unlikely places – mess halls, Nissen huts, campsites. This led naturally to a good deal of improvisation on the part of both writers and actors.

Two of the plays among the dozen that we turned out give the flavour of what we were trying to achieve. The first, *What Are We Fighting For?*, was presented in early 1944 when the assault on Europe was in full preparation and was designed to build morale and understanding among the troops who would take part in that historic liberation. The second, *Where Do We Go From Here?*, was written when victory was already assured and the question on almost every soldier's mind was what would happen after the war. Would the promise of a better life be broken as it had been after World War I?

We developed a technique which produced some of the most exciting theatre I have ever seen. Two or three of our actors were planted in the audience in uniform. The play would then begin on a rather superficial note, perhaps with a couple of actors talking round the problem without getting to grips with it. Then, at a given moment, one of our actors in the audience would rise to his feet and denounce the people on the stage, demanding that they give straight answers to straight questions.

The effect was often shattering. Ordinary soldiers in the audience were carried along by the heat of the argument: many of them intervened, some even mounted the stage and joined the action. On occasions a play that was scheduled to run for an hour would still be playing after two. It was an exhilarating experience, a tribute to the power of theatre to move and stimulate people.

The drift of these plays was almost inevitably towards the Left, so much so that the government of the day had ABCA investigated for political bias. But by the time the investigation had been completed the war was already won and the organisation, its work done, was in the process of being wound up.

There were those who claimed that ABCA was, in great measure, responsible for infecting the troops with the social-istic ideas which swept the Labour Party to victory in the 1945 general election. I think this is a massive exaggeration. The returning soldiers were simply expressing the feeling that there had to be some change for the better, that they did not intend to return to the pre-war depression years.

To some extent, ABCA helped to crystallise and focus these profound feelings and in that sense, in its own small way, it did help the process of change. In a personal sense it had helped me to learn a little more of my trade, for which I remain grateful. And, incidentally, it provided me with some very useful professional contacts. Many of the directors, producers and actors I met in ABCA went back after the war to jobs in the theatre, radio, cinema and a few even attached themselves to the largely unknown medium of television. In the next few years some of these, remembering my work for ABCA, were to call upon my services as a writer.

3

At this period, my time was being increasingly absorbed by Unity. I wrote as a free-lance late into the night but most of the days and the evenings belonged to the little theatre in Goldington Street. In 1945 and the early part of 1946 I wrote three new plays, the first of which, *The Yellow Star*, also marked my début as a director.

The Yellow Star was probably the best constructed of my plays to date, a sign that I was beginning to understand the elements of the craft. It is set in the autumn of 1942 in a small Polish town where the Nazis are planning the extermination of the Jewish population. The central character is a rabbi who is called upon to lead a resistance to the Germans but whose religious convictions forbid him to take human life. In the end, circumstances force him to kill a Nazi collaborator and, in his anger, he curses the Fascists:

> The Lord pardon them never: the wrath and fury of the Lord burn upon these men and bring them all the curses which are written in the Laws. Blot out their name under heaven. Let no man speak to them; no man write to them; no man show them any kindness; no man stay under the same roof with them; no man come nigh unto them. Set them apart for destruction, O Jehovah!

It was, though I say it myself, a powerful part and it was given a stunning performance by a young actor called David Kossoff. He added a subtlety to the character which was not always present in the writing and, evening after evening, when he pronounced the curse the audience listened in tense silence and then erupted into passionate applause. Small wonder, then, that when the play ended its run David turned professional and joined the BBC Radio repertory company. From there he went on to establish himself not only as a character actor of international repute and a portrayer of biblical characters, but also as a best-selling author and illustrator of biblical tales. A multi-talented man who also happens to be a fine, genuine, good human being.

The Yellow Star was a success for Unity and gained the added distinction of being performed at the Grand Palais, the centre of Yiddish theatre in the East End. On an impulse I entered the script in a playwriting contest whose purpose was to find new plays with Jewish themes. The first prize, I think, was fifty pounds and, a few weeks after entry, I received a letter informing me that this very useful sum was mine. I had won!

The anti-climax came when the organisers wrote to say that I had breached the rules of the competition, which clearly stated that only Jewish writers were eligible. Since I was a Gentile, they had no alternative but to disqualify me. There was, I understand, some outcry about this decision from some members of the organising committee, who argued that it represented in reverse the kind of discrimination to which the Jewish community so strongly objected. A compromise was reached. Another winner was chosen but I was sent a cheque for twenty-five pounds 'in recognition of an outstanding work by a non-Jewish author'. A very decent gesture, I thought.

My next play was less serious, reflecting the lighter mood that came with victory and the end of the war. Called *God Bless the Guv'nor* and loosely based on characters created by the Victorian novelist Mrs Henry Wood, its flavour can be conveyed by the programme note:

> A moral melodrama in three acts and a short epilogue, in which the twin evils of alcohol and trades unionism are alike shown in all their squalor and ugliness, as an awful warning to those misguided few who may be influenced by either or both; in which virtue is proved to be its own reward, justice to be ever-present and the employer to be the rock on which the sure foundations of our national life are based.

It was, in short, a sort of *East Lynne* in a new mix. An honest workman is duped into joining a trade union and led into drink by the wicked villain to the despair of his adopted daughter Millicent. The villain inevitably has designs on Millicent but, equally inevitably, he is foiled by the hero, Austin Danesbury, the handsome son of the local mill-owner. There is heartbreak when Austin realises that he cannot marry Millicent because of her humble background but all comes right when it is discovered that she is the long lost daughter of the Duke of Battersea. Curtain.

This little bit of nonsense was played by a superb cast in which Joe Levene as the villain and Hazel Vincent Wallace as Millicent were particularly outstanding. Hazel later set up a small theatre in Leatherhead which, due to her pioneering work, is now the well-established and highly successful Thorndike Theatre.

We had a lot of fun with *God Bless the Guv'nor* and it was well received by Unity audiences who hissed the villains and cheered the goodies with great gusto. One of the highlights came with the epilogue in which the cast lined up and, to the tune of the well-known hymn, sang this appealing ditty:

Yield not to temptation,
For yielding is sin.
Try drinking some water,
It's much better than gin.
Shun the Doctrines of Labour,
Trade Unions too,
Look to your employer
He knows better than you.

After this musical exhortation the audience were invited to tear up their union cards, deposit them in the receptacles provided and have a glass of water, courtesy of the management. *God Bless the Guv'nor* was one of Unity's successes, so much so that it was taken up by other Unity groups and revived successfully at Goldington Street on several occasions.

The Bells are Ringing, a comedy-drama about a working-class family facing up to the problems of adjustment to peacetime conditions, was written towards the end of 1945. It was not produced at the main theatre but had a limited success with the reconstituted Mobile Group and with Unity Theatres in other parts of the country.

It did, however, produce something quite substantial in the way of royalties. The play was taken up by the New Theatre, a left-wing group in Sydney, Australia, and they wrote to ask how I would like to be paid. Mindful of the severe food shortages which we were still suffering I suggested that they might pay me in food parcels.

For the next six months or so large parcels arrived at irregular intervals, packed with tinned fruit and meats and dried fruit. Our popularity with the neighbours increased accordingly!

4

Unity was buzzing at this time and I seemed to be at the centre of it. Old stalwarts were coming back from service in the forces and new members, attracted by the theatre's reputation, were pouring in. At times the sheer pace of development was breathtaking.

It was decided, for example, to set up a national network of Unity groups to add to those in London, Glasgow and Merseyside. We needed an organiser for this job and I recruited a very good one in circumstances that can only be regarded as unusual. One evening Oscar Lewenstein, an old friend and colleague from the Labour youth movement, turned up at our flat in Maida Vale. He wore a uniform which hung from his thin frame as if from a coat-hanger and his pallid, pasty appearance moved Audrey to invite him to share our supper. What she did not know was that this was Oscar's habitual appearance. In all the years I have known him he has always looked as if he were on his way to hospital. But the old adage that one should never judge a parcel by its wrapping applies in full measure to Oscar. He was to prove that he had enormous vitality and drive.

He announced that he was to be demobbed in two or three weeks and we talked late into the night to a point where it was realised that Oscar had missed the last bus and would be unable to get home. There was no alternative but to put him up for the night – but where? We had no spare room, no spare bed and very little in the way of spare bedding.

Audrey, in her straightforward way, came up with the solution at once. We had a large double bed and somehow we would squeeze Oscar in. So it was. With me lying uneasily in the middle between the other two we passed an uneventful night, with Oscar sleeping like a baby. This was the first and last time in our married life that we got anywhere near a lit-à-trois.

In the morning I offered, and he accepted, the post of national organiser for Unity for a six-month period at a weekly wage of two pounds ten shillings. Like so many members of Unity, Oscar later branched out as a professional and went on to become an outstandingly successful theatre impresario and film producer. His first step along the professional path came when he brought Glasgow Unity Theatre to London's West End in a riveting production by Robert Mitchell of Maxim Gorky's drama The Lower Depths.

The next item on the agenda was the relaunch of the magazine New Theatre. In its earlier form it had been snuffed out by the outbreak of war and we decided to revive it, though on a broader base. To this end we recruited such luminaries as Sybil Thorndike, Sir Lewis Casson, Benn Levy – dramatist and MP – Peter Ustinov, Beatrix Lehmann, Patrick Hamilton, Walter Hudd, George Devine, Alec Guinness, J. B. Priestley and others either as patrons, contributors or members of the editorial board.

New Theatre was a lively little magazine. Apart from the usual articles about theatre technique, national and international news and play reviews – Peter Ustinov was our theatre critic for the first eighteen months – we tried hard to give the magazine a campaigning edge. We wanted the government and the local authorities to do more, much more, for the ordinary playgoer. One of our main platforms was that every town of reasonable size should have its own civic theatre, arguing that the theatre should enjoy the same status and degree of support as libraries.

Our proposal to convene a British Theatre Conference to debate and take action on this and other issues drew wide support from all sides of the profession. With J. B. Priestley in the chair, delegates and observers, among them some of the most glittering names in the business, gathered at Caxton Hall in London in February 1948. Surprisingly, for such a temperamental audience, the discussions were disciplined and the verdicts near unanimous. The press was there in force and the next day the theatre received front page attention.

It was a triumph, emphasised by our having managed to get Sir Stafford Cripps, then the Chancellor of the Exchequer, to address the closing session. In his speech he promised that the government would enact legislation to make it possible for local authorities to support their civic theatres financially. Governments do not always keep their word and Cripps, a sick man, had to retire not long after the conference, but the torch was picked up by Aneurin Bevan and the change of law carried into effect.

If for nothing else than this, the existence of *New Theatre* was worthwhile. It kept going for three years under four editors, Elkan Allen, Alec Bernstein, Oscar Lewenstein and myself, with sturdy support from the ever-present John Collier. But its finances had always balanced on a razor-edge and, rather than run it into debt, we ceased publication in July 1949. We felt quite pleased to come out at the end with a credit balance of one pound and fivepence!

5

As if all this were not enough, we launched two other initiat-
ives – a film company and a photographic studio. Crescent
Films was designed to complement Unity Theatre and, as a
beginning, we decided to film one of the theatre's most successful shows, a kind of old-time musical called *Winkles and
Champagne*. I managed to persuade a Wardour Street producer
to put up a thousand pounds, with Unity supplying the script
and the talent. Alec Bernstein, who under the name Alexander
Baron was soon to make his début as a novelist with the best-
selling war novel *From the City, From the Plough*, wrote the
screenplay for our film and also produced it.

Sadly, the film never saw the light of day. My backer
got cold feet and took possession of the negative, presumably
to protect his investment. My principal regret is that Audrey,
who had a feature role as a singer, never saw herself on screen.
After this débâcle, Crescent Films sank with scarcely a ripple.
Unity Studios, the photographic venture, lasted much longer,
thanks largely to the talents of its two chief photographers,
Cyril Bernard and Leo Kruks.

In February 1946, we embarked on the most ambitious
project yet – the launch of Unity's first professional theatre
group. The idea had first been mooted before the war and,
in the mood of confidence that had come with victory in
1945, we judged that the time was ripe to turn it into reality.
We had contacts with the famous American Group Theatre
and our aim was to create a theatre collective which would
follow its style and approach.

It was never easy to reach a decision at Unity and this
plan split the theatre into warring factions. On one side stood
the old stalwarts who saw the move away from amateur status
as destructive of all that Unity stood for; on the other, those
like myself who saw the creation of a professional company
as a logical development of the theatre's success; and in the
middle, a few wise, cool heads who could see the arguments
in favour of a professional group but were concerned as to
whether we had the ingredients to make it work, that is talent
and money.

In the end the wise heads were proved right. We had not
done our sums properly and the painful facts soon became

clear. The theatre was too small and if we had filled every
seat every night we would still have run at a loss. And we
had not got the artistic sums right either. My appointment
as artistic director was a fundamental error for which I must
take the major share of blame. My imagination, which is active
enough, runs on different lines from that required for a stage
director and I lack the patience for this demanding job. My
direction of the plays for the new company was never more
than competent which, at any time, in any theatre, is never
good enough. The audiences, voting with their feet, stayed
away and after eighteen months we wound up the company.

That was, more or less, the end of my association with Unity.
I wrote two more plays, in 1947 and 1949, but gradually, as my
writing commitments developed in other areas, I slipped out
of the committees and the administration until, finally, I went
no more.

But that shabby little theatre, lingering at the end of a dingy
alley, will always occupy a corner of my heart. At its best it
crackled with life and energy, far removed from the 'Anyone
for Tennis' school of drama. Dozens of now successful actors
took their first faltering steps on its creaky stage and it was
here that the fuse which ignited the post-war explosion of John
Osborne, Arnold Wesker, Sheila Delaney, Eric Paice and other
playwrights was first lit. And Unity's famous satirical shows
like *Babes in the Wood* and *Alice in Thunderland*, established the
base for such later shows as *Beyond the Fringe* and television's
That Was The Week That Was.

Unity's strength lay in its passionate political commitment.
Given a play in which the actors whole-heartedly believed, the
fervour of the ensemble playing could and did transcend any
limitations of experience and technique. In footballing terms
it was rather like a lowly fourth division club meeting one
of the first division giants in a cup match. On the day, the
passion and commitment can make them the equal of their
superiors.

I have many enduring and warm memories of Unity.
In view of what happened to me in 1963, one incident
seems particularly prophetic. It came during a production of
Spanish Village by Lope de Vega. In the play the villagers are
in revolt against their landowners and there was a wonderful
moment when the actress Maxine Audley, as a rebel leader,

burst through the audience brandishing a sword and shouting,
'Let me die killing lords!'

6

'I am very sorry,' said the little man from the Czech Ministry
of Culture, 'but it is August, you understand. There are no
theatres open in Prague at this time.'

There had, it seemed, been a great bureaucratic cock-up.
Oscar Lewenstein and I had been invited to visit Czechoslovakia for a week to meet the leading people in the theatre
to see and discuss their work and most of them were on
holiday! I was not in a good mood because my pocket had
been picked on the day we arrived and all my money stolen;
the news that the theatres were closed did nothing to raise my
spirits.

Seeing that I was not best pleased, the official, who
had the sad eyes of a hungry Labrador, came back later
with a suggestion. Emil Burian, their finest and most famous
director, was rehearsing his company in a new play at a castle
in Bohemia. Perhaps we would like to visit him there, no? But
yes, we replied.

Castles in Bohemia are pretty numerous and no match for
Windsor in scale or grandeur. The one we came to was suitably
turreted and not much bigger than an English country house
but what it lacked in size it more than made up in beauty. Set in
the heart of the rolling Bohemian countryside, with lush lawns
sweeping down to a crystal river, it sparkled like a gem in the
summer heat.

As our car drew up, we heard voices and merry laughter
coming from the back of the castle. Our guide and interpreter
smiled and led us towards the sound, murmuring that a
rehearsal was in progress. There was indeed. A company
of about thirty people, of varying ages and all shapes and
sizes, was gathered on the lawn before the fiercely bearded
Emil Burian.

And at least half of them were stark naked! Burian, wearing
nothing but his beard, greeted us courteously and introduced
us to the artists, who applauded enthusiastically. One well-
endowed young actress, who had apparently seen *Buster* at

Unity Theatre, embraced and kissed me with a warmth that lifted my temperature and almost everything else.

It was all quite casual and natural as if rehearsing without benefit of clothes or costumes was the normal procedure. In the following year the Communists took power and the long night of darkness descended upon the Czechs. One of their early victims was Otto Schling, an old wartime friend who went home after the Liberation with a song in his heart and was executed for no other reason than that he had spent too much time in the West. Another was Burian, whom they dismissed from the theatre as a 'bourgeois counter-revolutionary' and who died, probably of a broken heart, two years later.

But I shall never forget that sylvan scene in Bohemia where there was more freedom in the air than you could shake a stick at.

Chapter Five

1

My work as a theatre director may have had its faults but in the spring of 1946 I was partially responsible for a production which defied criticism. On 4 April as a result of an earlier collaboration between Audrey and myself our son John was born. To our pleasure and relief, he turned out to be a bonny, sunny-natured, seven-pounds-plus baby but it was a damn close-run thing. For some reason, probably the severe immediate post-war conditions, there was no space for Audrey in a maternity hospital and she had to go into a down-at-heel nursing home in North London. The doctor, no doubt wishing to be helpful, yanked the baby out with forceps and the instrument came perilously near to John's eyes. Fortunately there was no serious damage but he is the only member of a family that is noted for its good eyesight who has had to wear glasses from his early youth.

My first reaction on hearing the news that I had become a father was to mount my trusty bicycle and ride up and down Delaware Road without holding the handlebars, shouting to all and sundry, 'It's a boy! It's a boy!' Our good neighbours came on to doorsteps and balconies to applaud my progress and when mother and child at length arrived home they greeted them with rare gifts. Alf, the genial black-marketeer, brought a chicken and a half-dozen eggs; Millie, the call-girl, screwed some babywear out of a wholesaler who was one of her customers; Mrs Benjamin, the mighty Jewish momma on the ground floor, delivered some of her famous fish, fried in matzo meal.

The coming of this new responsibility prompted me to move up a gear in my search for writing assignments. What I was paid at Unity when it went professional just about covered the rent and I had to get money from somewhere. Perhaps one of the reasons that I was not a better artistic director lay in that after a long day at the theatre I would come home and work into the night on scripts for Jimmy Carr and World-Wide Pictures and anything else that came my way.

Anything else just about sums up my desperate need to earn the housekeeping money. There was, for instance, a famous band at the time called Sid Seymour and His Mad Hatters and through the good offices of a neighbour I was introduced to the great Sid himself. A raucous, likeable Cockney character, much in the mould of Max Miller, he had a line in spiel which would have done credit to a Petticoat Lane market salesman and a capacity for drinking tea which kept our kettle constantly on the boil.

Sid's act was more of a comedy show than a band performance. His humour was broad and unsubtle but immensely popular with the music-hall audiences of the day. One of his specialities was to present parodies of popular songs and he asked me to try my hand at a couple of these. Since he offered to pay three guineas for each one that he accepted, I agreed to become a lyricist-cum-parodist on the spot.

I took my first efforts to Sid in his dressing-room at the Old Metropolitan Music Hall in Edgware Road one evening. He was not impressed and handing them back he said, 'Rough 'em up a bit, boy. Give 'em a bit of the old you-know-what.' I interpreted this as best I could and tried again. One of my efforts pleased him better and I went away with three pound notes and three shillings burning a hole in my pocket. Thereafter he took to coming to our flat, usually late at night, when he ordered Audrey to 'Put the kettle on, missus,' and briefed me on his future requirements.

All in all, I must have written about thirty parodies for Sid. I did not keep copies for I had a shrewd suspicion that they would have no place in posterity's files, but one did survive, a parody of the song *Red Sails in the Sunset*.

Red knickers on Monday
On Tuesday they're blue
On Wednesday and Thursday
She varies the hue.
By Friday the colours
Are beginning to pall
So over the weekend
She wears nothing at all.

Dreadful stuff but reasonably harmless and in those days three guineas in cash bought a lot of groceries.

2

Around this time an old ABCA associate who had gone back to work at the BBC got in touch and asked me if I would like to try my prentice hand at radio. During the war the Corporation had broadcast a daily serial called *Front Line Family*, which, as its name indicates, chronicled the daily life of a group of Londoners facing the hazards and problems of wartime life.

This was now considered to have run its course and a decision had been taken to revamp the series and give it a new name, *The Robinsons*. Each episode ran for fifteen minutes. Would I care to submit a sample script? The producer was prudent enough to protect his back by stressing that this did not represent a commitment on the part of the BBC.

I jumped at this opportunity and wrote not one but three scripts. Apparently they were good enough for before long I became a regular member of the small team which supplied the series with the words. Another regular writer was a delightful lady called Jonquil Anthony who remained cheerful despite a desperately unhappy marriage. She consoled herself with the company of animals, sharing a house in the country with a noisy selection of cats, dogs, pigs, goats, chickens and donkeys on whom she lavished much tender loving care and a fair slice of her earnings.

I contributed about eight episodes each month at a fee of seven and a half guineas per script – like Sid Seymour, the BBC always reckoned in guineas in those days. This averaged out at over ten pounds a week so, for the time being at least, we were in reasonable nick financially. I even contemplated the purchase of a second-hand car.

The BBC then decided that *The Robinsons* was a little too down-market and plans were made to cut its throat and replace it with a new series. Jonquil and I were given a half-page of notes setting out the requirements. All it boiled down to was that the central characters should be a London doctor, his wife and their two children, with the action centred around his home and practice.

I went to Jonquil's house, we cleared all the animals except one persistent cat from the living-room and after a couple of hours emerged with a full outline for the new series. We named it *Mrs Dale's Diary*. It was accepted by the BBC, I wrote some material for the auditions and within three months the series went to air. There were the usual complaints from listeners who demanded that we bring back *The Robinsons* and it took some time for the Dairy as we called the new programme to settle down but eventually it took hold and, in those pre-television days, pulled in five or six million listeners.

Jonquil and I were the only writers and we each took responsibility for one month of programmes. This seemed to be an admirable arrangement at the time but, mainly due to the differences in our backgrounds and personalities, it proved disastrous. Jonquil came from a middle-class background and her inclination was to push the Dale family up the social scale. My approach was precisely the opposite.

The amazing thing was that there were no script conferences to iron out these differences. Indeed, Jonquil and I seldom met. Thus when she had completed her monthly assignment I might, for example, discover from her scripts that Dr Dale was about to open a practice in Harley Street, that daughter Gwen was engaged to a wealthy aristocrat and that Mrs Dale had taken up bridge.

I would immediately reverse this process when it came to my turn. Poor Jonquil would learn that Dr Dale had decided to open a free clinic in darkest Stepney, Gwen had abandoned her rich fiancé and was now working on the Underground calling out 'Mind the doors' and Mrs Dale was organising an outing for underprivileged children. I'm sure all

this must have confused the listeners but not half as much as
it confused us!

3

It was while working on *Mrs Dale's Diary* that I first experienced the hypnotic power that the media can exert over its
audience.

I had written an episode in which daughter Gwen, now
happily married, is in her fifth or sixth month of pregnancy.
Clothes rationing was in force at the time and Mrs Dale, armed
with as many clothing coupons as she can collect, sets out to
buy a layette for the baby. After a gruelling day in the shops
she comes home triumphant but exhausted, declaring, 'For
heaven's sake, don't ask me to go through all that again.'
Whereupon Gwen informs her that she has just come back
from an ante-natal check-up and that she is to have not one
baby but two. Twins. Another layette will be needed. A groan
from Mrs Dale as the episode ends.

Within a week bundles of baby clothes addressed to Mrs
Dale began to arrive at Broadcasting House, all sent by sympathetic listeners. One of our actresses who was cheerfully
pregnant swooped on this unexpected bonus and took her
pick. The rest went to a children's home.

This incident fired my imagination and I thought up
another ploy. In a later episode I established that it was
soon to be Dr Dale's birthday. Gwen and her mother have
a conversation in which Mrs Dale bemoans that she will be
unable to make a cake for the occasion due to the chronic
shortage of dried fruit. Once more, within days, our faithful
audience responded with gifts of sultanas, currants and icing
sugar. One lady from Epsom even left a cake decorated with
Dr Dale's name at the reception desk of Broadcasting House.
Hundreds of listeners wrote in with recipes for birthday cakes
which did not include dried fruit.

It was really rather touching for most of these presents came
in small packages and were sent by people who had saved the
offerings from their own limited rations. The accompanying
letters addressed Mrs Dale as if she were a living person,
chatting on about the dreadful problems of running a home

with so many essentials on ration. Some, sadly, wrote to her as a friend who had done much to relieve the loneliness of their lives.

All this not only made me realise how thin can be the line between illusion and reality, but it brought home the need for the writer to recognise that he has a responsibility to the members of his audience, a responsibility that arises from his ability to influence their conduct and emotions. The truth, whether we like it or not, is that many people are gullible. Why else would advertisers spend millions of pounds in successful campaigns to persuade us to buy one washing-powder in preference to another? So, whether an author is writing a mighty masterpiece or the humblest episode of a soap opera he should take care not to abuse either his craft or his audience. Which, of course, I had done with the birthday cake episode of *Mrs Dale's Diary*.

Faced with a table laden with packets of dried fruit I felt rotten. I had conned a lot of decent, generous, if credulous women. To send the stuff back was impossible and, in any case, it might have compounded the crime by destroying the illusion. We sent it all round to a hospital and in a subsequent episode of the series I wrote a scene in which Mrs Dale proudly carried in a birthday cake and announced that she had been able to bake it because so many kind friends had rallied round with the necessary ingredients. I can't say that honour was satisfied but it was a gesture which went some way towards salving my itching conscience.

In any case, the series was to take its own revenge on me and impose a sort of back-handed justice. One weekend, when the programme had been running for about a year and steadily increasing in popularity, I sat down to write the last two episodes for my monthly quota. When these were finished some quirky sense of humour – or it may have been boredom – prompted me to add a short additional script.

Mrs Dale decides to take her family and her friends and neighbours – the key characters in the series – on a day trip to Eastbourne. She hires two or three coaches and they all set off. Unfortunately, on the way home, the coaches accidentally reverse over Beachy Head. Total disaster, total end of Mrs Dale and her Diary. With one blow, so to speak, I had killed off a soap opera.

A new producer had recently been appointed to replace
my friend and in the foolish belief that he might enjoy a small
laugh from time to time I sent him the extra script along with
the rest. I could tell he was not amused when he rang the next
day and, in a voice that crackled like breaking ice, asked me
to go in and see him.

No, he did not think my little script was funny. What
it revealed was that I did not have the proper respect for
a series which had won a place in the heart of the nation.
His tone suggested that what I had done was only marginally
better than fornicating in church.

He went on to say that he had been worried about my
work for some weeks. My persistent efforts to give the series
a working-class slant were not helpful – there was a half-hint
here of sinister political motives on my part. In any case, said
the producer, he had decided to make a fundamental change
in the series. Dr Dale was set to acquire a practice in a leafy
middle-class suburb and this would require a new approach.
And a new writer. One who knew more about this sort of
background than I did.

I walked back to Maida Vale and my family in a black
mood. I had lost a job, a regular income, and I had blotted
my copybook with the all-powerful BBC. It was back to the
starting blocks again.

4

Jimmy Carr seemed to have a sixth sense when it came
to other people's problems and, although I never mentioned
that money was in short supply in the Willis household, he
came galloping to the rescue with a series of commissions for
documentary films. I wrote several commentaries at a fee of
ten pounds a reel while, for turning out a full shooting script,
the money increased to three times that sum. The pay may
seem low in today's market but it was the going rate then and
to me it came like manna.

With the decline of my commitments to Unity, I was
now able to undertake the research which is the basis of
all documentary film-making and this called for a good deal
of travelling. In the space of two or three years, I tramped

over farms in search of material for a film on agriculture, toured workshops for a film on the clothing industry, sailed from Aberdeen to Iceland on a trawler to gather background facts on fishing, went up to the annual conference of the TUC at Blackpool to research a script for the Amalgamated Engineering Union and down to Cornwall for a documentary on the lifeboat service. And these were only a few of my assignments.

It was an exhilarating time and one that did a great deal to shape my approach to writing. I found that the closer one got to the people involved in a particular industry or enterprise, the easier the eventual writing became. It was not necessary to invent characters, they were there, in real life, in rich and colourful abundance. Quite often their dialogue was better and sharper than anything I could devise. The basic purpose of documentary is to present facts, but facts on their own can too easily bring on terminal boredom. Presented in the framework of a story featuring lively, interesting characters the audience can absorb the facts without pain and, perhaps, be stimulated to action. In recent years, John Cleese, with his training films for industry, has demonstrated the truth of this time and time again. Long after I had left the documentary field I still found that the writing came more easily and was better if I went and lived for a while among the people in the location which was to provide the background to my story.

The trip to Cornwall for the lifeboat film proved a case in point. I spent a glorious week in the little village of Coverack just north of Lizard Point. I put up at the local pub, the Paris, which is named after – and, I believe, partly built of material from – a ship that was wrecked off the Manacles, the menacing rocks that lie in wait just off the coast.

I struck up an immediate rapport with Archie, the skipper of the lifeboat crew. He was a gem of a character, a sturdy wag of a man, built like a brick oven, with dark laughing eyes and skin burnished by a thousand winds. Never before or since have I met a man with such smouldering sexuality. As far as I could see he did not use it consciously – the girls, especially the summer visitors, seemed to scent Archie at a hundred paces and made their way with flushed, expectant faces up to the loft where he kept his fishing nets. Somehow he was able, with his broad mahogany smile and gentle wit, to withstand their breathless approaches and send them away unsatisfied but as starry-eyed as if they had been in the presence of a god.

The man had more than his fair share of courage too, although he was decently reticent about his exploits. The hero of dozens of lifeboat rescues, he held the Royal National Lifeboat Institute medal for bravery and several commendations. Years after I met him he was featured on the television programme *This Is Your Life*.

I went out on the lifeboat with Archie and his crew, I ate and drank with them and, perhaps the greatest compliment of all, I was drafted into the darts team for a match against their great rivals from the nearby village of Cadgwith. A regular member of the team had gone sick and Archie had observed that, while I was pretty useless in normal circumstances, when I had taken on board a couple of pints of mild and bitter I was capable of throwing a mean dart. I wish I could record that I won the game in glory by getting the final double but, adequately fuelled by the anxious Archie, I managed not to disgrace myself.

Leaving Coverack was like saying goodbye to dear friends. I kept in touch with Archie for some time but he was not a man for writing letters and, as these things go, the contact slipped away. Without him and the other locals my film could never have been written.

5

I believe that I can claim the doubtful distinction of being the only man to be called up twice for the British Army. It had happened in the usual way, in 1940, when I was mustered into the 22nd Battalion of the Royal Fusiliers. There was a repeat performance in 1948 in curious circumstances.

The Army Kinema Corporation (AKC), for which I had done some work in the past, was anxious to have a film which would help to smooth the path of young men being called up for National Service. I was invited to meet the Colonel in charge of the project and he told me the basic idea – a documentary which would illustrate and dramatise the first six weeks in the life of a recruit. Would I write it?

I could not afford to turn down the assignment but, on

the other hand, I could not see how it would be possible
to undertake the kind of face to face, on the spot research
that such a film would require. Without thinking, I shook my
head and replied, 'I like the idea, but I don't think I could do
it. It's years since I was a recruit and it must all be different
now.' Remembering that in my first six weeks in the Fusiliers
we had been forced to drill with broomsticks, I almost added,
'Presumably they have rifles now.'

The Colonel, a dark cadaverous man, so tall and thin that
he looked as if he had been stretched on a rack, gave a small
ominous chuckle rather like bones being rattled in a bag and
said, 'We've thought of that. We can arrange for you to spend
a few weeks with the Buffs at Canterbury. You would join a
new intake and train with them.'

From then on there was no going back. We discussed
dates and details. The assignment was to be kept secret:
only the commanding officer at Canterbury and the regimental sergeant major were to be told that I was not a genuine
recruit. And the Colonel gave me a stern warning, 'When
you are issued with your paybook don't, on any account,
sign it. More important, do not draw any pay. If you do, we
may have some difficulty in getting you out of the army.' The
bones rattled once more as he spoke and mine responded with
an encore.

So it was that I turned up at Canterbury Barracks one fine
morning to report for National Service. From the beginning I
had to do some fast talking for I was at least ten years older than
the other recruits and looked it. In answer to their questions I
replied that I had been on essential work in industry and my
call-up had been deferred.

I was issued with denims, uniform, army regulation boots
and a rifle and for the next six weeks went through the ritual
of square-bashing and physical training. New recruits were
not allowed leave in this initial period of their army lives but I
confess that I used my privileged position to wangle a couple
of Sundays off. I changed into my civilian clothes in the CO's
office and he smuggled me out of the barracks in his car. When
I arrived home on the first Sunday, Audrey declared that not
only had I lost weight but she had never seen me looking so fit.

Surprising though it may seem, I quite enjoyed my second taste of army life. The lads were a decent bunch and I

made some good friends among them. My previous military experience, though not extensive, proved to be quite useful and I showed them how to cut a corner or two when it came to kit-cleaning, but my greatest accomplishment was to introduce my platoon to that most desperate of all gambling games, Blanket Brag.

Relief from the rigours of the barrack square came at fairly regular intervals when, by prior arrangement, I visited the CO in his office. The ostensible reason for this was so that I could question him and thus further my research, but the truth lay deeper. He was a hospitable man and I enjoyed the refreshment he provided.

There was a dramatic and ironic change of roles from the moment he closed the door and we were alone together. I was no longer the sweaty denim-clad recruit but a guest and he became the host rather than the commanding officer. In many ways he even treated me as a superior, deferring to my views politely and plying my glass with malt whisky. He seemed to be very anxious to make a good impression.

When the time came for me to leave, I bought drinks all round for the lads in my platoon and confessed my masquerade. It took them some time and several pints to absorb this information and more to believe it. They watched in startled envy as I got into the CO's car and, as we drove away, broke into cheers of farewell.

Back at the offices of the AKC, I met the long thin Colonel again and went over my experiences. He asked me how I had got on with the CO at Canterbury.

'He couldn't have treated me better,' I replied. 'I didn't think the army would have too much respect for a scriptwriter but he leaned over backwards to be helpful.'

I heard that graveyard laugh once more and his answer explained a great deal. 'I was a bit concerned about that myself. I was anxious that he should give you complete co-operation, you see. So we played it safe and told him that you were an officer in Field Security Police making a special undercover investigation.'

The material I had gathered was so rich in incident and character that the script practically wrote itself. When I delivered it my connection with the army effectively ended, but I still have a little bit of military property. I managed to hold on to the khaki beret which was part of my Buffs uniform and I have it still, a permanent reminder of one of my strangest assignments.

6

It was around this time that I ended my brief association with the Communist Party. Before the war I had been the leader of the Labour Party League of Youth but in 1939 the national executive of the party carried out one of its regular sweeps against the left wing and Sir Stafford Cripps and others were expelled for advocating a united front against Fascism. Conscious of the axe hovering above my own head, I got out before it could fall.

I became editor of *Challenge*, the young Communist weekly paper and, for a couple of years, drama critic for the party's daily newspaper, the *Daily Worker*. But writing began increasingly to absorb my energies. Slowly I slipped out of the mainstream of political activity.

It was the case of the Soviet war brides which triggered my final break with Communism. During the war a number of British servicemen had been posted to Russia and about a hundred and fifty of these had fallen in love with, and married, Russian girls. Not unnaturally, when the war ended they expected to be able to bring their wives home with them but, to their astonishment and anger, Stalin refused to let the women leave. The Foreign Office begged, pleaded and threatened, the press railed, but the Soviet dictator remained adamant.

I could hardly believe this and I whipped off an angry letter to the *Daily Worker*. What I said, in essence, was that this incident had done more to turn ordinary people against the Soviet Union than a thousand anti-Soviet speeches and I went on to argue that Stalin had missed a marvellous propaganda opportunity. He should have given the women a generous dowry and free travel and sent them off with a fanfare.

The editor refused to publish my letter because it was critical of Stalin. I argued to no avail and that, effectively, was the end of this particular road for me. I wanted nothing more to do with a regime and a philosophy which could treat people with such calculated disregard for their human feelings. My reaction was an emotional one but, as developments in Russia were to prove, my political instinct was not far off the mark. After a year or so with no party affiliation, I applied to rejoin the Labour Party and I have remained within that broad fold ever since.

Chapter Six

1

A call from Sydney Box, the producer who had briefly been interested in making a film of *Buster*. Would I go out to the Gainsborough Studios in Lime Grove to discuss a film idea? I would have dropped everything at that moment and gone immediately but the appointment was made for two days later and I had to contain myself in hope and patience.

Sydney, whom I was to get to know well, gave an instant impression of glistening roundness. The face was round, the stomach globular, the fair pink skin shone like a polished apple. He had a bad, painful hip and the effort of walking emphasised the roundness and increased the shine. Behind the shrewd eyes, as I was to discover, lay an even shrewder brain and a warm, generous spirit. Like all producers he suffered from telephonitis – a telephone in hand or sometimes one in each seemed to be essential to his survival. It probably was.

I was introduced to his wife Muriel, a delicately attractive, gentle and talented lady and to two men, one of whom wore an expensive shirt with the letters GW embroidered on a top pocket. I didn't catch the name at first and, not recognising the gentleman, I thought for one startled moment that I was in the presence of a representative of the Great Western Railway. A little later I established that this was the author and journalist Godfrey Winn, who at this time was practically a household name. The other man was Peter Rogers, a writer, who blossomed later as a film producer in his own right with the successful *Carry On* films.

The idea, which I think came originally from Godfrey Winn, was to write a story set in a holiday camp. There were to be four stories, woven together into a single script, each dealing with a different set of characters. Holiday camps were much in the news and Billy Butlin, sensing the increasing post-war need for family holidays, was already a jump ahead of the field.

I went up to the Butlin camp at Filey at the height of the season and stayed for three or four days doing a fair imitation of a holidaymaker. I went as a Doubting Thomas but came away a convinced supporter. It was impossible not to be impressed by the sight of hundreds of people so clearly enjoying themselves. For most of them this was the only kind of holiday they could afford; it also represented a glorious release from the narrow tyrannies of seaside landladies. Thereafter I had little patience with the sneers of critics, who from their lofty perches belittled the concept of such mass holidays which, after all, were simply the working-class equivalent of the more up-market and snobbish ocean cruises. Holiday camps may have had their day but in the years after the war Billy Butlin, Fred Pontin and others provided millions of people with good affordable all-in holidays and entertainment.

During the filming I met the actor Jack Warner, little realising that this was to be the beginning of an association which would stretch over thirty years. Kathleen Harrison – who later starred in my television series, *Mrs Thursday* – teamed up with Jack as a Cockney couple, Mr and Mrs Huggett and their twelve-year-old daughter was played by the young Petula Clark. This inspired casting was so successful that it spawned a series of other films featuring the Huggetts, as well as a radio series. I contributed one film to the catalogue, *The Huggetts Abroad*.

Holiday Camp was streaked with the sentimentality which seemed to go with film-making in those days but it proved a popular box-office success. And for me the greatest satisfaction was to see my name on the screen credits of a feature film for the first time. It did not matter that I had to share the distinction with Sydney and Muriel Box and Peter Rogers. At least I had my toe in the door.

2

It is an axiom in the film business that out of every six screenplays written only one will be filmed. Many writers have survived for years on commissions for films or television pilot scripts which have subsequently remained buried in a studio office. Even when a screenplay is accepted it can often take a frustrating two or three years before the cameras start rolling and by that time, his head down on other projects, the writer has almost forgotten the subject.

I had my share of unproduced scripts. At Sydney Box's behest I spent ten days on the canals with a family of narrow-boat people and emerged with a screenplay called *Streets Paved with Water*. This I thought, was one of my better efforts but financial problems were gathering around Gainsborough, part of the larger J. Arthur Rank film empire, and the film was never made.

Another unfulfilled project, the screen adaptation of a book called *Streetwalker*, actually landed me in some personal danger. The novel told the true story of a girl who finds herself penniless in London and slips into prostitution. A suicidal urge to check out the background for myself led me to the streets of Soho and to some weird encounters.

I talked in a dingy room in Lisle Street with a vicar's daughter called Marylin who wore a crucifix. She told me that she charged extra if the client wanted her to take all her clothes off but never, not for a million pounds, would she remove the crucifix, which had belonged to her grandmother. At the time I did not have enough cash on me to test her resolve.

Another attractive blonde prostitute confessed to being a male transvestite. Several of the girls had an understandable contempt for men and found solace in lesbian relationships, usually with other prostitutes. Some were sadly, pathetically, in love with their pimps, the shady unsavoury creatures who both protected them and preyed upon them.

One of the most candid was a woman called Mona, whom I met in Hyde Park. A housewife from wealthy Windsor, married to an older man who owned a small engineering business, she came to London three or four afternoons a week to ply the trade.

'I enjoy my outings,' she said, in a cheerful cut-glass accent. 'I like money and sex. I don't get much of either from my husband so this is an ideal solution. Call it mixing business with pleasure. Mind you,' she added, looking at me suspiciously, 'I'm very particular. I don't let just anyone fuck me.'

Word of this young man who was wandering around paying the girls their fees and more simply for the privilege of talking to them must have spread through the dark underworld of ponces. One evening I approached a girl in Greek Street with my usual opening line to the effect that I would pay the full fee for a half-hour of her time but that I only wished to talk.

I had scarcely got this out when she put two fingers in her mouth and produced a whistle of which a train might have been proud. I swear it rattled the windows on the other side of the street. She followed this up by screeching at the top of her voice, 'He's here! He's here! The bloody copper's here!'

Three sinister characters who looked as if they had stepped straight out of an American gangster movie appeared as if by some sleight-of-hand from various directions and advanced towards me. My blood felt as though it had been injected with ice-cold water. I looked around desperately, ran across the street and crashed through the door of an Italian restaurant, narrowly avoiding the grasp of one of my pursuers.

The manager registered mild surprise at my noisy entrance but, making no comment, led me to a table. I sat there for an hour, toying with some food, wondering whether the three men were waiting. Clearly they thought I was an undercover member of the vice squad, a busybody who had to be taught a painful lesson. Then I had an inspiration. Jimmy Carr had an office in Soho Square not far from the restaurant and I knew that he usually worked late. I called him on the restaurant telephone.

He told me to stay put and in ten minutes he arrived, a diminutive figure flanked by two burly men, a cameraman and a film editor. I fancied that I saw the enemy lurking in doorways on the other side of the street but, surrounded by my escorts, I got safely out of the danger zone and took a taxi home.

After this encounter Audrey insisted that I had done

enough research into street-walking and, ever anxious to please, I agreed. Even so, it was a year or so before I could walk through Soho without looking over my shoulder.

3

On the whole, I was reasonably lucky with the film scripts I wrote for Gainsborough. In quick succession I scripted *Good Time Girl*, starring a rising young actress named Jean Kent, and *A Boy, a Girl and a Bike* in which John McCallum, Honor Blackman and Diana Dors played the leading roles. They were decent little films which enjoyed some popular success. Neither of them cost a fortune to make and I was somewhat surprised some twenty years later when, in a New York hotel room, I tuned the television to the Million Dollar Movie and saw a rerun of *Good Time Girl*. My recollection is that the budget was less than a tenth of this sum. Again, later still, I saw it on television in Hong Kong in a series labelled *Classics of British Cinema*. That it never was.

The idea for *A Boy, a Girl and a Bike* came from Sydney Box who, on a Sunday drive in the country, became impressed by the number of brown-legged young cyclists on the roads. We decided to build a story around a cycling club and set it in Yorkshire. So off I went on yet another mission of research. I made contact with a club in Shipley, bringing back memories of the time when I had tramped through the Dales and sold my first article. I had not ridden a bicycle more than half a mile for some time and the research began painfully. My legs and backside were out of practice and both became so sore and tired that for a day or so afterwards I walked like a bandy-legged jockey.

Most of the film had to be shot on location in Yorkshire and from the beginning this created problems. We needed to shoot in sunlight, a commodity in very short supply that summer. For long periods we were holed up in a hotel from which crew and cast made short, fitful forays to take advantage of any brief break in the weather.

After a while boredom set in and the handmaiden of boredom is mischief. When a local farmer came in for a drink, leaving a truckload of pigs outside, one member of the crew accidentally on purpose released the squealing animals who promptly invaded the village. It took half a day to round them up and the producer Ralph (Bunny) Keene had to pacify the farmer with a hefty payment from the cash float. One of the small-part actors, having taken a glass or two, went up one flight of stairs too many and was discovered by the furious landlady snoring on her bed. Unwisely, he had removed all his clothes.

Perhaps the most mischievous of all was Diana Dors. She was still a member of the Rank Charm School at the time, being paid a pittance, and this was to be one of her first films. I have an enduring memory of an afternoon when Diana and I went for a spin round the lanes on a tandem. She took the front seat and, from my position at the back, the view was breathtaking. The places were reversed after a while for we wobbled off the road and she landed on the grass verge with me on top of her.

A young farmer of the locality began to seek out our unit and it soon became obvious that he had become smitten with Diana. A decent simple lad, he could not keep his eyes off her – that she teased him without mercy made no difference. Nothing, it seemed, could shift the adoring look that lit up his eyes like those of a devoted puppy. It all came to a head one evening when she snatched his cap and ran off with it. He cornered her at last, whereupon she lifted her skirt and tucked the cap between her thighs. As the poor boy grabbed at it she slapped his face and loudly accused him, in so many words, of invading her privacy. I think 'touching me up' was the phrase she used.

On this occasion she kept the teasing up for too long and went too far. The more the lad protested his innocence, the more angry became her accusation until he too lost his temper. The sea-change in him was both amazing and frightening and Diana backed off. When the noise of battle brought in the landlady he turned to her and shouted, 'You want to get rid of this lot, missus, or you'll lose all your regulars.'

Which is what she did. The good woman knew on which side her bread was buttered and she'd had enough of our madcap behaviour anyway. We were given until the next day to pack up and get out. But it is right to record that Diana asked me to find out the young man's address and in the morning we went to see him. She put on a performance which promised much for her subsequent career as an actress, apologising to such effect that, as we left, I could once more see the love light shining in his eyes.

4

It was midnight and the police car was cruising the White-chapel Road in East London on one of its regular patrols. A young constable was at the wheel, a sergeant sat beside him and I had the back seat to myself. The driver had just given me a breathless demonstration of the power of the car, racing down the shadowed road at a speed of over a hundred miles an hour, often screaming past other vehicles on the wrong side of the street. I was relieved when we slowed to a more respectable speed.

The sergeant was the first to see the young man moving uncertainly along the opposite pavement. He seemed to be having some difficulty with a long, heavy bundle which was slung across his shoulder. At the sergeant's instruction the driver did a U-turn and we drew up alongside the man. The sergeant wound down his window and barked, 'Here, you. Here! Come here!'

The young man stopped, turned and moved in a weary, resigned fashion towards the car. He was wearing a navy blue roll-neck sweater, a donkey jacket and corduroy trousers and, on his face, a look which suggested that he'd had a bad day and that being stopped by the police was the last straw.

'Where are you going?' demanded the sergeant.

'Where do you think? I'm going home.'

'You can cut the lip!' said the sergeant smartly. 'Where's home?'

The young man sighed and gave an address. The sergeant nodded. 'Name?'

'Stanley Martin.'

'I see,' said the sergeant. 'Well, Stanley, tell us what you've got there.'

'Where?' asked Stanley, who seemed genuinely puzzled.

'Now, don't bugger me about,' snapped the sergeant. 'What's that bloody great bundle you've got round your neck?'

'This?' said Stanley. He dropped the bundle on to the pavement. 'See for yourself. It's a carpet, innit?'

It was indeed and, in the next few minutes prompted by the sergeant, young Stanley told the tale of how he came to be carrying this object along Whitechapel Road at midnight. He was, he said, a deck-hand on a merchant ship which had docked that afternoon, a day earlier than expected, with a cargo from Argentina. He had signed off that evening and hurried towards the loving arms of his young wife, whom he had married about a year before.

The trouble was that when he arrived home he found those same loving arms around another man, whom he promptly and violently ejected. After a long and unpleasant scene with his wife, Stanley decided to cut the painter and go home to Mother. Which was where he was going when the sergeant had so rudely interrupted him.

The sergeant's face registered a mixture of amusement and doubt as he listened. He was a tough old China hand and he knew from experience that your average Cockney can spin a plausible yarn at the drop of a cloth cap.

'OK, Stanley,' he said, 'but where does the carpet come into it?'

Stanley shook his head. To him, it all seemed so simple. 'Look,' he said, 'it's my bleeding carpet, innit? I brought it back from Istanbul on my last trip, didn't I? Bloody good carpet, too good for that bitch. So I'm taking it to my mum. OK?'

'I see,' said the sergeant. 'Where does this wife of yours live then?' Stanley gave him the number of a house in Cable Street. 'Right,' continued the sergeant. 'Let's go and check, shall we?'

A few minutes later we were on our way, Stanley sitting in the back with me and his carpet stretched across our knees. We pulled up outside a terraced house in Cable Street and the sergeant, Stanley and the carpet went to the front door. Not wishing to miss the climax of this domestic drama, I followed.

The door was opened eventually by a sharp-faced young woman with lank blonde hair under which black roots were struggling to assert themselves. She wore an old raincoat over a nightdress. A smile of sorts eased the sharpness of her face when she saw Stanley and, grabbing his arm, she shouted, 'So you're back! Come in, you silly sod.'

With that, she pulled the bewildered Stanley inside and made to close the door.

'Hold on a minute, missus,' said the sergeant. 'You've forgotten this.' He threw in the carpet and the door slammed in his face. Turning to me, he added, 'That's police work for you. A matrimonial agency and a bloody furniture remover rolled into one.'

Later, back in the car when he'd had time to think, he said, 'Did you get a good look at the wife? A right little scrubber. Poor Stanley, I don't reckon we did him any favours. We should have let him go home to Mum.'

This incident was part – a small part – of my research for a new assignment, a film about the life and work of the police to be called *The Blue Lamp*.

5

The idea had come from Sydney Box and his script editor at Gainsborough, a writer named Jan Read. Up to that time the British policeman had usually been portrayed as a bumbling simpleton who habitually licked the stub of a pencil, was respectful to the Squire and left the investigation and solution of serious crime to brilliant, educated amateurs like Sherlock Holmes and Lord Peter Wimsey.

Sydney decided that there had to be a little more to it than that and Jan and I were asked to do some research and knock together a script. A policeman had been murdered some weeks before by two young hoodlums and Sydney suggested that we should take this as a starting point, telling the story from the point of view of the police not of the criminals. A writer develops a nose when it comes to stories and, from the beginning, I sensed that this had all the makings of a major subject.

I spent six weeks living in the pockets of the police at the old Leman Street station, in Arbour Square which housed the motorised units, and at Paddington Green. I pounded the beat by day and night, sat behind the station counter, in the charge room and dropped in at the homes of officers of all ranks to talk to patient, long-suffering wives.

I became particularly attached to an Inspector Mott, a

middle-aged officer who had risen through the ranks. He had spent years in his East End manor, seemed to know every crack in every pavement and was instantly recognised and greeted respectfully by half the population. Today, I suppose, he would be called 'one of your old-time coppers'.

I walked many a mile with Mott, threading our way down those mean streets. He talked to me of his interest in the stars, which he had studied as a constable on the beat, in music, and in people. Above all, in people. The man had more understanding of people and their motives than a dozen Harley Street psychiatrists.

There was an old lady, a Mrs Heslop, who came into the station at regular intervals and she always asked to see Mr Mott. I was lucky enough to be there on one of her visits and once Mott had introduced me as one of his best friends she allowed me to stay for the interview.

'It's back again, Mr Mott,' said Mrs Heslop.

'Oh, I'm sorry to hear that,' said Mott.

'There's a spot on the wall of the kitchen. It watches me from there. Follows me with its eyes. All the time.'

'Just follows you with its eyes?'

'Yes.'

'In the kitchen?'

'Yes. I've got the Security Shield up in the living-room. The one you gave me last time. It wouldn't dare go in there.'

'Well, then, Mrs Heslop, we'd better let you have another one for the kitchen, hadn't we?'

Mott reached in a drawer and removed the silver foil from a cigarette packet. He smoothed this on the desk and solemnly handed it to the old lady.

'Has it been treated?' she asked cautiously.

'Treated specially at the police laboratory,' he replied. 'Stick it up in the kitchen and you'll have no more trouble. Come back and see me if you do.'

She went away, chirping as happily as a box of birds, and he explained. 'Poor old girl. She's a bit round the twist. She imagines that an odd creature from outer space is watching her. I gave her some silver foil the first time, telling her that it had protective qualities and would frighten off any alien who came near it. When I saw her later, she was delighted. Said it had worked. She comes back every so often for more.' He looked at me and smiled. 'Well, it's better than locking her away in a loony-bin, isn't it? She's quite harmless.' And he added perceptively, 'She's also lonely. It does her good to pop in for a chat and a mug of tea.'

Once we visited a man who had been arrested for assault to check on his family. Home was a damp squalid room, family a beaten-down woman with three young children. As we left, I saw Mott quietly leave a half-crown on the cluttered table and back at the station he telephoned the welfare department at the town hall to alert them of the woman's need.

But he could be tough too. On one occasion, a drunken six-foot man with the brawn of a stoker went on the rampage in the market, upsetting stalls and threatening customers and stallholders. Mott darted in, put the man's arm in a lock so painful that he screamed aloud, and frog-marched him to Leman Street.

Walking round the manor one day he remarked, 'You want stories, Ted? Knock on any door round here and you'll find one.' Years later this phrase come back to me and I used it for my television drama anthology, *Knock On Any Door*.

I didn't have to look any further for the central character of *The Blue Lamp*. I modelled him on Mott, named him George Dixon and he was eventually played by Jack Warner. Although Dixon was killed off halfway through the film and thus played no part in the climax, Jack's performance was so effective that he won most of the accolades. A young actor named Dirk Bogarde, who was in the early days of what was to become a distinguished film career, played one of the young criminals to riveting effect.

Sadly, the completion of the screenplay by Jan Read and myself coincided with one of those periodic crises which afflict the British film industry. The great Rank film production empire all but collapsed. Savage retrenchment was the order that went out from the boardroom: Gainsborough Pictures, with its famous trademark of the Gainsborough lady, was wound up and the Lime Grove studios were bought by the BBC.

Michael Balcon, head of Ealing Studios, became overall chief of what was left of Rank's production arm and he took on *The Blue Lamp*. His first step was to turn the script over to Ealing's star writer, T. E. B. (Tibby) Clark, author of such gems as *Passport To Pimlico* and *The Lavender Hill Mob*.

After our months of work and given our enthusiasm for the subject this came as a galling disappointment to Jan Read and myself. But Tibby had been in the police force and he brought to the rewritten screenplay not only this experience but all his great skill as a scriptwriter. He honed, refined and improved our material and added much more that was uniquely his own.

And we managed to rescue something from the wreckage of Gainsborough. Before he passed our screenplay to Michael Balcon, I persuaded Sydney Box to let Jan and me have the stage rights in the story and to allow me certain other rights to the character of PC George Dixon. I don't know what instinct persuaded me to do this but it proved to be a pretty useful move.

I wrote the novel of *The Blue Lamp* and later, with Jan, adapted the story for the stage. The play ran for a wildly successful summer season in Blackpool and came from there to the old Hippodrome Theatre in Leicester Square. And, later still, I was having a drink in the BBC Club with Ronnie Waldman, Head of Light Entertainment at the Corporation, and he asked me if I could come up with an idea for a police series . . .

But that story must wait a little while.

Chapter Seven

1

Somehow, despite long periods away on research followed by weeks of work on the screenplays and regular visits to Lords to watch Edrich and Compton at the wicket, I still managed to find time for the theatre. I wrote what was to be my last play for Unity, a short piece for the Mobile Group called *The Jolly George*, and thereafter turned my sights on the professional scene.

A dynamic and dedicated couple, Anthony and Marjorie Hawtrey, had opened up the Embassy Theatre in Swiss Cottage and in successive years they produced two of my comedies. The first, *The Magnificent Moodies*, told the story of a Cockney family who, having won the football pools, move into the Dorchester Hotel for a holiday. It was comedy with a broad brush and that it came off at all was largely due to a cast which was headed by two former Unity stalwarts, Bill Owen and Alfie Bass and directed by another, Peter Copley. Among the supporting players, all on minimal salaries of around ten pounds a week, were three actors who would soon be topping bills themselves, Leslie Phillips, Warren Mitchell and John Neville.

I found the idea for the second play, *The Lady Purrs*, in an old Egyptian legend which tells of a sacred cat with the ability, at certain times, to transform itself into a beautiful woman. I brought the theme up to date, creating a plot in which a pompous local mayor who is up for re-election finds that his family cat is now a sexy girl – moreover, since she has been around as a cat for some time and often slept under his bed, she knows most of his guilty secrets.

This piece worked out well and at the end of its short run

74

at the Embassy it went out on a reasonably successful tour. Directed by Henry Kendall, one of the top comedy producers of the time, it showed the madcap Eleanor Summerfield at the top of her form and, down among the also-rans, at least two more artists who were to find greater fame, Dandy Nichols – who played Alf Garnett's wife in Johnny Speight's brilliant TV series, *Till Death Us Do Part* – and Joss Ackland.

But my most ambitious stage project around this time was a play called *No Trees in the Street*. Loosely based on characters I'd met in childhood in the dingy back streets of Tottenham, I think I wrote it to exorcise certain ghosts. The central characters are a mother and daughter – the mother an evil, foul-mouthed woman without a decent motive to her name, the daughter a young woman who is struggling to escape the lower depths of poverty. The mother mocks her efforts and, in the end, creates the circumstances in which she can sell her daughter to the local bookmaker for a cash payment. I had seen this happen as a teenager and I had been a little in love with the real-life girl.

It was very strong stuff and used some very strong language, although I avoided the more blunt four-letter words. My instinct told me that this would be pressing reality too far for the tolerance of the times. Much of the scene where the girl is raped took place off-stage but what I did show was pretty daring by the standards then prevailing. It was, I suppose, one of the first of what came to be known as kitchen-sink dramas and, in that sense, was almost a decade ahead of the trend. When I had finally got it out of my system, my overwhelming feeling was that the only theatre which might even consider it would be Unity.

I had escaped from Rita Cave by this time and gone to the sheltering arms of an altogether more reasonable and professional lady named Margery Vosper. She read *No Trees in the Street* overnight, fell in love with it and announced that she was going to submit it to a Mr Basil Dean. Producer, director, manager, impresario and former head of ENSA, the wartime entertainment organisation, Dean was a formidable almost legendary figure in the theatre, a man with a reputation for toughness which bordered on ruthlessness. It was said that his failure to get the knighthood that his services to the theatre and ENSA should have made virtually automatic was due to his having made so many enemies.

I was a member of the executive committee of the League of Dramatists at this time, a very junior member, sitting with such giants as James Bridie, J. B. Priestley, Esther McCracken and Emlyn Williams and fast-rising stars like Peter Ustinov. We met every quarter in a comfortable boardroom at the offices of the Society of Authors under the gentle eye of Elizabeth Barber, the secretary, to discuss the problems of playwrights. Tea, in delicate bone china cups, accompanied by a selection of Huntley and Palmer biscuits, was always served promptly at four o'clock.

They were a shrewd and surprisingly militant bunch. On one occasion, a firm of play publishers proposed a reduction in the fees paid to authors by amateur theatre companies. Bridie bristled at this, seeing it above all as a threat to those minor dramatists who relied on their amateur fees for a living, and the committee agreed. Strong representations were made to the company, coupled with a veiled threat from a dozen leading writers to withdraw their plays from the firm's catalogue. Nothing more was heard of the matter.

It so happened that, at his suggestion, I had sent Priestley a copy of *No Trees in the Street* and he had commented upon it in very flattering terms. After one of our meetings I told him that the play had gone to Basil Dean. The old lion shook his head. 'Waste of time. Not his kind of stuff – not his kind of stuff at all.'

As it turned out, he was wrong. To my astonishment, Margery Vosper rang to say that Mr Dean was interested and that she had made an appointment for me to see him on the following Saturday morning at eleven in his office in the St James's theatre.

2

The interview almost ended before it had begun. Audrey had arranged to go to Dublin for the weekend with Elsie, her friend from Unity days, and Elsie's new husband, Charles Warren, and I was left to look after John, then aged almost four. He was a gentle, well-controlled child and I decided that he should come to the St James's with me and after, as a treat, I would take him to see a Walt Disney movie at a West End cinema.

We arrived in good time and were shown to Basil Dean's office above the theatre, a large, tastefully decorated room which, apart from the desk, looked more like an elegant sitting-room than a place of work. And, similarly, the silver-haired man in the severe spectacles, dark grey suit and impeccably knotted club tie who rose to greet us from behind the mahogany desk had all the formal dignity of a senior diplomat. I was relieved to think that my sportscoat and flannels were in reasonable shape and that I had made young John look presentable.

'Come in, come in,' said Dean courteously, stepping around the desk. Then he beamed at John who was clutching my hand as if he felt that life and limb were in danger, and added, 'And what is your name, my little man?'

I have never been able to explain or understand what happened next. Perhaps it was some trick of light glinting from those spectacles which frightened him or perhaps he was obeying some primeval instinct but my gentle, non-violent, well-controlled son released my hand and, charging across the room like a deranged goat, buried his head with sickening force in Basil Dean's solar plexus.

Basil gasped and staggered back against the desk, his face drained of colour, his chest heaving like a pair of overworked bellows. My first thought was that he might pass out, my second that this spelled the finish for *No Trees in the Street*. John trotted back to me and looked up as if for approval. I scolded him as convincingly as I could, apologised to Basil and thereafter kept a tight hold of my errant son.

For some reason, after this incident Basil seemed anxious to conclude the interview with as much speed as possible. Keeping a wary eye on John, he explained that he liked my play but that, in his view, it was not the sort of piece which would go down well in the sophisticated West End theatre. What he proposed to do, if I agreed, was to send it out on an eight-week tour to four provincial theatres. While we were occupying their stages, each of these theatre companies would bring a play to the St James's for two weeks. He proposed to direct *No Trees in the Street* himself.

I accepted gratefully. And then he raised a spectre which had not entered into my calculations. 'It's – er – a very – er – bold – play. Our first hurdle will be the Lord Chamberlain's office. If we can't get it past him – well . . . ' He spread his hands as if to indicate that this would mean the end of his interest in the play.

'I suppose I could tone down the language a bit,' I said.

'No, no. Not at this stage. Let him see it as it is. In fact, what I'd like you to do is work up the rape scene, make it more explicit. And it won't hurt if you throw in a few more juicy swear words.'

I couldn't understand how this would help and said so.

'It's a simple question of tactics,' said Basil. 'If you can beef up the rape, the Lord Chamberlain will certainly demand that it be cut. He may then decide that he has done his job and let a lot of the other raw stuff through. We offer him a sprat, he leaves us with a mackerel.'

In the face of this cunning I agreed to give him a rape which would shake the Lord Chamberlain's office to its foundations.

As he stood up to shake hands in farewell I noticed that Basil kept the desk between himself and John.

3

The Lord Chamberlain's power of censorship over the theatre was abolished in the sixties but before that no play could be given a public performance without his licence. He was the censor, the guardian of the nation's morals and standards, protecting the innocent playgoer from playwright hooligans like myself. Looking back, it is incredible to think that one man should hold such dominion over the nation's drama. Unity had avoided his clutches because it was a club theatre and its productions were open only to members. Even so, the police had kept a close eye on the theatre to ensure that we did not break the rules.

Basil Dean had been right. The revised rape scene had clearly shaken the Lord Chamberlain and the play came back with the comment that no licence would be forth-coming unless the scene was cut. He made a list of other undesirable items of which the following are typi-cal:

Page 3   First speech: Cut 'bloody'.
Page 5   Fifth speech: Cut 'My God'.
Page 9   Sixth speech: Cut 'bloody hell'.
Page 14   Third speech: Cut 'Jesus Christ'.
Page 26   Middle of scene. The character Wilkie should
             not be seen fastening his trouser buttons on
             stage

The list of proscribed words and incidents went on for three and a half pages. It was serious but it also had its funny side. I had a mental picture of the austere gentlemen civil servants in the Lord Chamberlain's office poring over our plays with Irish linen handkerchiefs held to their noses, extracting naughty words and scenes for all the world as if they were fishing in a sewer.

It seemed to me that if I agreed to all the cuts I would be left with something colourless, far removed from the slice of raw life that I had attempted to portray. Basil Dean was less pessimistic. In fact, he was positively cheer-ful.

'It's not bad,' he said, 'not bad at all. Leave it to me.' With that he waltzed off to see the Lord Chamberlain. A couple of hours later he came back in triumph, a winner's smile shining on his face.

It seemed that the Lord Chamberlain had fallen for the ploy. The exaggerated rape scene that I had inserted at Basil's request had to be cut back as we expected but the trimmed version was more or less what I had written originally. Simi-larly, the other cuts still left us with a great deal – the wily old devil had emerged with 95 per cent of the play intact and we were in business.

Beatrix Lehmann, an actress who had starred in a string of West End successes, agreed to play the leading role and rehearsals began. From the beginning Basil let it be known, without equivocation, who was the boss. He did not draw performances from the actors, he imposed them.

He knew exactly how he wanted a speech to sound and insisted that it should be spoken his way, even down to the tiniest inflexion. If an actor strayed from Basil's concept of how a line should be delivered he would order him to stay behind and drill him like a sergeant-major, making him repeat the line endlessly until he was satisfied. At times he would conduct a rehearsal with his back to the company, simply listening to the speeches and making changes in the way they were delivered. He called this 'orchestrating the play'.

He was scornful of the Stanislavsky school of acting which puts the emphasis on inner motivation. Once, an actor in one of the smaller parts had the temerity to ask why he was required to move across the room to put out a cigarette in an ash-tray.

'I don't think he would do it, Mr Dean. It's not in character. He's the type who would drop the cigarette on the floor and stamp it out.'

Basil fixed him with a glance that would have withered an oak. 'You want a motive for the move, is that it?'

'Yes, please, Mr Dean.'

'The motive is very simple,' Dean replied, 'and I hope you have the wit to comprehend it. You move across the room because I want you to. I need you over there for the rest of the scene. So don't agonise about it – just move!'

The last word exploded like a bullet and the quivering actor hastily headed for the ash-tray.

The only member of the cast who had the standing and the spirit to stand up to Basil was the talented Miss Lehmann. There were many head-on clashes between the two and, I suppose, at the end, honours were pretty even but there were moments when I feared that the whole project might collapse.

Miraculously, it did not. I would not recommend Basil Dean's style of direction but he knew the theatre and he knew his craft and by the dress rehearsal the play looked to be in good shape. Then it was off to the Playhouse, Liverpool, for what Basil, with unusual flamboyance, insisted on calling the world première.

4

It did not take me long to discover that Maud Carpenter, the formidable lady who ran the Playhouse, did not approve of my play. She came into the rehearsal on the afternoon before opening night and went away stunned and horrified. She told Basil that he had betrayed her trust. He was such a distinguished figure in the theatre that she had accepted the play sight unseen – had she known what it was like she would never have allowed it within a mile of her theatre. I was quite sure that if there had been time she would have cancelled the production. She looked at me as if I were something that had fallen out of a dustbin.

Not an auspicious beginning and my jangling nerves were not eased at the first-night performance when, after about thirty minutes, a trickle of people began to leave the theatre in evident disgust. Little protesting murmurs came from some of those who remained. I turned to Audrey, who had bravely come with me, whispered that I would not be long and fled outside to the refreshing night air and thence to the nearest pub.

I did not return until halfway through the second act and I sensed at once a major change in the atmosphere. The murmuring, the impatient coughing had stopped: the audience sat in a tense collective silence as if afraid to miss a word or a move. The silence continued for a second or two when the curtain fell and then came the applause, tremendous thunderous applause that fell on my ears like the sweetest music. The company was called back for curtain after curtain and a steady, excited buzz came from the customers as they filed out of the theatre.

This taste of success had a strange effect on Basil Dean. He had pages of critical notes about the performances and was in a foul mood, raging on about a wrong move here or a changed inflexion there. Ordering the stage manager to call everyone in for an additional rehearsal, he swept us off to the Adelphi Hotel for what was intended to be a celebratory supper.

I realise now that people in the theatre have different ways of showing their first-night nerves. Basil's method of relieving his own inner tension was to turn on other people. He was right, of course, to be critical, to aim at perfection but, on occasions, his criticism was expressed in terms which were savage and humiliating for the person concerned. At the supper, he transferred his attention from the actors to the waiters and to one elderly waiter in particular. He barked orders and harassed and harried until the poor man's hands were shaking. I could feel Audrey tighten in her chair until after one especially sarcastic assault she could take it no longer. Quietly but firmly she said, 'Mr Dean.'

'Yes?'

'Why do you keep picking on that waiter? He's doing his best.'

'Well, his best isn't good enough!' Basil's eyes glinted behind the austere glasses as if he were looking at some impertinent student. He did not know that when Audrey has a full head of steam on she is not easily derailed.

'Neither are your manners!' she replied sweetly. 'If you want to take it out on someone, why don't you choose a person who is in a position to answer back?'

There followed a long, icy pause and an audible gulp as Basil glared at my beautiful young wife and attempted to gather himself. Beatrix Lehmann intervened, tactfully changing the subject, but from then on he addressed the waiter as if he were a human being. This was Basil's second encounter with my family – John had rammed his stomach and now Audrey had, just as effectively, taken the wind from his sails.

By the next morning his mood had changed and he behaved like a benevolent uncle. He was influenced, I think, by the lengthy queue at the box office when we arrived at the theatre. That night the house was packed and the House Full boards were in frequent use for the remainder of the two-week run. When we moved on to Sheffield, Birmingham and Bristol the business was equally good, often breaking the box-office record.

The notices in the local papers veered between two extremes. 'Do we really want to see this sort of depravity in our theatres?' demanded one reviewer. Another wondered whether the Lord Chamberlain had been asleep when he gave the play a licence. Yet another expressed sorrow that such a distinguished actress as Beatrix Lehmann had lowered herself so far as to appear in this 'shocking drama of the gutter'.

On the other hand, there were reviews which described

the play as 'stunning and provocative' – one went as far as
to say that, after this, 'drama will never be the same again'.
The distinguished critic of the *Birmingham Post*, T. C. Kemp,
described me as 'the poet of the slums', a pioneering playwright who had broken new ground and should be regarded
as 'London's own Sean O'Casey'. Over the top, maybe, but it
did wonders for my self-confidence.

There could be no doubt that *No Trees in the Street* was
a huge popular success. Two weeks before the tour ended
Basil rang me up. 'I've changed my mind,' he said. 'I think
the play might do well in London. I'm going to put it on at
the St James's.'

5

Sadly, the St James's Theatre has now gone, having been
demolished in favour of a commercial development in the
late fifties, but it was one of the most illustrious playhouses in
London. Olivier, Richardson, Ashcroft, Gielgud, Thorndike –
almost every distinguished artist in the British theatre – had
graced its stage at one time or another. It was hard to believe
that this graceful, beautiful old theatre was now going to be
home to my gritty, down-to-earth drama of the slums.

The first night followed much the same pattern as when
we opened in Liverpool. A certain restlessness at first, a
few people making for the exits in disgust, and then the
play seemed to take a grip. I did my usual disappearing act,
returning towards the end to find an audience that seemed to
be totally engrossed in the performance, the silence broken
only by little telltale gasps of shock or surprise as the drama
moved to a climax. Up in a box attending the West End theatre
for the first time in her life sat my Cockney mother, beaming
proudly down on the scene.

When the curtain fell she led the applause which went on
and on, for something like fifteen calls, with some members
of the audience standing and cheering. It was the custom in
those days to call for the author and I was ushered on stage
to take a bow with the company.

On this occasion, Basil's mood was one of cautious elation.
He would not commit himself until he had seen the morning's

reviews but he seemed confident that we had a winner on our hands, so much so that he asked me to go in to see him the following day to talk about my next play.

I went home in a kind of exhausted glow with Audrey and my friend from the London Philharmonic, Tom Russell. We took a cab as far as Regent's Park and walked the rest of the way in the cool night air to Maida Vale. Tom was buoyant, confident of success, and he cautioned me about the future.

'Tomorrow you will be famous,' he said. 'That's the time to be careful. You will be asked to dinners, cocktail parties, all sorts of things. They are a waste of time. Turn them down, Ted. Go to a good accountant and get him to look after your money. And just get on with your work. Don't let anything turn your head.'

I fell into bed with this well-meant advice drumming in my head and, almost at once, sank into a deep sleep. It was late morning when I awoke and went to the kitchen in search of Audrey and a cup of tea. She rose and put her arms around me as if in protection and I felt her tears on my cheek as she pointed wordlessly to the pile of newspapers on the table.

The notices were not simply bad; they were savage, cruel, dismissive, contemptuous. Not one critic had a single good word to say for the play, not one even suggested that there was a hint of promise in the writing, or mentioned the favourable audience response. They were virtually unanimous in their condemnation of what one called 'this dustbin drama'. The general view was that what I had written constituted an insult to decent theatre. Significantly, there were several vicious references to my left-wing connections.

It was devastating, the more so because of the build-up that had gone before. The successful tour had raised my hopes to the skies and given an extra dimension to my ego. Now the hopes had come crashing down like a rotten oak and my ego lay flattened. And, of course, there was nothing that could be done, no effective way to answer back. For a few hours I was in the depths of such despair that only the comforting support of Audrey and the presence of little John kept the thought of suicide at bay.

It took me a long, long week to pull back to some normality. By then the notices had gone up and *No Trees in the Street* ended its West End run after sixteen performances. Did it really deserve such an instant death?

Looking back, I can see now that the play did err on the side of melodrama and that its message was too bleak and uncompromising for the times. Even so, I do not believe that it deserved to be so utterly and ruthlessly destroyed, or that the applause I had heard in Liverpool, Sheffield, Birmingham and Bristol had been a trick of my imagination.

Adversity is a good training ground and I learned a great deal from my experience with *No Trees in the Street*. The theatre may be a palace of illusion but, for those involved, it can be a hall of delusions also. Self-deception is an occupational hazard: the warmth and camaraderie of a company working in enthusiastic harmony can induce a misguided optimism about the show's possible success. This is dangerous. One should never entertain any expectations about a play's prospects until the audience has pronounced judgement. Never again would I allow myself to be trapped in sunny dreams of overnight success. There would be no more false dawns.

Three developments helped to restore my spirits. The first came in the form of a telegram which read, IGNORE THE CRITICS. GET ON WITH YOUR NEXT PLAY. GOOD LUCK – JACK PRIESTLEY. I cannot attempt to explain what that meant to me.

The second was a call from a producer called Stanley Williscroft. He had bought the set of *No Trees in the Street* from Basil Dean and would like to send it out on a provincial tour. Would I agree?

The third came with an important announcement from Audrey. She had some news which, typically, she had kept from me during the past stressful week. Our visit to Liverpool for the opening night at the Playhouse had yielded an exciting bonus. She was pregnant again.

6

My delight was tempered by the thought that our top-floor flat in Maida Vale would be quite inadequate for a family of four. Bumping the pram up and down five flights of stairs to take young John in and out had already proved to be a major problem and I did not want to go through it all again when the new baby arrived. I had dreams of a house with a decent bit of garden in which the children could play but very little money with which to make those dreams come true.

I went along to the offices of the old London County Council – of blessed memory – and asked the housing department if they could do anything to oblige. A kindly grey-haired lady in a twin-set informed me, with a certain sadness, that the waiting list was so long that it would be at least six or seven years before my name came up for consideration. But then she threw me a life-line. Glancing at my application she said, 'I see you are a writer. I wonder if you would be interested in one of our Higher Income Group houses?'

I gave her all my attention as she explained that the LCC had decided on an imaginative experiment. Large estates were being built on the fringes of London and the Council wanted them to be balanced communities. To that end, each estate would have a certain number of four-bedroom houses which would be available to professional people like myself at a higher rent than the smaller ones. If I were interested it was possible that a house might be allotted to me in about eighteen months.

The words Higher Income Group rather frightened me. I certainly did not consider myself to be in that category and nervously I asked what the rent was likely to be. She explained that she could not be explicit but that the figure would probably be about four pounds ten shillings a week. Double what I was paying for the flat in Maida Vale!

I took a deep breath and asked her to put my name down for a Higher Income Group house on the estate at Loughton, Essex, praying inwardly that by the time it was ready my income would live up to this description of my status.

One other seemingly insignificant incident which occurred at this time was to have a profound influence on my life. Audrey made the mistake of sending me to the Edgware Road to buy a new plug for the electric iron – a mistake because I was, and still am, an impulse buyer. Left alone in one of today's supermarkets I am quite capable of emptying the shelves. Couple this with a reckless tendency to spend the money in my pocket before it has time to settle down and you have a recipe for disaster.

Television was only just beginning to get into its stride after the wartime shut-down and programmes were only broadcast for four or five hours a day on one channel by the BBC. There were few sets around. However, the electrical store in Edgware Road had just taken delivery of this very rare commodity – a television set made by Pye with a tiny nine- or ten-inch screen on which I could see Hopalong Cassidy in full pursuit of a band of renegades. Fascinated not so much by the film as the technology I enquired the price. It was ninety-eight pounds. Naturally I bought it, a transaction which left us with exactly four pounds in the bank.

Audrey was furious. As the price of domestic peace I had to accept an arrangement which holds good to this day and which, I must admit, has saved us from financial disaster on many occasions. I agreed that from then on any cheque over a certain specified amount had to be countersigned by my wife.

The television set was a great social success. Evening after evening the local kids crowded into our flat to see the children's programmes, to be followed later by their parents who casually dropped in to pass the time of day and inevitably stayed for an evening's viewing.

It wasn't long before they bought their own sets and, watching this mushrooming of interest, my enthusiasm increased. This was the creature of the future, one which would reach into millions of homes, and it would have to be fed. It would need programmes and that meant writers.

For me, that would be some time ahead. In the meantime *No Trees in the Street*, though critically dead, was stubbornly refusing to lie down.

Chapter Eight

1

Stanley Williscroft, the man who had been foolhardy enough to propose another tour for *No Trees in the Street*, turned out to be a gentle ex-actor who seemed too frail and decent for the harsh world of theatre management.

His plan was to put the play on at a series of what were then known as number two theatres: in other words, not the prime provincial dates but smaller theatres in less favourable venues. With engaging honesty, he explained that it would be a tight operation on a very low budget and if it did not work out in four weeks he would have to pull the show. To help him, would I forgo the usual percentage royalty and accept a fixed weekly fee of twenty pounds?

This is not an arrangement that I would recommend to any dramatist today. My excuse is that there was then no trade union like the Writers' Guild to advise me and, in any case, it seemed sensible to try to make what I could out of my West End disaster. What it boiled down to was that I needed the money. I persuaded Stanley to raise the fee to twenty-five pounds, payable weekly in advance and we were in business.

We opened in a modest theatre in Barnstaple, Devonshire, to an equally modest house. There was not a name among the actors and they were all on minimum salaries. Yet once again this seemingly indestructible play worked its strange magic and by the end of the week we were playing to full and enthusiastic houses. What had been so summarily rejected by the West End clearly had an appeal to plainer, less high-flown audiences.

This experience was repeated at a dozen other venues and a delighted Stanley Williscroft kept booking new dates. The tour stretched into its sixth month and there was a distinct danger that we might run out of suitable halls and theatres. As an experiment Stanley booked the play into Barnstaple again with the most extraordinary result. It seemed as if the whole town had been waiting on our return for a week before we arrived every seat had been sold.

News of this unusual phenomenon naturally trickled back to London and some of the bigger theatre managers began to take an interest, among them the brothers Lew and Leslie Grade and Jack Hylton, the impresario. On this occasion, Lew, the former dancer, proved to be quicker on his feet than Jack, the ex-band-leader, and he struck a deal with Stanley Williscroft. He would put *No Trees in the Street* into the New Cross Empire for a trial week; if this worked he would take the play to other similar theatres. The financial arrangement, which I only got to know about later, stipulated that Lew and Leslie Grade would pay Stanley a fixed sum to cover all his costs, including my weekly payment, plus a guaranteed fee for himself. The Grades would cover the hire of the theatre, publicity and all other charges. Stanley thought it was a fair gamble and anyway he was running out of number two dates and needed the muscle of the Grades to get into the bigger theatres.

A garage now stands on the site once occupied by the New Cross Empire, just as a hotel has replaced the Old Metropolitan in Edgware Road. It was, I suppose, an inevitable process for even forty years ago the dismal signs of decay were already evident. The New Cross Empire was a huge seedy barn of a place with seating for over fifteen hundred customers; star attractions were in short supply and when these were not available the theatre kept itself ticking over with twice-nightly shows like *Nudes on Parade*. Impossibly expensive to maintain, the old place looked like something left over from another age, a dejected relic of the great glittering days of Victorian music-hall. It even smelt of the past, a curious mixture of the scent of oranges, paraffin and damp.

No Trees in the Street was scheduled to play two performances each night and Audrey and I decided to go to the second performance on the Friday evening. I had heard nothing from Stanley and, as a consequence, we were totally unprepared for the bewildering scene that greeted us. A long bustling queue stretched from the box office all the way round the theatre and halfway down a nearby street. Two mounted policemen were patrolling the crowd, edging them into line, and two constables stood guard at the entrance.

As we watched, a harassed but happy house manager came out with the House Full sign. A groan went up from those who could see this but most continued to queue in the hope of getting tickets for the Saturday matinée or for one of the last two evening performances. These people were clearly not your usual theatre-goers but plain, unsophisticated working-folk, the sort whose mothers and fathers had once thronged the music-hall: they looked and sounded more like a crowd of fans queuing for Cup Final tickets than a potential theatre audience.

I managed to steer Audrey across the road to the entrance but further progress was blocked by a policeman who demanded to know where we were going. I tried to explain that I was the author and that I wished to see the manager about getting a couple of seats. He was unimpressed, 'I don't care whether you are the Sheik of bloody Araby, sunshine. They're hanging from the chandeliers in there. There's not a seat to be had.'

Audrey and I watched the crowds for a while and then, consoling ourselves *en route* with some fish and chips, we went home.

2

This was the beginning of yet another fairy-tale lease of life for dear old *No Trees in the Street*. Lew and Leslie Grade reacted with understandable enthusiasm and booked it into almost every major provincial theatre in the country. Quite often the play went to a theatre two or three times and, whether the venue was Edinburgh or Bristol, London or Newcastle, the people came in their thousands. In all, the tour lasted almost two years and only towards the end did the audiences show signs of falling away.

Not unnaturally, after a few weeks of such success, I began to get restless about my small weekly fee. I calculated that, had I been on a normal touring royalty of 5 per cent of gross takings I would have been earning between a hundred and two hundred pounds each week instead of twenty-five, and I decided that it was time to take action. Stanley Williscroft could do nothing to help – he too was on a fixed fee and any extra payment to me would have to come from his own pocket. The difficulty was that my contract was with him, not the Grades, and I could find no loophole in it. He suggested that I should go and see either Lew or Leslie and discuss the problem with them.

A day or so later I went to their offices in Regent Street where, after a few minutes, I was greeted in an offhand way by one of the assistants who explained that Lew and Leslie were tied up with a client. He had been deputed to help me. What was the problem? His expression made it plain that he really did not want to know the answer and that he was doing me a favour by being there at all.

After I had explained he set off on a complicated rigmarole of excuses. The Grades were not responsible since my agreement was with Williscroft – in any case, they had taken the initial risk and the overheads were enormous, all that sort of thing. What became clear was that the answer to my request was in the negative. I sat there in glum silence wondering what my next move should be and then, suddenly, he made a ghastly miscalculation. Taking my silence as an admission of defeat he smiled patronisingly and said, 'Listen. Leave it with me. Christmas is coming. You won't find two more generous men than Lew and Leslie. They'll look after you, don't worry.'

This was adding insult to injury – the equivalent of lighting the blue touch-paper on a firework – and I exploded with fury and flew at him. 'I've had enough of this. You can stuff your Christmas presents! I didn't come here for a bloody tip! I want my rights and I am not leaving here until I get them!' I sprayed him with a volley of four-letter words and announced, finally, that I would not move until I had seen Lew and Leslie in person.

Within a few minutes I was led in for my first ever meeting with this extraordinary pair of brothers. Lew, who is still striking deals to this day, is perhaps the last of the great showmen. Cast in the same rainbow mould as Goldwyn or Ziegfeld, he bounces through life like a beach-ball. His voice has the penetration of a road drill, his whisper would be another man's shout. In business, he flies, as they say, by the seat of his pants, impulsively making decisions by instinct rather than considered thought. That his instinct is right more often than wrong is proved by his success. Yet although Lew has made a lot of money out of show business – and lost quite a lot at times – money is not the engine that drives him. He just loves playing the game and he will go on playing it to the end.

Leslie, who died in 1979, was a much less flamboyant figure, a quietly spoken, smiling man with a mind as sharp as a razor who seemed happy to play clarinet to Lew's trumpet. He was the organiser, the one who often tightened the nuts and bolts on his brother's impulsive deals. Leslie also suffered from telephonitis and it was not unusual to see him conduct two or three phone conversations at the same time. He drove himself without mercy and, in the end, the stress was too much. He fought back from a massive stroke in 1966 but thirteen years later a double heart attack killed him.

I got to know them both well in later years but on that morning in 1950 they were just names to me. Lew walked up and down with the light, spring-heeled Jack tread of a dancer, Leslie faced me from behind a desk. Still steamed-up and prepared for a fight to the death I ran through my complaint yet again, stressing the injustice of the situation.

'Everybody is making money out of the play except me!' I said. 'I created it, and all I get is a pittance!'

To my astonishment, Lew nodded. 'No argument. I've talked it over with Leslie. On takings up to two thousand a week we'll pay you a hundred. Over two thousand, one hundred and fifty. Back-dated one month. Does that suit you?'

He held out a hand and I grasped it thankfully. The interview had lasted no more than five minutes and I had come out of it with a very satisfactory increase. I was to shake that hand on a deal many times in the future and to learn that a handshake from Lew was more than a promise, it was a contract.

Some years later Leslie told me that the tour of *No Trees in the Street* had come in the nick of time for the Grade agency. The brothers were overstretched financially and the profits from the play, around two thousand pounds a week, had provided them with a cash flow which put them back on an even keel.

3

With the cushion of this extra money behind me I decided to invest in my first car. New cars were still at a premium so I consulted Charlie, an old friend who had once been the getaway driver for a gang of smash-and-grab merchants and who, among other things, dabbled in the second-hand motor trade.

After a few days he took me along to a decrepit garage in Kentish Town and introduced me to a pre-war Austin Seven Ruby saloon. It had, he said, been the property of a vicar who had looked after it like one of his flock. Charlie assured me that he had checked it over carefully; it was in perfect nick and a snip at two hundred pounds. The owner of the garage, on Charlie's say-so, agreed to accept half of this on the spot, the rest to be paid over three months.

Settling in cash to save the embarrassment of asking Audrey to countersign a cheque, I explained later that a car was an absolutely vital necessity, a statement that left her unmoved. She gave me a hard time over my extravagance but after a while she became as fond of the little car as I was and even christened it Ruby.

It soon became obvious to me that the vicar still exercised a sort of long-distance influence over Ruby. I was sure that she had strong religious convictions and resented being driven by a pagan non-believer like myself. From time to time, for no apparent reason, she would stop – presumably to pray – and the only thing to do in these circumstances was to respect her desire for privacy and leave well alone for a few minutes. Her orisons concluded, she would start again quite happily as if communication with the Almighty had somehow recharged her batteries.

Apart from this crotchet, Ruby was a brave little thing who gave sturdy service and put up with a good deal at my hands. At regular intervals I used to load her from bow to stern with children from the street and drive off to the river Chess near Watford where we could picnic in a farmer's field and splash about in the stream. On one famous occasion I put five children aboard plus some gear and supplies and the gallant Ruby hauled us down to Sheepcote Valley near Brighton where we set up camp for a week.

I am not the Boy Scout type and it was pretty rough and ready stuff. Baked beans and milk for breakfast, fish and chips and ice-cream for lunch and in the evening a fearsome concoction known as Ted's Stew, the full recipe for which is a trade secret, though I can reveal that the principal ingredients were tomato soup, chips and turnips boiled until they become a pink goo. The children, who would not have touched such slush with a bargepole in their own homes, fell upon it with all the enthusiasm of hungry tigers. I was the only one who didn't touch it – I knew what it was made of.

A relief column arrived mid-week in the shape of a heavily pregnant Audrey and Mrs Benjamin, who brought vital supplies and an extra camper. Mrs B's young daughter Betty was so impressed with the outdoor life that she begged to be allowed to stay and so my little company became six. No doubt with the thought of the journey back seething under her bonnet, Ruby stood silent beside the tents, deep in prayer.

I coped with most of the problems reasonably well. At night, after we'd had a singo round the camp-fire and I had told a story or two about my exploits on the moon or how I had won the war more or less single-handed, I tucked the children away in their sleeping bags in the big tent and sat outside, eating the ham rolls that I'd bought surreptitiously during the day and reading by the light of a hurricane lamp. From time to time, a little voice would cry out urgently and I passed in the seaside bucket so that the pressures of nature might be relieved. Each morning I was aroused by a swarm of hungry children.

The only thing that really defeated me was little Betty's hair which hung in two dark plaits – I could not get these right no matter how I tried and was forced to send her over to a neighbouring family of campers and the skilful hands of the lady of the house. Ruby brought this full load home safely to Maida Vale at the end of the week, although she was so exhausted by the end that for two days after she refused to start.

These and other exploits earned me the local title of King of the Kids and so it was with mixed feelings that I received a call from the twin-set lady of the LCC to say that a house might be available sooner than expected. Would we care to go and look at it?

4

The house was not in Loughton, Essex, as we had expected but at Petts Wood in Kent. We were North Londoners who naturally viewed anything or anyone south of the river Thames with dark suspicion. It was widely rumoured in Tottenham and Camden Town that the denizens in the south ate their babies for breakfast. We were surprised and relieved to find that the folk of Petts Wood seemed, in every way, to be as human as those superior beings who had the wit and good taste to live on the northern side of the river.

I had been told that one has an instant reaction to a house, either positive or negative, and this was certainly our experience. With us it was love at first sight. Set at the end of a little close it had a huge garden which dipped away from the house and then rose again; a magnificent old oak commanded the scene and all around it the ground was green with bracken. It took us a few minutes to realise that the unfamiliar but exhilarating fragrance that we could scent all around us was actually fresh air.

The house had a simple no-nonsense appearance which was attractive in itself and, to flat-dwellers like ourselves, the interior was a delight. Four bedrooms of decent size, one of which would be ideal for my workroom, a fitted kitchen big enough to eat in, a large, light sitting-room, plus the luxury of two toilets and central heating. I tell you, the old LCC did things well in those days!

I signed a seven-year rental agreement at four pounds ten shillings a week, praying inwardly that *No Trees in the Street* would keep up the good work. We were told that the house would be ready for occupation in about six weeks which, since Audrey was due to yield up our second child in a month, was pretty good timing. In fact, she gave birth to a daughter in Queen Mary's Hospital, Hampstead, three weeks later.

John and I were keeping each other company at home while this was happening and I heard the news early in the morning when I rang the hospital. John stood beside me in his pyjamas, as eager to know about the fourth member of our family as I was. I'd wanted a daughter to complete the set and I could hardly contain my delight when the nurse told me that

Audrey had kindly obliged. Turning to John, I said excitedly, 'You've got a sister! A little sister!'

His face fell and the bottom lip began to tremble. I remembered then that, despite all we could say, he had set his heart determinedly on a brother.

'I don't want a sister!' he wailed. 'I want a brother!'

I needed to do some quick thinking. 'I'll talk to the hospital,' I said, 'and see if they can change her for a boy.'

Surreptitiously holding the bar of the telephone down, I went through the charade of speaking to the hospital. 'I am afraid there has been some mistake. We ordered a boy. Is it possible to change?'

After a minute or so of this imaginary conversation, I put my hand over the receiver and turned to my waiting son. 'There's a problem. They've run out of boys and they won't have any in for ages and ages. Maybe a year. Do you want your mum to stay there and wait for a boy or shall we tell her to take the girl and come home? It's up to you, son.'

A dreadful moment while he considered this. I felt as if I were standing at the edge of a big black hole. Then he sighed, and shrugged his shoulders in resignation. 'I want my mum to come home. We'll have the girl.'

I hugged him, delighted that the pull of his mother was stronger than his desire for a brother. But more trouble was to follow. Over breakfast, having given the question of his new sister some thought he said, 'I want to call her Ginger.'

'Oh, I don't think we can do that,' I said carefully. 'It's not a proper name. It's a nickname.'

'Yes, it is,' he insisted. 'What about my friend at school? She's called Ginger and she's nice.' I recalled that he did indeed have a little carroty-haired friend at nursery school whose actual name was Eleanor.

We discussed the issue for a while. Audrey and I had already decided that if the new baby were a girl she should be named Sally Ann. Not wishing John to feel that he had not been consulted on this important family matter, I did not mention this choice. Instead I decided on another desperate gamble and made a second spurious phone call to the hospital.

'My name is Willis,' I said. 'I rang a while ago and agreed to accept a girl. We will need to give her a name. Can you tell me what names you have left on the list?'

I nodded and murmured as if taking in the reply. My wells of inspiration were fast drying up. I turned to John. 'They have only three girl's names left. We can have either Diphtheria, Chloroform or Sally Ann. Which would you like?'

He evidently did not care for any of them but the natural good taste of the Willis clan prevailed and he replied, 'Sally Ann, I suppose.'

He was content after this, feeling that he had a proprietary interest in his new sister since he had both picked and named her. God knows what I would have done had he chosen one of the other names!

Sally Ann was two weeks old when we said a sad farewell to our friends in Delaware Road and moved into number 2 Sefton Close, Petts Wood, where we were to spend ten happy years.

There must have been some special essence in the air of that friendly little close. When we first settled there our immediate neighbours were a young barrister, a junior civil servant, a newspaper reporter and a fledgling accountant. Thirty years later, when we had all moved on, the barrister had become the Honourable Judge Finlay and his wife the deputy chairman of the Equal Opportunities Commission; the civil servant was transformed into Sir Frank Wood, Permanent Secretary at the Ministry of Defence; the reporter had made it to features editor of a national newspaper and the accountant was financial controller of a major publishing company.

But all that was in the future. In the meantime we were all struggling to make our way. I knew that the tour of *No Trees in the Street* could not last much longer and that I now had an enlarged family on my hands. However, 2 Sefton Close proved to be a lucky house. Within a week of moving in, Jack Hylton's office rang and asked me to go in and see the great man, a call came from BBC Television at Alexandra Palace with an offer of work and Margery Vosper telephoned to say that *No Trees in the Street* was to be produced in Hamburg and Sydney, Australia. The late Jimmy Hanley, who had played a young policeman in *The Blue Lamp*, headed the cast for the Australian presentation.

These two overseas productions were, to all intents and purposes, the end of the line for the play which had survived against mighty odds. It did not receive another professional outing. I went over to Hamburg for the German opening and found myself seated next to one of the actors at the after-show supper. In the course of conversation I asked if he had ever been to London.

'Dozens of times,' he replied, 'but I never stayed.'

It turned out that he had served in the Luftwaffe during the war!

Chapter Nine

1

Alexandra Palace had been a happy hunting ground for me as a boy: it was under its domed ceilings and on its sweeping terraces that I had acted out my fantasies, transforming myself at a stroke of swash and buckle into such heroes as Richard the Lionheart returned from the Crusades, the Black Prince, Robin Hood and Douglas Fairbanks. Now I had come back to a fantasy world that, paradoxically, was real, to a world where dreams and stories were turned into images and beamed out to thousands of homes by means of an electronic miracle.

This was then the production centre for BBC Television. The great mast, set at the highest point, loomed on the skyline like some watchful iron sentinel and below, in parts of the palace that had been converted to studios, the producers, directors, writers, actors and technicians struggled to come to terms with and master the complexities of this new medium. In those faraway days we were all learners and it was exciting – and a privilege – simply to be there.

I had been called in to do some work on a comedy series called *The Handlebar*. Originally conceived by writer and composer Joe Shellard, the BBC felt that the concept needed another pair of hands and I was asked to work with Joe. The central idea was a simple one: the mishaps and adventures of two ex-RAF characters who, without previous experience, take over the running of a country pub. Jimmy Edwards and Humphrey Lestocq were to play the leads and the title referred not only to the name of the pub but also to Jimmy's famous handlebar moustache.

A simple idea, as I said, but fiendishly complex to work out. Tommy Handley was then at the height of his popularity with

ITMA on radio and our task was not made any easier when the producer blandly told us that he saw the series as 'television's answer to ITMA'.

Joe and I laboured long and hard over the scripts but almost from the beginning I had an inner sense of doom. In the first place, neither of us had the wit or experience of Tommy Handley's writers and in the second, the series asked too much from television's infant and limited resources. Today a programme can be shot in colour on video or film, edited and transmitted later; modern techniques and cameras make it possible to move easily from scene to scene, to mix in reaction shots, to create all kinds of special effects.

No such luxury for *The Handlebar*. We went out in black and white live on the night with no margin for error and no time to correct any that were made. We had three sets in the studio and when a character had to move from one scene to another it was necessary to write in a few lines of 'covering dialogue' to give him time to hotfoot it to the next set and to allow the heavy cameras to be manhandled across the studio floor. Comedy on television needs flexibility and this we did not have.

The best of the six episodes that went out owed much to the irrepressible Jimmy Edwards. Feeling, no doubt, that things needed livening up a bit he went into the studio early and surreptitiously laced the substitute and innocuous pub 'beer' with whisky and brandy. He poured with a generous hand as always and the effect on the cast was exhilarating. The custom then was to do a full rehearsal of the episode first and then go straight on to the live performance. By the end of the rehearsal the actors were moving and speaking with a freedom which gave promise of a very interesting evening ahead.

One actor, who was playing the role of an ancient and regular customer, got so carried away that, without benefit of script, he began to sing 'Roll Out the Barrel'. It so happened that another scene was being shot at the other end of the studio and the dialogue was accompanied throughout by the lusty voice of the ancient. This so disconcerted another actor that he jumped his lines and effectively cut three minutes from the programme's running time. When the bewildered director finally called for the final fade out, the entire company, in

roaring mood, made a concerted rush for more of Jimmy's
lethal cocktail.

The Handlebar ran for its allotted six episodes and then
faded into oblivion. But the experience had further whetted
my appetite for television. I knew that I had a long way to go
before I could write with confidence for this new medium but
at least I had my feet on the learning curve.

2

I had now completed the dramatisation of *The Blue Lamp*,
using some of the material originated by Jan Read. It was
an ambitious effort with many scenes and requiring a large
cast – it would need a big theatre and the backing of a major
management. Jack Warner had expressed enthusiasm for the
project and, at his suggestion, we sent the playscript to Jack
Hylton.

Hylton had now established himself as one of London's
leading producers, specialising in large-scale musicals, revues
and variety. During his career he mounted dozens of successful productions, among them the famous Crazy Gang shows
which ran for years with comedy stars Flanagan and Allen,
Nervo and Knox, Naughton and Gold and the inimitable
Monsewer Eddie Gray. He bought the hit radio programme
Take It From Here, written by Frank Muir and Denis Norden,
and promoted it to an equal success on stage. Another venture, a revue called *La Plume de Ma Tante* also packed in the
audiences.

I was well pleased, therefore, when a call came from
Hylton's office indicating that he was interested in *The Blue
Lamp* and inviting me to see him. At the meeting he was brief
and business-like. He would put the play on in Blackpool for
a summer season and if that proved successful he intended to
bring it to London. Terms were agreed with Margery Vosper
and we were in business. This, for me, was the beginning of
a ten-year roller-coaster association with Jack Hylton.

Jack is a difficult character to fix on the page. A working-
class lad from Lancashire who had begun his career as a
clog-dancer, he appeared to have two consuming interests in
his life, show business and women. Money was important too

but principally as the means to fuel these twin pursuits. He did not look at all like a great lover – he was no Cary Grant or Clark Gable. Short and plump without actually being fat, he had fair pinkish skin, blond eyebrows, wavy marmalade-coloured hair and he never appeared publicly in anything but immaculate Savile Row clothes. The eyes were shrewd and penetrating, the brain as quick as a computer and by nature he was an extraordinary mixture of generosity and ruthlessness. A legally signed contract meant little to him. If he wanted to break one he simply did just that, defying the other party to sue him while knowing full well that few could afford to do so.

I had some personal experience of this. The production of *The Blue Lamp* at Blackpool filled the Grand Theatre to capacity and proved itself to be just as great a success as the film. The weekly take was about six thousand pounds, a big sum in those days; Jan Read and I were on 5 per cent of the gross and were well satisfied. However, after about a month, Jack invited me to lunch and asked me to reduce this royalty by 1 per cent, claiming that the play was cripplingly expensive to run. There were, he said, four big stars to pay, Jack Warner, Gordon Harker, Susan Shaw and Bonor Colleano; in addition, he had been forced to install a revolve to cope with the scene changes and since this had to be operated manually there were extra back-stage staff to pay. Unless he could cut costs, he argued, there was no possibility of bringing the play into London after Blackpool.

It was no use my pointing out that he had signed a contract stipulating a royalty of 5 per cent on tour and more when the play came to London. Nor did it make any impression when I said, mildly, that I had it on good authority that he was making well over a thousand pounds a week profit from the Blackpool run. He denied the figure and insisted that costs had to be cut. Later I learned that he had approached Jack Warner and other members of the cast with a similar demand.

I had to think fast. Jack was a powerful and influential producer and at this stage of my career I could not afford to fall out with him. Deciding to play for time, I told him that I could not take the decision alone; my associate, Jan Read, would have to be consulted since he was financially involved. A week or so went by as I tried to postpone the moment of decision but eventually I had to come face to face with Jack again. I told him that I had spoken with Jan and that he was totally opposed to any reduction in his share of the royalties.

Jack smiled a lot, and he was smiling when he replied, 'Too bad. But never mind, we'll take a half per cent from your share.' Which is exactly what he did – from then on, while *The Blue Lamp*, a play which I had written in its entirety, was at Blackpool I received a 2 per cent royalty and when it came to the Hippodrome, London, and the royalties increased, Jack still imposed a $1/_2$ per cent cut on my share. I had neither the nerve nor the resources to fight him.

This was the business face of Jack, the tough operator at work; in private, by contrast, he was a man of almost careless generosity. Some of his acts of kindness were out of this world. I once saw him, without a second's thought, write out a cheque for a thousand pounds to pay for medical care for the crippled daughter of one of his stage managers.

I happened to mention one day that Ruby, my gallant little motor-car, had reached the end of her tether. New cars were still hard to come by and I asked if he had any influence with the main dealers. His reply shook me to the roots.

'I can do better than that. Go and see Nicky, my chauffeur. There's a brand new Ford Prefect in the garage. If you like it, you can have it.'

I was off to see Nicky like a streak of lightning. Sure enough, there in the garage was this spanking new blue Ford which, after the limitations of Ruby, looked to me like a Rolls-Royce. The only thing that puzzled me was that it had been built for export and had left-hand drive. Nicky unravelled the mystery.

'The guv'nor bought it for one of his lady friends. She was French, wanted the car to drive over there. But the guv'nor found out that she was having it away with someone else, took the car back and told her to get lost.'

I went back to Jack and told him that I loved the car but I could not accept such an expensive gift. He simply shrugged and suggested that I give him what he had paid for it, a sum of three hundred pounds. I could not pay this all at once and said so. 'No hurry,' he replied. 'Pay me as and when you can.'

When I showed the new car to Charlie, my smash-and-grab driver friend, he valued it at eight hundred pounds and, when I sold it four years later, I made a 100 per cent profit on my original investment.

Jack's generosity spilled over when it came to his girl-friends on whom he lavished cars, clothes, jewellery and even apartments. He put some of them on the pay-roll of his shows, listing them ironically as wardrobe mistresses. What they had to do in return was pretty obvious for Jack had a voracious sexual appetite. He was, as I learned from one of his ladies, a sexual performer *par excellence*; another girlfriend described him, with evident satisfaction, as the male equivalent of a nymphomaniac. In addition to whichever regular mistress was currently enjoying his favours, it was said that he kept a girl in a separate flat with instructions that she be there between two o'clock and five each afternoon just in case, after lunch, he felt in need of further refreshment!

3

We held the auditions for some of the supporting roles in *The Blue Lamp* at the Adelphi Theatre in the Strand. These thespian ordeals are sometimes referred to in the business as cattle markets and there is a lot to be said for the description. A selection of hopeful actors and actresses followed each other on stage where they read a few lines of script and occasionally answered questions posed by the director, Richard (Dicky) Bird. Then, for all but a few, it was the usual show business words of farewell. 'Lovely, lovely. Thank you. Next!'

Dicky Bird was a large, rumbustious character with a considerable reputation as a producer of comedy and musicals. Heavily built, gravel-voiced, with a face the colour of a ripening plum, he was constantly breathless and seemed to me always in imminent danger of a seizure. Despite this, while he could not come anywhere near Jack Hylton, he had a sex drive of which your average buck rabbit would have been proud.

Towards the end of the auditions he suddenly turned to me in some alarm and murmured, 'How many more girls do we need?'

I consulted the list. 'One. We need a girl of between twenty-five and thirty to play a policewoman.'

'My God,' he said breathlessly, 'I hope I haven't left it too late. We're in Blackpool for over three months and I haven't fixed myself up with any crumpet.'

The girls came on stage one by one for inspection with Dicky leaning forward from his seat in the stalls watching with keener interest. When the fourth or fifth entered his breathing quickened and, when she had read her lines, he called, 'Come on down here, dear. Here.'

She descended from the stage and, taking her arm, he drew her into the dim light of the gangway. I heard an exchange of whispers and then, like the explosion of an inflated paper bag, a sharp slap. Her voice rang out in the empty theatre, 'What's my name? You fucked me night and day for two weeks in Birmingham last year and you have the bloody cheek to ask my name!'

Dicky came ruefully back to his seat, breathing dangerously. He looked at me and shrugged, 'Well,' he said, 'I didn't see her with her clothes on very often.'

The auditions continued. He did not fill the part of the policewoman that day and when the full rehearsals began I wasn't really surprised to discover that the girl who had slapped Dicky down had got the role. They spent a lot of time together in Blackpool and, as far as her name was concerned, he became word perfect.

The Blue Lamp duly opened in London in November and received some very good notices. Unfortunately, a real old-fashioned pea-souper fog descended on the streets on the third night and, infuriatingly, hung around for almost a week. The box office never really recovered from this setback for, by the time the fog had lifted, we were into the pre-Christmas period which is a notoriously bad time for theatre.

The play clung on until early March and then the notices went up. On the last night Audrey and I had supper with Jack who seemed quite cheerful – he was always a good loser. During the course of the meal he turned to me and said casually, 'I'm going to Paris next week to look at a new comedy. Would you like to come? If you're interested maybe you can adapt it for the English stage.'

He brushed aside the fact that I spoke only a few words of fractured French, assuring me that he would provide a literal translation for me to work from. All this actually came to pass. I saw the play, which I did not understand but which had the Parisian audience splitting their sides, and expressed some doubts about its chances in England. However, Jack was more enthusiastic and eventually in collaboration with Talbot Rothwell – who later wrote many of the *Carry On* films – I made the adaptation. The English title, I think, was *A Kiss for Adèle*. It opened at the Royal Court Theatre in Sloane Square and after a brief, undistinguished run faded from view. I cannot even recall what it was about.

But if the play did little to rivet my attention in Paris, there was another real-life comedy that did. It was performed for the most part in Jack Hylton's suite at Claridge's Hotel on the Champs-Elysée.

4

There were times during those three or four days in Paris when I felt superfluous to requirements, like a spare groom at a wedding. Jack kept insisting that he would discuss the play with me but never got round to it. He was too busy making deals and bedding the available talent.

Exchange controls were in force at the time which meant the amount of money one could take out of England was limited by law. This did not seem to deter Jack, who had a large attaché-case stacked to the brim with French francs, so much so that when he flicked the latches the lid sprang open as if on springs and the money spilled over. Soon after our arrival he introduced me to the case, gave me a fistful of notes and said, 'You're in Paris now, lad. Make the most of it. Enjoy yourself.'

I did not need to go out to find entertainment. A bubbling stream of volatile French and Italian producers flowed through Jack's suite all eager to do business. Any translations were done by Gino Arbib, Jack's international manager, a tall, grave, courteous man with the thin-lipped look of someone who was on the way to a funeral. From time to time Pat Marlow, the current mistress-in-residence, floated in and out, leaving behind a faint drift of expensive and provocative perfume.

Pat was a stunningly beautiful girl. The daughter of a Chatham taxi-driver, Jack had selected her for the chorus of one of his shows and then rapidly promoted her to the role of girlfriend. I admired his taste, for as well as beauty she had wit, intelligence and a graceful charm which could illuminate any dinner-table. In a previous age she might have been a great and famous courtesan.

Jack once confessed to me that Pat was the only woman he had ever truly loved. He had a sentimental streak to his nature – and this might well have coloured his words – but it is certainly true that long after their affair had ended he kept in touch with her, helped when she was in trouble and when she tragically committed suicide leaving a small baby, Jack stepped in and made provision for the child's future. That he was not the father was of no consequence.

On the second afternoon of our stay, Pat took me aside and exploded a small bombshell. She said that she was leaving for New York the next morning to get married to a young South American businessman. The trip to Paris had been in the nature of a farewell to Jack.

'Please,' she begged, 'keep an eye on him for me. He's fond of you, he trusts you. Don't let him get too upset.'

'Does he know that you're leaving to get married?' I asked.

'Of course. We talked it over. He said he won't stand in my way.'

'And are you in love with this man in New York?'

She shrugged. 'I don't know. What is love? I like him a lot and he's very kind.'

'And rich?'

'Of course,' she replied gravely, 'very rich.'

A subdued Jack came back from the airport the next afternoon having seen Pat on to her transatlantic flight. Within a few minutes of his return there was a knock at the door of the suite and when I opened it I found myself facing two lovely girls who looked so alike that they had to be twins.

'We have an appointment with Monsieur Jack,' one said, in English that was certainly better than my French.

There followed a few minutes of giggling and slap and tickle then the three of them disappeared into the bedroom. I went to my room to do some work and left Jack to it for a couple of hours. When I returned to the suite the trio was just emerging – the two girls looked exhausted but Jack seemed to be as fresh as ever, his spirits completely recovered. He opened the famous case and gave each girl a handful of money. When they had gone he smiled with satisfaction and said, 'I needed a tonic.'

That night, after a long and cheerful dinner, I went thankfully to my bed with the rather naïve thought that the revels were over. It was not to be. Just before midnight the telephone rang.

'What are you doing?' asked Jack.

'I'm in bed,' I replied. 'I was almost asleep.'

'In bed!' He sounded almost indignant. 'Look, I'll meet you downstairs in five minutes. We'll go to the Piano Club – it's only round the corner.'

5

A heavy gentleman who looked as if he doubled in his spare time as a hit-man for the Mafia ushered us respectfully to a table just in front of the tiny stage. He clearly knew Jack or had heard of him for he treated him like a visiting Emir. The heavy gave us each a menu and with a little bow said, 'If there is anything that Monsieur Jack or his friend likes to fancy, please to let me know.'

'After that dinner, I couldn't eat a thing, Jack,' I said putting down the menu.

'It's not a bloody menu, lad,' he said. 'It's the programme.'

Wine was brought, the room lights dimmed and the show began. A parade of exquisitely shaped young ladies stripped and dressed and stripped again, sometimes with the help of a man who invariably kept his clothes on. Various items of flimsy underwear descended on our table from time to time. I had never seen a strip show before and I have to admit that this one was impressive, it had a certain style.

During the performance, Jack took out his gold fountain-pen and ticked off two or three of the acts on the programme. When the lights went up again he offered me the pen.

'Did you see anything you fancy?' he asked.

I had indeed. One would have had to have ice-water in one's veins not to be turned on by some of these performers. On the other hand, I'm hopeless at one-night stands and the stuffiness of the crowded room had increased my exhaustion.

'Not tonight, Jack,' I said apologetically. 'I'm too tired, I couldn't manage it.'

'That's easily settled!' He pulled on a long thin gold chain and hauled a small gold pill-box from a trouser pocket. Inside were some ominous-looking off-white pills, tiny things, like grains of rice. 'Put two of these on the tip of your tongue and let them dissolve. In a few minutes you'll feel like a young buck.' He demonstrated by putting two pills on his own tongue and I followed suit.

I regret to say that they did nothing for me. Eventually as Jack began to entertain one of the performers, a lovely girl in a chic suit, I managed to make my excuses and slip away. Jack's farewell look indicated that he was deeply disappointed in me. When I went to his suite the next morning, the lovely was just leaving and Jack, looking as fresh and chirpy as a newborn chick, reproached me with a shake of the head, 'You must be daft, Ted. You don't know what you missed.'

Some months later I met Jack's doctor at a social gathering and out of curiosity I asked him if he knew anything about those little white aphrodisiac pills. He had taken a drop and leaning towards me he whispered, 'Aspirin. Tiny aspirin. I make them up for him.' He tapped his forehead. 'It's all in his mind.'

This, I would submit, was only a half-truth. Jack had an awful lot elsewhere.

6

I was lucky in that I could escape from this sort of madness to the sanity of my home in Petts Wood. Audrey shares my abhorrence of cocktail parties, night clubs, film premières and the synthetic razzle-dazzle which seems to be an inseparable part of show business and, as far as possible, we avoided such activities. I was warned more than once that I ought to be seen at the favourite watering-holes of fashionable and powerful producers but I have never regretted ignoring this advice. I was away so much that I snatched at any chance to be with Audrey and the children.

By working late into the night I was able to organise a good deal of time with them. When at home I often met Sally and John from school and took them and their friends to picnics or to the cinema. I put up a cricket net in the garden and bowled to John for hours – he would never allow me to bat!

At night I supervised their baths, put them to bed and spun them stories which I usually made up as I went along. Then, as they slept, it was back to writing, which was no hardship – there is nothing like the telephone-free peace of the small hours for getting the creative juices flowing.

I have always been able to write almost anywhere – in hotel rooms, on aeroplanes, even in the library of the House of Lords – but I am happiest in the private and personal space of my own workroom. Here, untidily surrounded by shelves of books, playbills, photographs and mementoes, and facing a framed film poster of Mary Pickford in *A Beast at Bay*, I can take refuge from outside pressures and work in tranquillity. When I close the door and go to my old desk I feel a kind of unity with the crowded room, a surge of warmth, as if it has been waiting to welcome me.

Audrey always stood guard over my privacy, repelling all boarders, and the children had been taught not to disturb Dad when he was at work. But I remember one occasion when John, who was about five at the time, slipped the net and came in to me with a furrowed brow and a question which clearly to him was of grave importance.

'Dad,' he said, 'what is the rudest word in the world?'

After a moment's thought I decided to be a progressive parent and answer boldly, truthfully. 'Fuck,' I said. 'Fuck is the rudest word in the world – and you must never, never use it.'

Some weeks passed and he toddled off to a friend's birthday party from which he returned after only an hour in tears. The friend's mother, it seemed, had sent him home in disgrace.

'What did you do?' I asked.

'I don't know.' He seemed to be genuinely perplexed and went on, 'Dad, is sugar-bugger rude?'

'It isn't very nice.'

'Is bacon-bonce rude?'

'Not very nice.'

'Well, Jimmy Kirby said sugar-bugger is the rudest word in the world. Ian Martin said it's bacon-bonce. But I told them that fuck is the rudest word in the world – my dad said so. That's when the lady made me come home.'

I took him to the cinema to make up for his disappointment and that ended my experiment in progressive parenting!

Chapter Ten

1

In the mid-fifties a number of so-called independent producers were working out of the Rank film studios at Pinewood. I qualify their status because in the film business, and to some extent in television, it is difficult for any but the mighty to be truly independent. The small producer who is enthusiastic about a subject often has to go, begging-bowl in hand, to a major company to get the money just to start – even if he can raise this initial sum himself and get a script written he still has to convince one of the big distributors to put up the mountain of dollars needed to get the movie on to the screen.

With so much money at stake, the backer makes demands. He may be an illiterate in film terms, scarcely able to read a screenplay with a magnifying glass, but he has to demonstrate his power and protect his investment. So he might well ask for changes to the script, the signing of a big box-office star for the lead, a different title, a more stringent budget, an exorbitant share of the profits. The producer may disagree with all these proposals but, desperate to get his picture into production, he is often forced to bow the knee.

Many a stubborn independent has spent years going from distributor to distributor in the hope that he can make the picture he wants to make without crippling concessions. Independent production is a war-game – nobody actually dies but it is frazzling to the nerves, hazardous to health, perilous to private life and a financial disaster area. Only the fittest survive in a world in which a promise is like a piecrust, made to be broken.

Of one financier in the business it used to be said that from him 'a firm handshake on a deal was a flabby maybe'.

I knew of one small producer who had bought an option on a novel and who was promised a deal if he came back with a screenplay. The poor unsuspecting man took the promise at face value and remortgaged his house so that he could pay a leading screenwriter to adapt the book. He delivered the draft script to the distributor and waited three agonising months for a reply. Finally, the script came back with a flat rejection. The desperate producer sought an interview to discover the reason, only to be told, 'It's a great subject, a great screenplay. I liked it. But we must think of the women in the audience. I gave it to Lesley to read and she hated every word.'

Lesley was the great man's eighteen-year-old mistress.

That was some years ago but I don't believe things are all that much better now. There are too many accountants at the top of the business who think that their experience of creative accounting qualifies them to be the final arbiters of what will make good cinema. The wonder is not that so many bad films get made but that so many good ones get through.

The independent producers at Pinewood were a very mixed, not to say mixed-up, bunch. There was one I remember who seemed to have found a way to beat the system for in three years he survived handsomely without even getting near the making of a film. Another informed Alan McKinnon, a well-known film writer, that his screenplay was too short and told him to pad it out with 'Hello-Goodbye' dialogue. When Alan enquired what this meant the producer replied, 'You've got six people in a room, OK? A woman comes in. She goes around the others greeting them, OK? Hello, George, hello, Mary, hello, David and so on, OK? Then someone gets up to leave. So it's goodbye, George, goodbye, Mary – all that stuff, OK? You can fill up a couple of pages like that.'

Alan told this story at a meeting of the Screenwriters' Guild when he was speaking on the craft of screenwriting! A variation on this was the 'Up periscope' and 'Down periscope' dialogue that featured so prominently in the war pictures of the time. And, years later, when soap operas on television became popular, writers made frequent use of what came to be called 'By the way' dialogue. One character addressing another will say, 'By the way, whatever happened to old George?'

The other character can then explain at some length and the conversation about old George will fill up a couple of minutes.

I cannot remember why or how I got work at Pinewood. The first assignment was to collaborate on the screenplay of Norman Wisdom's first film, *Trouble in Store*, in which my main task was to invent 'sight gags'. If Norman's ice-cream is somehow catapulted across the table and falls into the ample cleavage of a stout lady, that is a sight gag. Charlie Chaplin was a master of such situations – by comparison ours were fifth-rate stuff.

Thereafter I was called in to write in the same vein on two more such comedies, *Top of the Form* and *Up to his Neck*. I cannot say that I enjoyed the experience and longed to get my teeth into some serious screenwriting. I wrote one decent little picture about a miscarriage of justice called *The Long Rope* for Julian Wintle, another independent but, this apart, Pinewood had me firmly tagged as a gag-man.

It was television that gave me the chance to escape. And my incurable habit of impulse buying which added an additional member to the family. On the way home from the studios one afternoon I pulled in at a kennels and, for five pounds, bought a puppy, a cross between a Labrador and an Alsatian; we named him Buster. He had a gentle and forgiving nature allied to a libido compared to which Jack Hylton rated as a monk. Buster's great-grandchildren are still padding around Petts Wood.

A fierce guardian of our children, Buster was the first in a line of dogs whose company brought us nothing but pleasure and whose passing we mourned bitterly.

2

Caryl Doncaster was a producer at the BBC and an early pioneer of the documentary on television. A handsome intense girl with a consuming passion for her work, she had been greatly influenced by the post-war Italian cinema and the naturalistic real-life approach of such films as *Open City* and *Bicycle Thief*. Caryl was the first person I heard use the term drama-documentary.

She had been given a free hand and much encouragement from her boss, Laurence Gilliam, a craggy, talented man under whose guidance a string of mould-breaking documentaries came out of the BBC, both on radio and television.

Aware of my work at World-Wide Pictures, Caryl asked me to write a one-hour programme about young apprentices in an engineering factory. I spent three or four days in a car plant at Luton and eventually presented her with a script which, to all intents and purposes, was a play. Transmitted with moderate success, she asked me to think up other ideas.

Before I could get back to her she rang me to say that she had a stunning, brilliant, wonderful plan for a series of six programmes. All Caryl's ideas, at least in the initial stages, were stunning, brilliant and wonderful, but I did not know this at the time and expressed suitable enthusiasm.

She operated out of the studios at Lime Grove where I had once worked for Sydney Box so, for me, it was a little like going home. Television had got into its post-war stride by now: it was rapidly overtaking radio in terms of popularity and the first lobbies for commercial TV were forming in the wings. Lime Grove buzzed with excitement and activity.

To my surprise, Caryl's stunning idea for the new series turned out to be mine. Three or four years earlier I had written a play for Unity called *What Happens to Love?* which dramatised in a documentary style the rise and decline of the relationship between a young man and a girl. It showed them meeting, falling in love, getting married and eventually, because of various social and personal pressures, heading for the divorce court. Suitably adapted, the play had recently gone out on radio and Caryl had heard the broadcast. She proposed that I should take this theme and develop it into a six-part series to be called *The Pattern of Marriage*.

Some statistics had been published around this time indicating that an alarming number of marriages were breaking down after a year or two and Caryl asked me to dig rather deeper into the reasons than I had been able to do in the play. I spent three weeks talking to marriage guidance counsellors, churchmen and a few recently married young people and sat in the divorce courts for two days listening to some sad and often weird stories.

My admittedly limited investigations put sexual problems as the number one runner, with financial hardship, housing and social pressures close behind. All this may sound obvious today to an audience which has been drenched in explicit documentaries about this and other issues but forty years ago we were hemmed in by tighter moral frontiers and the subject was a ticklish one.

How, for example, could we dramatise sexual ignorance? One marriage guidance counsellor in the East End told me of a young couple whose marriage had reached breaking point because for six months the husband had been trying to enter his wife through her navel. Nobody had told him that there was another, easier, route. On the other hand, in the divorce court I heard a wife complain of her husband's unreasonable sexual demands. When at home he insisted that she walked around wearing nothing but a brief apron so that he did not have the chore of undressing her if the urge came upon him. Which, she said, could be five or six times in the course of an evening.

I wrote the scripts over eight painful weeks and, when I'd finished, I felt the inner glow that comes to every writer when he senses that he has touched the hem of something good. Caryl was delighted with the work and she signed Billie Whitelaw and Peter Byrne for the leads, two brilliant pieces of casting. The series fulfilled all our hopes: it was successful and controversial, and it brought in hundreds of letters, many of them so poignant that reading them was an agonising experience. The Marriage Guidance Council had an instant upsurge in business and in Parliament an MP put down a motion which led to a debate on the need for better sex education. The programme was a portent of what lay ahead for television. This powerful new medium was flexing its muscles and becoming an influential social force.

An extra bonus came my way as a result of my researches for *The Pattern of Marriage*. The Franciscan friars were noted for their unselfish social work and I went to their East London headquarters to discuss my programme with them. Two little West Indian children sat huddled together in the outer office, looking so lost and forlorn that I enquired about them. The kindly friar told me that their mother had been taken to hospital with tuberculosis and that they could not trace the father: they were looking for someone to care for the children for a few weeks.

To say that Audrey was astonished when I arrived on the

doorstep with two little black children would be to understate the case but, as usual, she took my eccentricities in her stride and the children to her heart. It was hard going at first for the little boy, Horace aged three, was so terrified that he would not leave his sister, who was five, for a single moment. He clung to her as to a life-line. The little girl, Margie, old beyond her years, comforted him like a mother and watched us warily.

Gradually, however, they relaxed, making friends with Sally and John and, as the days passed, became part of the family. The weeks stretched into months but eventually their mother was well enough to take them back. It was a wrench to part with them.

3

With *The Pattern of Marriage* I felt that my career had gone up a notch. The offers came in more frequently, my bank manager at Petts Wood began to greet me with a smile and I even acquired an accountant. For the first time I was able to pick and choose a little, to turn down a subject that did not appeal to me. And despite the increase in work for film and television I continued to serve my first love, the theatre.

It was Sydney Box who pointed me in the direction of my next play. We were lunching one day and the conversation came round to Richard Gordon and the runaway success of his book, *Doctor in the House*. Sydney mentioned that he had thought of adapting it for the stage but had abandoned the idea as impractical.

'It has no plot,' he said, 'dozens of characters and far too many scenes. Even if it were adapted, the cost of putting it on the stage would be ruinous.'

I argued that almost any novel could be shaped into a play but instead of stopping there I went on rashly to boast that not only could I adapt *Doctor in the House* but that I could do it with just one set and not more than ten characters. I think I must have taken a drop too much of the wine for I had not the slightest notion of how to back up my bluster. At any rate, Sydney called my bluff and bet me twenty-five pounds that it couldn't be done. I shook hands on the wager with a confidence I did not feel.

Richard Gordon readily gave his agreement although he too expressed some doubts about the feasibility of the project. I shut myself up in my room, already regretting my moment of impetuousness, and set to work. In the first two days nothing came, nothing at all. I just could not see a way to pull the material together into a dramatic whole but late on the third night something clicked in my head and the play came flowing out. I finished it in a week and, miracle of miracles, it had only one set and nine characters. Sydney paid up with a smile.

The first production of *Doctor in the House* was at Morecambe in Lancashire and Richard Gordon and I went up for the opening. We arrived in the evening of a bitterly cold day and the townsfolk seemed to be in winter hibernation; the summer cafés, fish shops, amusement arcades and ice-cream parlours were darkly shuttered as though in mourning. We found a small restaurant which was optimistically open and Richard, with equal optimism, asked for a dish of the famous local shrimps. The bored waitress looked at him as if he were a creature from another planet and we settled for egg and chips.

A little light relief came when we asked the way to the theatre and modestly revealed that our play was showing there.

'Your play!' she cried with unexpected animation. 'Which one is Richard Gordon?'

Richard made suitable acknowledgement whereupon she rushed into the kitchen and emerged with his famous book. Brushing me aside as if I were the mere hod-carrier and he the master bricklayer, she begged him to inscribe the book to Marlene. He wrote some generous words on the flyleaf and then, never a man to miss an opportunity, asked her what time the bookshop next door would open the next morning. I hadn't even noticed the existence of the shop but his keen medical eye had picked it up and he asked the now admiring Marlene to inform the proprietor that he would look in before returning to London and autograph his stock of *Doctor in the House*.

We made our way in the teeth of a fierce east wind through deserted streets to the theatre. My spirits, as chill and raw as the weather, were not improved by the sight of a handful of people waiting at the box office and a near empty foyer. Almost immediately, the bell went for curtain-up and we slipped dolefully into the auditorium. To our utter astonishment and delight the place was packed from floor to ceiling! What is more the audience stopped the show with laughter and applause at the moment the curtain went up and they saw the crazy cluttered set that represented Tony Grimsdyke's room. This sent the play off at a gallop and by the end of the evening we knew that we had a champion on our hands.

Jack Hylton bought the rights and presented *Doctor in the House* at the Victoria Palace where it played for eighteen months. In that cast were Anthea Askey, daughter of Arthur, and a young actor who was to make a considerable reputation on stage and become a popular television star in such roles as *Callan* and *The Equaliser*, Edward Woodward.

There followed tour after tour. Jimmy Edwards took the play to Canada where it repeated its English success; Robin Nedwell played the lead in Australia, in a production directed by a former star of *Emergency Ward Ten*, Charles (Bud) Tingwell, which ran for six months; there were productions in Hong Kong, New Zealand, Singapore, Kenya, South Africa, Scandinavia and even Iceland. The first British tour was succeeded by others at regular intervals. The play has been performed by almost every repertory theatre in the country, often two or three times, and by hundreds of amateur groups. Thirty-five years later, Richard Gordon and I still enjoy a small trickle of royalties from this enduring comedy.

Over a period of years I tried my hand at adapting two more of Richard's books. *Doctor at Sea*, starring Nicholas Parsons and Peter Jones, had a fair success and, more recently, Linda Lusardi and Peter Duncan did well with *Doctor on the Boil*, but neither of these plays enjoyed the runaway triumph of their predecessor.

While *Doctor in the House* was still playing at the Victoria Palace I received an unexpected call from a learned judge. The caller, His Honour Judge Leon, using the pen name Henry Cecil, had written a book which tried to do for young lawyers what Richard Gordon had done for medical students. It was neither as funny nor as good as Gordon's stories but it had achieved some success and the film rights had been bought by the Boulting Brothers. Harry Leon, as I came to know him, wanted me to adapt his book for the stage and, still floating on the euphoria of *Doctor in the House*, I agreed to have a crack at it.

Harry, as befitted a judge, cut an imposing figure but he had an engaging warmth and an impulsive generosity which negated a certain outward pomposity. It did not take me long to realise that he was both stage-struck and star-struck. His delight at being in the theatre, even if only on the margin, was like that of a child who has been given the key of a sweetshop, and this led to certain difficulties.

Whereas Richard Gordon had left me severely alone and accepted my playscript without question, Harry Leon wanted to be involved in the writing at every stage. The trouble lay in that he had no real dramatic instinct and he drafted lengthy scenes and literary dialogue which just would not work in the theatre. Eventually I had to put my foot down and insist that he left me alone to do the job I knew best. He was a man without malice and he retired gracefully to the wings.

But when the play was bought by a well-known touring management and went into rehearsal, he popped up again, bubbling with enthusiasm. He took time off from his legal duties to attend rehearsals and was never happier than when he shared a coffee break with the actors. On the opening night at Wimbledon he bought bottles of champagne for the startled cast who were unused to such lavishness and on the last evening of the week's run at that theatre he took them all out to supper after the final curtain. Since I was an equal partner in the play's earnings I felt that I ought to share the cost with him and coughed up 50 per cent of the bill.

Unfortunately it did not stop there. Harry went to the play at regular intervals while it was on tour and on each occasion, beaming like Pickwick, he invited the entire company – which included a very young Susan Hampshire – to join the authors for supper. When I suggested that perhaps this was gilding the lily a little too much, he said, 'But they are actors, dear boy, they don't eat very well – it's the least we can do.'

The tour was not a great success, partly because I hadn't got the play right, and our royalties didn't amount to much. When it was over I drew a rough balance and discovered that, thanks to the stage-struck judge, my income from *Brothers-in-Law* exceeded my expenditure only by a mere ten pounds.

4

Abroad again with Jack Hylton and his entourage, this time to Cannes and the annual Film Festival. This, you may remember, was the occasion when Peter Ustinov put his foot down – on me. The current lady-in-waiting to Jack was a nubile and volatile young Italian singer named Rosalini Neri; their relationship had lasted some time despite frequent pitched battles and Jack had tried, without much success, to advance her career on the London stage. Rosa was in her early twenties and there was about thirty years' difference in their ages. I liked her and we got on well together.

Film and television festivals have their uses but they are really no place for the writer. These jamborees are best suited to the wheelers and dealers of show business, to the money men and their sycophants who would not recognise a creative instinct if it bit them on the ear. I felt as out of place among the moguls at the Carlton Hotel as an office boy at a party for his bosses.

I got off to a bad start on the first evening when I wrecked a deal Jack was trying to set up. He introduced me to a Jewish-American couple who were interested in investing in his shows and while he talked business with the husband I was left to entertain the wife. I am not much of a judge of women's ornaments but even I could see that the jewellery that glittered on her fingers and around her throat did not come from Woolworth's.

For some reason we got on to the subject of her background and she launched into a long and complicated story about her escape to America from Nazi Germany. It involved an angel who appeared to her in a dream just as she was about to be arrested by the Gestapo and guided her to the home of a Belgian Roman Catholic archbishop who gave her shelter and papers and arranged her passage to the USA. She added that she came to Europe each year to see and thank the Archbishop, who was now a cardinal, and, as if to prove her story, produced a beautiful old cross from her handbag which he had given her as a present.

'So you see,' she said in conclusion, 'I was saved by a miracle. God sent the angel to lead me to safety.'

It was then that I said the wrong thing. 'What,' I asked, 'is so special about you?'

'I beg your pardon?' she said icily.

'What was your God doing when all the other millions of Jews were being driven into the concentration camps and gas chambers? Why didn't he send an angel to save them? Or at least to save the little children among them? Why select you? What had you done to deserve such divine intervention?'

I thought, and still do, that it was a reasonable question, though perhaps I put it too bluntly, but I had inflicted a serious wound. She jumped up from the table flapping her arms as if trying to ward off a swarm of hornets and strode away, her high heels clacking on the terrace. Over her shoulder she shrilled at her husband – the poor man must have thought that I had tried to touch his wife up under the table for he gave me a look which had 'Why on earth would anyone in his right senses want to do that?' written all over it and scuttled after her. They left Cannes two days later without speaking either to Jack or myself.

On the Saturday, Jack, Rosa, Arthur Wilcox, his personal assistant and I went along the front to the famous Felix restaurant for lunch. As usual, the place was crowded and we were seated at a small table crammed against the wall. Scarcely had we ordered our meal when a stunning girl, tall and graceful as a model, came drifting across and, putting her arms around Jack from behind, kissed him on the ear and neck.

'Ah, Jack, chéri. How beautiful to see you again,' she murmured in a sexy French accent.

Jack rose to greet this perfumed vision and I felt Rosa stir beside me. After a moment or two of conversation, the model gave Jack a kiss which hovered between friendship and passion, waved frostily to Rosa and moved on.

'Who was that?' breathed Rosa.

'That?' said Jack with careful carelessness. 'Oh, that's a girl who was in one of my shows.'

'Did you fuck her?' asked Rosa, who was ever one for directness.

'Rosa, Rosa!' he protested. 'She worked for me, nothing more.'

She glared at him, her breasts heaving like twin ferrets trying to escape from a sack. It would have been possible at this moment to cut the air with a blunt knife. Then she stood up and announced in a voice that hit the far wall of the restaurant and bounced back, 'I want to make pee-pee!'

This entailed a certain shifting of the chairs and the table but eventually she extricated herself and headed for the lavatory which, in those days, had to be approached via the kitchen. We rearranged ourselves, sat down again and waited. Five minutes passed, ten minutes, still no Rosa. An anxious Jack sent a waitress in to look for her.

When the girl returned to say that there was no sign of Mademoiselle, Jack moved into instant and clamorous action. 'Wilcox!' he shouted. 'Get to the hotel and get the box!'

Wilcox sprinted off with Jack and me puffing in pursuit. Too late. As we reached the Carlton an open-top white Alfa-Romeo shot past us with Rosa at the wheel and rapidly disappeared into the distance. Wilcox confirmed that the box had disappeared with her. A distraught Jack explained, not without a certain bitterness, that not only had he just bought Rosa the Alfa-Romeo but the box contained most of the jewellery he had bestowed upon her, total value about fifty thousand pounds. That is still a lot of money today but thirty years ago it was a considerable fortune.

Jack's anger subsided and his sentimental streak took over: he declared that he loved Rosa, that he did not care about the car or the jewellery, he simply wanted her back. This went on for some time and since there was nothing that I could say or do I slipped downstairs to the television room where, by a lucky chance, the English Cup Final was being shown.

When I returned to the suite, there had been a development. Rosa had telephoned from Menton to say that she had left her passport behind and wanted Wilcox to take it to her. While Jack debated whether he should go himself the telephone rang again. It was Rosa again, calling from the Summer Casino in Nice, still demanding her passport.

Twenty minutes passed while Jack paced the floor of the suite in a strangely indecisive mood. Then, suddenly, he made up his mind. 'Come on, Ted, we'll go and get her!' Knowing Rosa's temper and temperament I did not altogether fancy this assignment but, as it turned out, my services were not needed.

As we reached the hotel lobby Rosa swept past us clutching the precious box, rushed into the lift and closed its door in our faces. When we reached the suite, Rosa was in the bedroom, making a considerable din as, presumably, she looked for her passport which, ironically, had been in the boot of the Alfa-Romeo all the time. Jack went into the bedroom and closed the door.

The fight went on for fifteen minutes, with much screaming and shouting but gradually the volume faded and other softer sounds could be heard. Remembering that I had gone lunchless I slipped away to eat. When I saw them again later that evening they were beaming at each other like a couple on honeymoon. The next morning I told Jack that I was wasting my time in Cannes and went thankfully home to Chislehurst.

I did eventually adapt the Italian musical and under the title *When in Rome*, with the late Dickie Henderson in the lead, it had a decent run at the Adelphi Theatre.

Chapter Eleven

1

So much happened to me in the frantic fifties that it is difficult to keep things in proper chronological order. Now I find that I have run ahead of myself and must go back a bit to two events which were to change my life and improve my bank balance very significantly: the birth of *Dixon of Dock Green* and, treading hard on its heels, the development of commercial television.

Dixon happened with astonishing speed. In March 1955 the idea of a home-grown police series for BBC Television was first discussed at a chance meeting between myself and Ronnie Waldman, Head of Light Entertainment. By summer of the same year the first series of six programmes went to air. They were so successful that Ronnie asked for more. And more. And more. We knew that we had a hit but even so none of us could have foretold that the series would run for twenty-one years, that it would become almost a national institution and that Dixon's regular opening line to the audience, 'Evening All', would establish itself as a popular catch-phrase.

The programme nearly went out under another name. It was originally called *Dixon of K Division* which somehow seemed to lack the necessary resonance and it wasn't until I had written the first four scripts that I hit upon a title which had the right feel to it. I had done research in the dockland areas of East London and at Paddington Green police station and I decided to put the two together to create the manor of Dock Green. Over the years this imaginary district became almost real, so much so that we had a map drawn to show the streets of the Borough of Dock Green and the location of such landmarks as the Star of India public house, the Empire Music Hall, the police station and George Dixon's home at number 17,

Dock Green Terrace. The map, I am afraid, was of little use to the many thousands of provincial viewers who thought Dock Green actually existed and wrote to say that they were coming to London and would like to visit the area!

If it were possible to define what makes a successful play, book or television series there would be no failures and no poor authors and, believe me, there are plenty of both around. There were several factors which drew millions of viewers to *Dixon of Dock Green*, not the least of which was Jack Warner and a supporting cast that fitted the series like a glove.

Jack would have been the first to admit that he was never an Olivier. One could not imagine him playing *King Lear*, *Othello* or *Henry V*, though I fancy that, given the chance, he might have made a very creditable Falstaff or an Alfred Doolittle in *Pygmalion* or *My Fair Lady*. Even then the real-life Jack would have been imprinted on the performance, for everything he did was based on and flowed from his own nature and personality. What you got on the screen was what you got in real life, straight and unadulterated. He had enough warmth, generosity, modesty and good humour for a dozen men and the unique ability, the quiet charisma, to project those qualities on screen. Through them he became a father figure to a huge audience.

It was no good trying to toughen the image. When Dixon had been going for some years, a few critics began to compare us unfavourably with the more recent *Z-Cars*, accusing our series of being too cosy and soft-centred. Stung by this, I approached my good friend Allan Prior, one of the creators of *Z-Cars* and borrowed two or three of his scripts. From these I selected a really tough scene in which Inspector Barlow abused and bullied a young tearaway in his own typically ferocious manner. With Allan's permission I reproduced this scene almost word for word in a Dock Green script, with Dixon taking the place of Barlow. I might well have whistled in the wind. The words came out in Jack's usual sturdy, decent fashion: the abuse became gentle reproach, the bullying little more than a slight raising of the voice. Of course I should have realised that you cannot make a sow's ear out of a silk purse, that Jack was your friendly neighbourhood copper and any attempt to change him would not only be useless but stupid. The fourteen million people who watched him on Saturday evenings could not all be wrong. We were supplying something they wanted.

Jack owed much to his training in variety from which he drew his matchless timing and unique rapport with audiences of all ages. One Christmas Eve he and his wife Mollie called in to see us on their way to their house in Broadstairs when John and Sally were about fourteen and nine respectively. I mentioned that they had never seen any of Jack's variety material, most of which he had written himself. He promptly entertained them for an hour non-stop, frequently provoking them to hysterical laughter and wild applause. I think he enjoyed it as much as they and, but for the need to get home, would have gone on all afternoon. I regret to this day that I did not have a tape-recorder running during this impromptu word-perfect performance.

Jack was already a big star when he came to *Dixon of Dock Green*. He had made his name in variety and radio before and during the war and then added to his reputation in a series of films which included such hits as *Hue and Cry*, *The Blue Lamp*, *It Always Rains on Sunday* and *Carve Her Name with Pride*. In 1950 and again in 1952 he was voted one of the Top Ten British Stars in a Motion Picture Hall of Fame poll. I considered that I was lucky to get him for my series but, modest as ever, he took the opposite view and never ceased to thank me, publicly and privately, for creating the role of George Dixon.

Ah, that modesty! So rare in so many actors, so much in evidence in everything that Jack Warner did. He would never alter so much as a half-line of one of my scripts without approaching me, full of apologies, to ask permission. Each week, before the first rehearsal of a new episode, Jack, who was famous and needed no introduction, went round to any newcomers to the case and presented himself with the words, 'Hello, I'm Jack Warner. Welcome to Dock Green.' It was not a gimmick or a pose, he meant it. Over the years hundreds not to say thousands of actors and actresses played supporting roles in the series – among them such future stars as Michael Caine, David McCallum, David Hemmings and Thora Hird – and I never heard anything but words of praise when Jack's name was mentioned. He had the gift of affection and he inspired it in others.

He drove an immaculate and elderly Rolls-Royce but this

was neither a showpiece nor a status symbol. Jack had started his working life as a motor mechanic and, quite simply, he loved good cars. And what other owner of a Rolls would fill the boot of the car with fish-fryers to help a neighbour?

He arrived at my house one day and, proudly displaying a stack of gleaming pans, asked Audrey if she was in need of one. Or perhaps two. They had been made by a craftsman in Broadstairs who had cash-flow problems and Jack had offered his services as an unpaid salesman!

2

The list of principal characters in the early episodes of *Dixon of Dock Green* read as follows:

PC George Dixon	Jack Warner
PC Andy Crawford	Peter Byrne
Mary Crawford	Billie Whitelaw
Sergeant Flint	Arthur Rigby
Sergeant Grace Millard	Moira Mannion
PC Barrel	Neil Wilson
PC Bob Penney	Anthony Parker

It was a formidable line-up and it had exactly the right chemistry. They were all superb artists but they played as a team – I cannot remember a single instance in which artistic temperament, that perennial and boring excuse for bad temper, raised its pretentious head. An author is lucky if he gets such a company a half-dozen times in his career and when he does he is thrice blessed.

I had worked with Peter Byrne on *The Pattern of Marriage* and already knew his quality. A charismatic actor on screen he was also utterly professional and reliable. He proved this one Saturday evening in the early years when the programme was transmitted live. Jack Warner had been suffering from a bad bout of influenza for two or three days and had only kept going by an effort of will. He seemed to be in control during the final rehearsal but during the transmission the bug decided to strike again: Jack was visibly in a state of collapse, shaking like a tree in a storm and, not surprisingly, his mind went blank and he blew his lines.

Peter, who was in the scene with him, reacted like a true professional. He fielded some of Jack's speeches so that the story made sense and improvised other lines, 'You look ill, George. It must be that flu bug that's going around. You shouldn't have come on duty tonight. The sooner you get home the better.'

It was brilliant and it saved the evening. Jack, the old trouper, was able to continue after an injection and the episode went out to the waiting masses without further incident. But many of the viewers were concerned about what they had seen and the BBC switchboard was assaulted by callers asking after Jack's health. Some indignantly complained that he had been the worse for drink, a slander if ever there was one for Jack never drank at all when working and was a very modest tippler at the best of times.

One positive outcome from all this was that the BBC decided that *Dixon of Dock Green* should be given the benefit of the new technology and all future episodes were recorded first and then transmitted.

Arthur Rigby, a massive corner-stone of the series, was another actor who imposed his own personality on his performances. Tall and portly with a face that God must have fashioned from putty and forgotten to finish, he had a blunt, crusty manner and enough natural authority to stop a charging bull with a look at ten paces. He had learned his trade in the theatre and made a name for himself alongside Tom Walls, Ralph Lynn, Robertson Hare and Winifred Sholter, the legendary comedy team which in farces like *Rookery Nook* and *Thork* by Ben Travers became almost a permanent institution on the West End stage.

Arthur made a perfect Sergeant Flint. It is, perhaps, a measure of how our policing methods have changed that Flint would mount his long-suffering bicycle and ride it through the darkened streets to check on the night-beat constables. If he caught one of them so much as having a puff on a cigarette he gave them hell.

Billie Whitelaw played Dixon's daughter only for the first half-dozen episodes and then, quite rightly eager to spread her considerable wings in the theatre, she decided to leave. The role of Mary was then taken over by Jeanette Hutchinson who stayed on for the next fifteen years giving birth to twins both on and off the screen.

Another actor who had a fear of staying in one role for too long and becoming typecast both professionally and in the public eye was Anthony Parker. After three or four years in the part of Bob Penney, a likeable young novice policeman, he decided not to come back for the next series and I decided that if he wanted to leave he might as well go with a bang.

The basic philosophy behind *Dixon of Dock Green* had always been to avoid the sensational. I wanted to dramatise the day-to-day work and life of an ordinary copper, 90 per cent of whose time is taken up by petty crime, routine enquiries and social problems. It may not be true today but back in the fifties a policeman was half law-enforcement officer and half social worker. A man could serve his whole career in the force without once being involved in a case of murder or even a major robbery. My aim was to show this, to demonstrate that a rift in a marriage can be just as interesting as a murder. I am sure that this low-key approach was one of the reasons for the success of the series.

However, there had recently been a rather brutal murder of a policeman and I felt that the departure of Anthony Parker from the cast gave me an opportunity to bring home to the viewers that police work had a little more to it than directing traffic or settling a domestic dispute. For the final episode of that particular run I wrote a script called 'Helmet on the Sideboard' in which the popular PC Penney was gunned down and killed.

Yet again I became conscious of the thin line between illusion and reality. There were millions of people out there who loved Bob Penney and felt that they had lost a friend. Many thought of him as a real person. Their wrath descended upon my head in an avalanche of letters and telephone calls. One typical letter consisted of my photograph, clipped from a newspaper, across which was written in red ink the single word MURDERER! Another came in the form of a Round Robin signed by all the women of a small West Country village warning me never to visit the place on pain of being tarred and feathered. Many correspondents begged me to devise some way of bringing the young policeman back from the dead and one ingenious writer, anticipating *Dallas* and Bobby Ewing by thirty years, suggested that I treat the entire incident as a dream.

The ring-master of the Dixon circus, the presiding genius, was Douglas Moodie, the producer-director. He set the programme up and lovingly cared for it during the first decade. It was Dougie who drew all the disparate elements together, creating order and entertainment out of apparent chaos, week upon week.

A thin, sharp-tongued Scotsman, he knew exactly when to flatter or cajole and when to bring out the whip. His attitude was the same whether dealing with Jack Warner, the star, or the humblest extra: he allowed no one to slack, simply to go through the motions. With a few well-chosen words he could reduce an actor to shivering silence or raise him to the heights.

On one occasion, at a first rehearsal, a young actor evidently decided that his part needed adjustment and he began to alter and paraphrase the lines. Dougie listened restlessly for a few minutes then stopped the offender in his tracks.

'Thank you so much for trying to improve the lines. However, the BBC pays the author a good deal of money for his scripts. Would you think it impertinent of me to ask you to speak what he has written?' There were no more problems from that quarter.

Once the work was done, Dougie could relax with the best. He liked a gin and tonic but insisted that the gin had to be Gordon's. I thought this a bit of affectation until one evening I bought him some other brand, thinking that he wouldn't know the difference. He took one small sip, slammed down the glass and glared at me. Tapping a new script that I had just brought in, he said, 'That's the second load of gut rot you've given me tonight!'

A number of young directors cut their teeth on Dixon, among them Robin Nash who went on to produce and direct many outstanding programmes and is now the Head of Comedy at the BBC. But Robin and all the others would agree, I think, that Dougie Moodie was a one-off, unique.

Among the millions of Dock Green fans there were some very distinguished people. I was told that the Royal Family were regular viewers and I had congratulatory letters from the then Archbishop of Canterbury, Cabinet ministers and many other public figures. But the most unlikely though avid follower of the programme was undoubtedly the late Field Marshal Montgomery of Alamein. His enthusiasm led to some interesting moments in the House of Lords.

On one occasion, for instance, I was entertaining some guests at lunch in the restaurant when, from a nearby table, I heard a thin sibilant call: 'Willish – Willish!'

I looked across and saw Montgomery motioning me imperiously to his table. Conscious of the fact that he was a Field Marshal whereas I had never risen higher than the rank of Local Acting Unpaid Provisional Lance-Corporal, I obeyed immediately and, resisting an urge to salute, stood before the great man who then introduced me to his table companions.

'This is Lord Willish,' he announced in his thin reedy voice which seemed incapable of getting itself around an R-sound or plainly pronouncing a simple S: 'Lord Willish who wites *Dixon of Dock Gween*. Best pwogwamme on the air. Always got a mowal, always got a jolly good mowal.'

The introductions over, he said curtly: 'Good show, Willish,' which was tantamount to a military dismissal and I returned to my guests. This sort of incident was to be repeated many times with that hissing call of 'Willish, Willish,' pursuing me down the corridors of the House of Lords.

At Monty's request I arranged to bring Jack Warner up to join us at lunch at the House. The two old gentlemen struck up an immediate accord and yarned on for hours while I was relegated to the role of silent listener. It was Monty's lunch but somehow this detail slipped his mind and I was left to pick up the tab.

3

Once the series was up and running my main job was to stoke the boilers, to keep the scripts coming. I had, and still have, a horror of falling behind and I made it a firm rule to keep at least twelve scripts ahead of the game. Apart from anything else, this gave me enough leeway to set Dixon aside for a few weeks and write something else. To help with the increasing burden I brought in a good friend, writer Rex Edwards, whose actress wife Hilda Fenemore I had known at Unity. Rex became my script associate and helped enormously with the supply of ideas and scripts.

Even this was not enough. We were using ideas faster

than we could think them up and something had to be done. In desperation I wrote to the *Police Journal* and offered to pay for any true stories which its readers cared to send me. The result was staggering. The letters came pouring in and, even better, something like 80 per cent of the stories were usable. I could not escape the impression that half the members of the police force were frustrated writers. After this I formed a panel of about twenty policemen of all ranks on whom I could call for advice and ideas. One of them, John Wainwright, went on to become a prolific and highly successful crime novelist.

Dixon of Dock Green had brought my name to the attention of a wider audience than I had known before and the press began to take an interest. I was written up as the 'man behind the scenes at Dock Green' and made the subject of many interviews. I was even invited to try my hand as a television interviewer on a programme which featured young people in the news. This departure turned out to be an unmitigated disaster and it taught me to keep my place – behind the cameras.

It so happened that the first person to come before me for an interview was the young Shirley Bassey. She had been born into a working-class family in Cardiff and, with exceeding foolishness, I asked her whether she felt any guilt when she compared the large fees she got paid for singing with the wages of a dock-worker.

Miss Bassey, quite rightly, would have none of that. Announcing that she had not come along to answer stupid questions she stalked off the set. After this I left the interviewing to my co-presenter, a young man named Robert Robinson who became quite good at it . . .

I had written a number of Dock Green short stories for the London *Evening News* and one day late in 1959 the editor, Reg Willis, asked me if I could go to the BBC Club at Lime Grove to have some photographs taken with Jack Warner and other members of the cast. I arranged to go the following Monday evening. Within an hour, Michael Barry, Head of Drama at the BBC, rang to say that he had heard about this photocall and that he would like to see me before I went to the club to discuss a new contract. The next morning Tom Sloane, who had succeeded Ronnie Waldman as Head of Light Entertainment, also telephoned to say that he too had some matters to discuss and that he would meet me in Michael Barry's office.

It did not occur to me that someone was very anxious to make sure that I turned up that Monday evening and I set out with a light heart. I spent an hour with Michael Barry and Tom Sloane discussing ideas for future programmes and then Michael suggested that it was time to go to the club. As we went across the brightly lit yard he said, 'I expect you're wondering about these lights. They're here because we're shooting a documentary on the work of the BBC.'

Into the club, where Reg Willis waited with a cameraman and all the principal actors in Dixon. A drink and a few photographs later I heard the familiar opening music of the programme *This Is Your Life*, and saw the titles come up on the club's television set. My first thought was that Audrey would be watching this at home.

Then I saw Eamonn Andrews heading for our group with the famous Red Book in his hands and my second thought clicked into place: the subject was going to be Jack Warner and I had been lured there to participate in some way in the programme. Then, as from a long way off I heard Eamonn: '. . . the man who created these marvellous characters. Ted Willis, tonight This is Your Life.'

Then I was hustled back across the yard, under those damned lights, which I now knew were there for a different purpose than I'd been told, with the cameras rolling while Eamonn talked and I answered I know not what. A car was on hand to take us to the Television Theatre and, as I learned later, the waiting audience was shown film which extolled my love of Tottenham Hotspur Football Club, suitably introduced by Jack Warner.

Audrey and the children were brought on early, Sally bright-eyed and eagerly curious as usual, John a little subdued and nervous. There was a touch of guilt in the look Audrey gave me – she had been working in cahoots with the producers for the past month, operating behind my back, and deception, even in a good cause, was never something that came easily to her.

As for myself, I felt as though I were locked in some bizarre and puzzling dream. The parade of people from my past – Alfie Bass, John Slater, little Jimmy Carr, ex-Inspector Mott, the two West Indian children, Margie and Horace – none of them seemed totally real and when they spoke I had the strange impression that I was standing outside myself, listening with amusement and a certain irony to the verbal bouquets they flung at the Ted Willis who was the object of their attention. It was a little like going to your own funeral to hear friends muttering rehearsed compliments about the dear departed.

Of course, *This Is Your Life* is designed to be entertainment and as such it is good, cheerful, sentimental stuff. There are no knives, the subject is not dissected, his faults are left outside the doors of the studio and no breath of criticism is allowed to foul the sweet emotion of the carefully prepared atmosphere. It must be taken with fingers crossed behind your back and, like most of show business, not too seriously.

The irony of one moment did not strike me until later when, having emerged from the dream, I read the transcript of what had been said. Eamonn introduced an old lady whom he referred to as Granny Budd. She had lived next door when I was a boy and I remember her as a tetchy nag of a woman who was forever complaining but the programme had her pegged as a kindly, lovable old trout and it was too late to argue. When Eamonn asked if she remembered me, old Granny Budd, aged 104, replied, 'Of course I remember him. We were at school together.'

4

After seven years I decided to turn my mind to other things and gave up Dixon. It was a difficult decision to make but the truth was that I had run out of road in terms of this particular programme. A new team of writers moved in to take over. Norman Crisp, Eric Paice and Gerald Kelsey, case-hardened and fine professionals all, gave the series the new look and fresh life it needed. From then on I watched its progress only from a distance.

Dixon of Dock Green finally ended its long run in 1976, twenty-one years after its launch. Thankfully, it is affectionately remembered by millions and, at dinners or meetings, I am still introduced as its author. But that will pass as all things must. The other day when the chairman of a youth club told his members that I was the man behind Dixon, a collective look of incomprehension appeared on their young faces.

It will have been obvious from what has gone before that I worshipped Jack Warner. As my mother used to say, when God made Jack he broke the mould. And so I cannot leave this chapter of my life without recounting two stories which give the humour and measure of the man.

Jack was a bit of a health freak and from time to time he subjected himself to some unconventional cures, such as allowing himself to be stung all over by a swarm of bees. And I mean all over. After one of these sessions I questioned the wisdom of this procedure but he insisted that he always felt on tiptop form after treatment. He added with a grin, 'You see, Ted, it's so marvellous when those bloody bees leave off.'

Years later I went to visit him in hospital following an enforced operation to amputate one of his legs. He was now very old and looked grey and weak but some of the old spark remained. Clutching my hand he murmured, 'Ted, when I get out of here we must have a talk. I've got a great idea for a series about a one-legged policeman.'

Two days later he died.

Chapter Twelve

1

'The characters are dull and lifeless . . . the dialogue banal in the extreme . . . there is no dramatic development . . . nothing happens, the play takes us nowhere.'

When I read the letter, a response to my latest television play, I felt as though I had been clubbed over the head with a shillelagh. It came from the drama editor of Associated Rediffusion and he went on, with a certain pompous condescension, to add, 'However, I think that if you and I were to sit down together, something might be made of it.' To which I replied angrily that if he thought that there was so much wrong with my play it must be beyond any such rescue mission.

The year was 1956 when, fathered by a powerful high-decibel lobby, ITV was born. For the first eighteen months or so there were doubts as to whether this scrawny infant could survive. The advertising agents, who so persistently call for boldness in others, stood back and watched cautiously, unwilling to commit their clients or their money, and the expected torrent of income from commercials emerged as a trickle. New capital had to be injected into the struggling companies and the butcher's knife was taken to the ambitious plans for programming on which they had won their franchises. Aeroplanes to the US were packed with executives desperate to buy television series at bargain prices to replace the ones they could no longer afford to make themselves.

Later, as ITV took a hold on the public and the advertisers developed some backbone, there was a dramatic turnaround. Commercial television became, in the immortal but ultimately fatal words of Lord Thompson, principal shareholder of the

Outside 55 Stanley Road, Tottenham, where I was born.

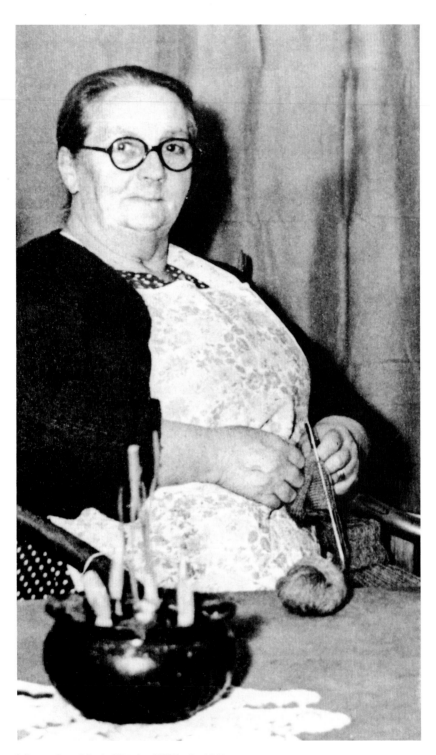

My mother, Maria Harriet Willis, in 1963.

Audrey singing 'Don't Go Out Tonight, Dear Father' in the Unity production *Winkles and Champagne*, 1944.

The première of the film *Woman in a Dressing Gown*.

Audrey and me with Jack Hylton and Rosalina Neri.

A typical comment
from Sid James, star
of my BBC series,
Taxi, 1965.

Jack Warner (Dixon) with his wife, Mollie.

Receiving the Writers' Guild Award for 'Outstanding writing contribution to films and television' from HRH The Duke of Edinburgh and Carl Forman, 1972.

Audrey and I receive the Variety Club award for distinguished service to show business, 1973.

With Roy Castle at the opening of *Mr Polly* at the Churchill Theatre, August 1977.

The National Film Development Fund Committee, 1978. *Back row, left to right*: Peter Coles (Secretary), Jack Gold, Richard Craven, David Puttnam, Jesse Lasky (Jr), Otto Plesches. *Front row*: Bob Hamilton (Vice Chairman), Sir John Terry, myself (Chairman).

Audrey and me with Lew and Kathy (Lord and Lady Grade).

With Googie Withers and her husband and co-star, John McCallum, at the first night of *Stardust*, 1985.

Scottish station, 'a licence to print money' – but in those very early days many of the leading lights of ITV were looking out of very high windows and wondering whether to jump.

In the mood of euphoria which followed its success in securing the London weekday franchise, Associated Rediffusion, the first commercial company to open up, set about corralling as much of the available talent as possible. They offered me a three-year contract to write and develop series. My new agent, Harvey Unna, negotiated a very satisfactory deal and I set to work.

The first project, a drama series called *Big City*, actually went into production and was successful enough for the drama department to come back and ask for more. But, in the midst of planning the second series, the panic began. The station was losing money like water out of a leaky bucket, cutbacks were ordered and *Big City* was replaced in the schedules by *Gun Smoke*, an American Western bought at a fraction of the cost of my series.

What to do? Harvey Unna had drawn up a watertight contract and Rediffusion had to pay me whether I worked or not. It was agreed that, instead of series, I should deliver a number of television dramas with the stipulation that these should be made on a tight budget. They were to be limited to ten or twelve actors, a minimum of sets and would be shot in the studios with a maximum of one minute of outside filming. Today these would appear to be stifling limitations on an author's creativity but I accepted them as unavoidable, even as a kind of challenge.

At this time a volume of television plays by Paddy Chayefsky, an American writer, came into my hands. This was the golden age of drama on US television when authors like Chayefsky, Reginald Rose, Tad Mosel and Rod Serling were producing plays which tellingly explored the possibilities of the new medium. Criminally, just as this school of exciting, pioneering drama came to a full flowering, the network moguls cut its throat. The single play on US television is now as rare as a soothing silence in a disco.

As I read the plays of Chayefsky and his introductory words I felt as though someone had kicked open a door. I had been struggling to get television into focus in my mind, trying to define how writing for this small screen differed from writing for the stage or the cinema. Paddy Chayefsky suddenly supplied most, if not all, of the answers.

Television, he wrote, could become a true theatre of and for the people, a theatre not for the middle class but for the masses. In describing two of his best plays, *Marty* and *The Mother* he said:

> . . . each represents in its own way the sort of material which does best on television. They both deal with the mundane, the ordinary, and the untheatrical. The main characters are typical rather than exceptional: the situations are easily identifiable by the audience: and the relationships are as common as people . . . I am just now becoming aware of this area, this marvellous world of the ordinary . . . television is the dramatic medium through which to expose new insights into ourselves . . . You can write honest dramatic literature for television, rewarding to your sense of pride.

This is what I had been stumbling towards in some of the episodes of *Dixon of Dock Green*. It was what the shrewd Inspector Mott had told me when he said of the people of the East End, 'Knock on any door and you will find a story worth the telling.' Chayefsky's phrase, 'the marvellous world of the ordinary' rang in my head like a bell. And with it his advice that in an hour's television drama it was essential to focus the attention preferably on one character and certainly not more than three, and that the central character should be caught at a moment of crisis, a turning-point in his or her life.

With so many technical facilities available to today's writers these admonitions may not hold so much validity, but it would be wise to remember them. Plays on the small screen cry out for a simple uncluttered approach, for a strong narrative drive and equally strong characters. There is a danger of overusing modern techniques. The most telling shot on television is still a close-up of a human face.

It is difficult to describe the glow of enthusiasm in which I sat down to write my first post-Chayefsky television play. Basing it on a situation I had come across in real life, I wrote of an ordinary, good-hearted, rather untidy, happy-go-lucky woman of forty and her reaction when she learns that her husband, a clerk in a timber merchant's office, has a mistress and wants a divorce. I called it *Amy* after the central character but halfway through, as so often happens, a better title flashed into my mind and it ended up as *Woman in a Dressing Gown*.

2

This was the play that I delivered to Associated Rediffusion under my contract and this was the play that came winging back like a boomerang with the curt and wounding rejection. Wounding because I felt in the marrow of my bones that the drama editor was wrong, that the play would work.

It was then that I had a bit of luck. Stung by my angry reply to his letter, the drama editor gave the play to a senior director for a second opinion. That director was Peter Cotes; he read *Woman in a Dressing Gown* overnight and rang me the next morning, brimming with enthusiasm. Within a month the play went into rehearsal with Peter's wife, Joan Miller, playing the part of Amy, Edward Chapman as the husband and Andrée Melly as the other woman.

When the play was eventually transmitted the public reception was breathtaking. Although there was no ITV network at the time and we were seen only in London by an audience about one fifth of today's television public it seemed to me the next morning that everyone in the metropolis had been looking in. This one play, fifty-five minutes of television, brought me more publicity and recognition than anything I had done before.

Woman in a Dressing Gown topped the ratings for that week and the critics, whom I feared would be waiting in ambush with the same clubs they had used on me after the production of *No Trees in the Street*, came out in a unanimous chorus of praise. Joan Miller's performance as Amy and Peter Cotes's direction were described as 'memorable' and 'magnificent'. They treated me kindly also, with such comments as, 'the most adult play on television since competition began', 'a television masterpiece' and 'a rare achievement, the true, complete and wholly convincing portrait of a woman'. I was delighted when one newspaper compared me to Paddy Chayefsky and referred to the 'Marty-style realism' of the script. The critic of *The Times* wrote:

In Britain television has not yet, on the whole, produced any comparable figure to those TV playwrights who, in America, have become household words. Practically the only exception, though a very distinguished one, is Mr Ted Willis.

But the comment that gave me most pleasure came from Bernard Levin in the *Manchester Guardian*:

> . . . what gave *Woman in a Dressing Gown* it's interest was the fact that somebody – presumably the author – had very clearly been doing some serious thinking about television in general and television drama in particular . . .

The play made such a mark that J. Lee Thompson, a young director who has since made his name in Hollywood, approached me about the film rights. He had some connection with the Associated British Picture Corporation (ABPC) which had its base at Elstree Studios and for whom he had directed *Ice Cold in Alex*. He was sure that they would finance the picture. I then made a near-fatal error: Lee and I got together with Frank Godwin, a producer and former financial controller with Rank films and formed a production company which, with great originality, we called Lee-Thompson-Godwin-Willis Productions Ltd. A deal was made with Robert Clark the head of production, by which ABPC put up the finance to make the film and our little company would get one-third of worldwide profits after deduction of expenses. There were two snags. We had to defer half our fees as director, producer and writer and we had no real control over that treacherous little word 'expenses'.

The film, starring Yvonne Mitchell, Sylvia Syms, Anthony Quayle and Andrew Ray, surpassed the success of its television original and was just as popular with the critics. In the *Daily Express* Leonard Mosley wrote:

> Wonderful! A film with the tang of truth. Comes under the heading: Must see.

The *New York Telegram and Sun* called it, 'Well-played, strongly written and surprisingly touching drama.' The *New York Post* described Yvonne Mitchell's performance as 'magic'.

And, with the thought of one-third of the profits in our minds we licked our lips when *Variety*, the Bible of American show business, told its readers:

> *Woman in a Dressing Gown* is a picture with obvious box-office potential which will reap returns when it goes the rounds.

The paper was right. The film had cost about £99,000 to make and on its first release it grossed £450,000 – a very good figure for those days. It continued to earn significant returns in other markets and when it had run its course the total figure must have been near £1,000,000. We won thirteen international prizes, including Best Film award at the Berlin Film Festival.

The result of all this was that, if anything, our pockets were lighter. The accountants assured us that the picture was not yet in profit and stressed the high cost of publicity and promotion. I went to Robert Clark in some anger to point out that the man who had served the drinks at the West End première, the men who had stuck up the posters, the projectionists and the ticket clerks – that all these and many others had been fully paid while I, the author, had still not received the deferred half of my fee, let alone a penny of profit!

This had some effect and a few weeks later we received cheques for the balance of our fees but still nothing in terms of profit. We should have learned a lesson from all this but, like innocent idiots, we put our fingers in the fire again. Anxious to follow up the success of *Woman in a Dressing Gown*, Lee Thompson proposed that we should film my play, *No Trees in the Street*. Robert Clark agreed, but imposed one extra condition. ABPC would finance the film but Lee, Frank Godwin and I had to agree that any profit we made from *Woman in a Dressing Gown* should be held back to offset possible losses on the new film. This, I understand, was common practice then and may still be today.

It was made very clear that unless we accepted this arrangement there would be no finance for the film and we had no option but to agree. So much for independence! The film, starring Sylvia Syms, Herbert Lom, Stanley Holloway and featuring Joan Miller and a young Melvyn Hayes, duly went into production. The mistress of the American producer who was the top man at ABPC also played a small role – Lee explained that he had included her to 'keep the peace'. She was a pretty girl but not very good.

No Trees in the Street did not match the success of *Woman in a Dressing Gown*. It was a decent little film and did quite well but the melodramatic faults which were present in my stage original seemed to be even more obvious on the screen. It took a long time to recover its costs and I waited two or three years before I was paid the deferred part of my fee. And my total share of profit from these two pictures, which arrived in dribs and drabs over the next ten years, was under a thousand pounds.

This experience finally cured me of film production. I decided that I did not possess the peculiar talent needed to be a producer, that henceforth I would stick to being a writer and that for any future film assignment I would take the money and run.

3

In the next year I wrote three more one-hour plays for Associated Rediffusion. *The Young and the Guilty* based on a real-life story which my agent, Harvey Unna, had drawn to my attention, dealt with an innocent first-love relationship between two sixteen-year old youngsters. Seen from today's standpoint, it seems as old-fashioned as a whalebone corset but in 1956, with Peter Cotes directing and with Andrew Ray and Jill Williams as the young lovers, it made an instant impact and topped the ratings. Robert Clark, at ABPC bought the film rights and it became a very respectable movie which, oddly enough, enjoyed a huge success in Japan.

The next play, *Look in any Window*, the story of a young girl trying to come to terms with the mother who had abandoned her as a baby, also enjoyed a measure of success and was rebroadcast three months later – a unique event in those days. The third play, *Strictly for the Sparrows*, a sort of British *Rebel Without a Cause*, made exciting television but, unlike the others, it divided the critics and angered some members of the public.

It was a study of the Teddy Boys of the time and I had researched it meticulously, spending a lot of time with a gang that operated around the Elephant and Castle area. Their leader was an intelligent but frustrated ex-grammar school boy named Billy Castle with whom, after an initial period of suspicion, I struck up a sort of friendship. It was often a hairy experience, culminating one Saturday at midnight when we ambushed the Deptford Teds and I had to prove my credentials by fighting shoulder to shoulder with Billy. I learned the dangerous lesson then that aggression and violence don't need to have a philosophy or a reason: they can be exciting in themselves, as stimulating as a sexual experience. Violence springs from the blood, not the mind, and the urge is most acute in the adolescent male whose body, tingling with strange juices, moves at times beyond control; ally this mindless violence to prejudice and you have the formula for Fascism, you construct a storm-trooper.

It is no part of the playwright's task to offer solutions and *Strictly for the Sparrows* had none. It merely held the mirror up to the problem and in effect said to the viewers, 'These young people are undisciplined and vicious. Why? What is going on in their minds? What has brought them to this and what do they think and feel about us?' Some reviewers understood this and praised the play for its courage in facing the problem – one described it as the 'most thought-provoking play I have seen in many a long year'.

There were others, however, who accused me of pandering to violence and several MPs signed a letter to the Independent Television Authority deploring this 'glorification of teenage violence'. The controversy continued for some weeks, the very first manifestation of a debate which still goes on today. The theme of violence on television has kept hundreds of academics and researchers in comfort, Mrs Whitehouse and her followers on permanent standby and used up several forests to provide newsprint. 'Ah, well,' as my mother used to say, 'it keeps them off the streets.'

It is interesting to record that I met Billy Castle some years later. He had become deputy headmaster at a state school.

4

I am not sure now how I crowded it all in but in 1957 I produced a new stage play, *Hot Summer Night*. It is a play of which I am rather proud, for I believe it to be the first drama to confront the problem of colour and race prejudice in Britain. Written at a time when the first wave of West Indian migrants was flowing in, it told the story of a radical trade union leader whose liberal attitudes are put to the test when his daughter falls in love with a young Jamaican.

I was a bit doubtful when Harvey Unna sent it to Emile Littler. Emile had a high reputation as a theatre producer but he had specialised in large scale musical comedies and pantomimes and I wasn't at all sure how he would react to a serious drama set in the backyard of a working-class home in Bermondsey. I need not have worried. Emile received the play one Friday afternoon and on the Saturday morning he rang Harvey Unna. He was clearly excited by what he had read and within three days we had exchanged contracts.

Emile did not at all live up to my mental picture of a producer of musicals. He had none of Jack Hylton's bravura and certainly did not share his habits. Happily married to Cora, a former musical-comedy star, and with two adopted daughters, he was a devoted family man who behaved more like a patron than a predator to the young actresses he employed. He loved to tell the story of how he had paid for extensive dental treatment for one of his female stars. Always quietly and impeccably dressed, he ran his office in St Martin's Lane, next to the Coliseum, with dedicated efficiency, avoiding the frenetic hustle and bustle which characterised Hylton's operations.

A shrewd and careful businessman, he had a rare eye for an opportunity. He was, for example, a regular customer of the Ivy restaurant with which establishment he negotiated a deal to supply watercress grown in the lake of his garden at Poynings in Sussex in return for a reduction in his luncheon bills. He delivered the watercress personally and I can testify that it was of superb quality.

Another of his investments had a rather macabre edge to it. He bought the insurance policies of elderly people who needed money – they got a reasonable cash sum from

Emile and, if there were any premiums still due, he under-
took to pay them while the policy-holders were still living.
When they died, he collected the insurance. It was, as he
explained, a sort of gamble. If the insured person died fairly
quickly the profit went up; if they lingered on, it went down.
By and large, he had done very well out of it. I believe there is
quite a well-established market in this kind of thing. He tried
to interest me in making an investment but the thought of
gambling money on some poor devil's early death stuck in
my throat and I declined politely.

Although careful with the pennies and the pounds there
was no meanness in Emile's nature. He honoured contracts
to the letter and could be thoughtfully generous. When the
time came for Audrey and me to move the family from
Petts Wood to our present home in leafy Chislehurst, he
sent us a valuable Victorian landscape with a note which
read:

> From Cora and Emile. We bought this picture when
> we first moved into this house. We hope it will bring
> you as much luck and happiness as it has brought
> us.

In addition to this handsome gift, he sent his designer,
Fyshe, down to Chislehurst to advise on the extensive redec-
oration needed to our new home. She not only advised but
helped actively, saving us a lot of money.

Emile set about the production of *Hot Summer Night* with an
enthusiasm which made me warm to him. Three old friends
were cast in the leading roles – John Slater, Joan Miller and
Andrée Melly. Among the supporting cast we had Harold
Scott, a marvellous actor whose portrayal of Duffy, an old
tramp, in *Dixon of Dock Green* had caught the public's fancy,
and Lloyd Reckord, a young Jamaican actor. Once again,
Peter Cotes was the director. There was no penny-pinching.
If the director wanted anything, Emile ordered that he should
have it.

The result was a production and performances of which I
was truly proud. And it paid off for when we opened at the
New Theatre – now the Albery – in Shaftesbury Avenue the
play garnered rave notices. 'Red Hot Summer Night' was a
typical critical response. Another less pleasant reaction came

in the form of some hate mail in which I was dubbed a 'nigger lover' and 'white coon'.

Sydney Newman, the dynamic Canadian who established *Armchair Theatre* for ABC Television and who was probably the most potent force in the development of British television drama, saw the play and as soon as we had ended the London run arranged to produce it for his programme. With some difficulty but with typical toughness he persuaded the programme schedulers to scrap the one-hour limit on plays for *Armchair Theatre* and allow us to run for ninety minutes. For the television production he made certain changes: John Slater remained in the lead but Ruth Dunning took over the role of his wife and Ted Kotcheff, a young Canadian, was appointed director.

Hot Summer Night on television became an overnight sensation. Universally praised by the critics, it soared to number one in the ratings, Ruth Dunning won an academy award for her performance and soon after Ted Kotcheff headed for Hollywood. The film rights were sold to Roy Baker, a producer with the Rank Organisation and, after various delays, the picture went into production at Pinewood Studios with John Mills and Sylvia Syms in the lead.

The delays caused me some anguish. I had to rewrite the screenplay so that the exteriors could be shot in winter and transfer the action from a hot summer night to a bleak Guy Fawkes night, 5 November. To match this we gave the story a new title, *Flame in the Streets*.

It emerged as a creditable movie, with excellent performances from John Mills and Sylvia Syms, but it had neither the bite nor tension of the original. And matters were not helped when Brenda de Banzie, a fine actress, appeared as John Slater's down-trodden working-class wife with painted fingernails, clothes which might have been bought in Bond Street and an accent that owed more to Mayfair than Bermondsey. Sydney Newman, in his brash Canadian way, was pretty scathing about the film version.

'Tell me, Ted, how could you let them do it? The idea of a hot summer night was central to the whole play. Setting it in winter ruined it. The film is shit, Ted, shit.'

He exaggerated but there was a deep core of truth in his judgement.

5

I wrote one other play for Emile, adapting a story by Rose-mary Timperley into a drama called *The Eyes of Youth*. This was produced at the Connaught Theatre, Worthing, and had a reasonably successful tour but it simply did not carry enough guns to make it a West End prospect.

I can see now that *Hot Summer Night* represented a sort of climax for me. I had been writing non-stop for fifteen years, turning out scripts and plays – in retrospect, the sheer volume of it all seems prodigious. Yet I still managed somehow to play badminton and tennis four or five times a week and to spend precious time with my growing family.

But, without realising it, I did need a break. It came shortly after the television production of *Hot Summer Night* when the chance came for me to make my first long-distance trip – to Australia. As a ten-pound emigrant!

Chapter Thirteen

1

'There's a bloody Pom over there, Bert,' said the first forestry worker, the one with the build of a bulldozer and great sunburned arms on which tattooed snakes and dragons wrestled each other for space.

'Too bloody right,' said the second forestry worker gloomily. Only marginally smaller than his mate, his tattoo, more modest in scale, showed a heart encircling the name Ruby.

'Where the hell are they coming from?' asked the third forestry worker, a round ball of a man with a beer gut that strained violently against his sleeveless blue singlet.

'Ah,' said the first man. 'Don't you know? They scrape the Poms off the keels of the ships in Fre-bloody-mantle harbour.'

Such was my welcome to Australia. I was standing with Bernie Freedman, an official of the Government Immigration Department, at the bar of a small country pub just outside Manjimub near the southern tip of West Australia. We had seen the words Counter Food painted in whitewash on the window and had agreed to try our luck with it, a decision promptly rescinded when we saw that the food consisted of a stack of tired, doorstep-size sandwiches. I thought at first that they were made of currant-bread until I saw the currants move on the surface and realised that they were flies. We contented ourselves with beer so cold it was like swallowing ice.

I had been told by an Aussie friend back in London that the basic survival kit for an Englishman going Down Under was a sense of humour. So I gave the three foresters what I hoped they would interpret as a warm and friendly smile and said to Bernie, 'Let's go and talk to them, shall we? Ask them to have a drink with us.'

He gave me a look which suggested that what I'd asked was the equivalent of an order to charge the Turkish positions at Gallipoli. So I asked the barman, who was languidly fanning the flies on the sandwiches with a dirty tea-cloth – no doubt to cool them off – if he would ask the three gentlemen at the far end of the bar to join me for a drink. Without stopping his efforts to lower the temperature of the flies he shouted, 'Bert, Johnnie, Kev – bloke over here wants you to have a beer with him.'

That was the beginning of a beautiful friendship. Bert, Johnnie and Kev joined us with all speed and we spent the next two hours swopping yarns and drinking. In spite of their remarks about Poms they spoke affectionately of England, which they called the Old Dart, and eventually Johnnie, the one with the snakes and the dragons, confessed that he had once been a Pom himself, having migrated from Enfield in Middlesex some thirty years before. When I told him that my wife Audrey was born and brought up there, I had to step back behind Bernie for fear that Johnnie would wrap me in those muscular arms.

Instead, he invited me to tea at his house in Manjimub for the specific purpose of meeting his wife, the daughter of a 'dinky-di Pom' from Edmonton, North London, who had settled in West Australia just before the First World War. Two days later, on our way back from Albany to Perth we took up his invitation.

I was taken aback when I saw what Johnnie called tea. It consisted of steaks the size of dinner-plates, adorned with two fried eggs and besieged on all sides by chip potatoes as thick as a man's thumb. Only later did I learn that an invitation to tea, at least from your honest-to-God working-class Australian, means come to supper.

I had told Johnnie previously that I was in Australia to collect material for a film about migrants from England and he had decided to help. After tea he took me to a local pub where, at his behest, a number of Poms had gathered. Some had only been in Australia a few months, others for years. They had nearly all absorbed the accent and it was impossible to distinguish them from the locals.

The result of all this was a drinking session that lasted beyond midnight. Bernie and I altered our schedule and stayed on in Manjimub for two days, moving from house to house, bar to bar. I contented myself with the thought that I was doing some genuine research. When we finally left for Perth, Johnnie came to the hotel to see us off and crunching my hand in his giant fist he said, 'D'you know, Ted mate, when I first saw you in the pub I took you for a bloody toff. But you're all right. You have all the makings of a bloody good Aussie, fair dinkum.'

I knew then that I was going to enjoy Australia.

2

It all began six months earlier in 1957 when I approached Associated British with the idea. At this time the Australian post-war immigration programme was just working up a full head of steam; thousands of British families, paying ten pounds per head, were leaving each month for what they hoped would prove to be the Lucky Country. By the time the Australian government wound up the scheme over a million people had migrated and of these only a minute proportion came back.

This vast exodus fascinated me. I felt in my bones that there must be a good feature film in the story of a British family which tore up its roots and travelled 12,000 miles to a new land and a new life. How would they be received? What problems would face them? How would they adjust?

Frederic Gotfurt, the script editor at Associated British, latched on to the idea at once. A refugee from Nazi Germany, he'd had some infinitely more painful experiences of settling in a new land and he approached Robert Clark, the boss, who gave the plan his seal of approval. The Australian government agreed to provide passage on a migrant ship and to give me all possible help when I arrived. I stockpiled a dozen scripts for *Dixon of Dock Green* which, together with the summer break between series, would give me at least four months' respite, and bought myself some lightweight clothing, charging the cost to essential expenses.

I left on a cold, miserable February morning; a chill drizzle wept from grey skies and, not to be outdone, everyone around me seemed to be weeping also. The dock at Tilbury was crowded with pale, sad-faced families who, suddenly conscious of the enormity of the step they had taken, were clinging tearfully to the loved ones they were about to leave behind. Audrey, who had come to see me off, became affected by the universal misery and she too began to weep.

'I'm only going for three months,' I said in an effort at consolation. 'I'll be back.'

But, in truth, in those first moments I had begun to regret the enterprise and to feel touched by the pangs of homesickness which were to become painfully familiar in the coming weeks. Almost the only condition I had made was that I should not have to share accommodation and Audrey and I said our farewells in the privacy of my small cabin. Such occasions are not notable for significant conversation and we disguised our sadness at what was to be our longest ever separation with reminders from me about how to handle calls from producers and what to do in the garden and injunctions from Audrey concerning my health and personal hygiene. I remember that when we heard the call 'All visitors ashore', she clung to me and murmured, 'Don't forget to change your underpants every day.'

As the SS *Otranto*, creaking like a second-hand bed, slipped out of the dock, I peered down at a mist of faces, among them the face of my lovely young wife and my heart dropped like a lift out of control. I was to leave her and the children many times in the next twenty years or so and, at the moment of parting, this overwhelming sense of loss always hit me like a blow in the solar plexus.

We waved ineffectually to each other and then she was lost behind a curtain of rain. I went below and lay down on my bunk. The engines were throbbing below but, this apart, the whole ship seemed to be wrapped in silence, the sad silence of farewell.

The next day showed little improvement. The passengers moved around the ship like condemned prisoners and meals were eaten in a sort of whispering gloom. The weather was not too bad and the sea merely choppy but many migrants were already being attacked by seasickness. The scene was not a cheerful one.

To all intents and purposes I sailed as a migrant, using

the cover story that I was going to a job as a tram-driver in Melbourne. Only the captain and the purser, Mr French who was known as Froggie, knew my true identity. The captain, a large pink-faced man with a stomach that was a perpetual threat to the brass buttons on the jacket of his uniform and an appraising eye for the ladies, had invited me to his table and on the second evening I remarked on the general air of misery among the passengers.

'Oh, it's always like that at the beginning,' he said cheerfully. 'This is the third migrant run I've done and it's been the same every time. But don't worry, by the time we reach the Med all the girls will look like Indian princesses.'

3

The captain had forgotten for the moment that we were not going through the Mediterranean. The Suez Canal was still closed to shipping, a legacy of the recent Middle East military fiasco, and we were going to Australia the long way round, via South Africa. Fortunately, he got the directions right in the end.

But his prophecy about the girls was spot-on. As the temperatures climbed, they shed both their gloom and their winter clothes and the decks bloomed like flower gardens as they paraded in their summer dresses and swimsuits. And it was not just the girls who changed. The sunshine and the relaxing, pressureless atmosphere of the sea voyage seemed to lift everyone's spirits and the whole ship came to life. It was as if the migrants, most of whom had never been further than Blackpool or Brighton, suddenly realised that they had been handed the holiday of a lifetime and decided to enjoy themselves while they could.

They were helped by the fact that the Australian government treated its future citizens handsomely, insisting that they should be fed, watered and entertained as if they were paying a full fare. All the normal facilities of a cruise ship were laid on – creches and playgroups for the children, concerts, film shows, competitions, deck sports, shore excursions and dances. The food was five-star and there were enough bars to service a small town.

Freed from work and domestic responsibilities, perhaps for the first time in years, the passengers forgot their fears of the future and lived for the moment. Middle-aged couples walked around the ship hand in hand, smiling secretly as if they had rediscovered each other and were in love all over again. Shipboard romances among the younger ones blossomed while the officers, handsome as film stars in their crisp white tropical uniforms, acted on the girls like a magnet to a box of pins. The officers had seen it all before and, concealing their cynicism, plucked the pick of the crop.

On her return to England the SS *Otranto* was due to be broken up and sold for scrap and there were times when I felt that she knew this and had decided to prolong the voyage. Like an old lady out for a Sunday afternoon drive she took her time. We called in at Cape Town and Durban and then made our leisurely way across the Indian Ocean to Colombo. For me this was the magical part of the trip, especially at night: sailing on a smooth dark sea under a velvet sky the ship seemed to be enveloped in a cocoon of peace, alone in time and space.

But, as we moved on from Colombo, another subtle change took place. Australian immigration officials had joined the ship for the last stage of the journey and, as they began to counsel the migrants about the new life that lay ahead, one could feel the nerves tightening, the tension growing. This came home to me rather poignantly when, two nights out of Fremantle, a concert took place.

A young Scots lassie, one of the passengers, sang with some success and, called on for an encore, gave us the ballad, *Oh, But I'm Longing For My Ain Folk*.

> . . . though I'm far across the sea,
> Still my heart will ever be
> At home in dear old Scotland
> With my ain folk.

The sentiment of the words struck home like darts releasing, from Scot and Sassenach alike, floods of homesick tears.

I was due to leave the ship at Perth and, in an impetuous moment, I told Froggie French that I would like to buy the officers and crew a drink. He looked staggered for a moment, then gently reminded me that the total muster consisted of about 420 people. In my simplicity I hadn't reckoned on such a number but, in the hope that the film company would pay, I told him to go ahead. I still have the chit, the wine card, which he presented to me afterwards.

Issue to Crew:	371 Bottles Beer	
	19 Minerals:	£19-3-8
Officers:	10 Bottles Veuve Clicquot:	£13-15-0

The price looks ludicrous now, but I think this might well qualify for an entry in the *Guinness Book of Records* as the biggest round of drinks ever bought by one man.

Another little snapshot of the voyage remains firmly in my memory. One evening I was sitting on deck when I heard two girls talking about their approach to love-making.

'What do you do when a chap starts to get fresh with you?' said the first.

'Oh, no problem,' answered her friend confidently. 'If I like him I let him. If I love him I help him.'

4

I spent the next two months in Australia travelling from state to state, capital city to capital city and covering hundreds of miles of outback: it was a unique once-in-a-lifetime opportunity to see the wide brown land. I fell in love with the bush and with the people, an affection which has not changed or dimmed with the years. I have been back about twenty-five times since that first memorable visit and fondly regard Australia as my second homeland.

Audrey's devotion and industry were fantastic. Each time I put down my bags at some new hotel a fresh batch of letters from England was there to welcome me. She wrote almost every day, sending all the news, press clippings, anything that might interest me. And there were letters from John and Sally. John usually gave me a blow-by-blow account of the latest match played by Tottenham Hotspur, while Sally wrote to her own special formula. Knowing my passion for football and cricket she always signed off with a reference to sport. A typical note from my seven-year-old daughter might read like this:

Dear Daddy – You will get all the news from Mummy.
I love you.
        Yours in sport – Sally.

Paradoxically, although these letters increased my homesickness they also raised my spirits.

In the course of the three months I spoke with hundreds of people from Britain. In each centre I went on the radio and gave interviews to the local papers, asking immigrants to write and tell me their stories. After such interviews it was not unusual for a queue of people to form at the hotel to see me. At the old Bellevue Hotel in Brisbane I talked with over fifty people in one morning. So many letters arrived at the Department of Immigration in Canberra that they assigned a secretary to answer them.

I gathered some amazing material. One Scotswoman travelled 300 miles to the Bellevue Hotel to tell me how her husband had brought her and their six sons from a hill farm in Scotland to Queensland because he had seen a barren valley in a dream. God, he had told her, wished him to go there to 'make the valley green'. Which, after surmounting enormous difficulties, is exactly what he did.

A Wiltshire man described how he had set his feet on the road to fortune by buying a hole in the ground. He had noticed this great hollow near the centre of the town in which he had gone to work as a garage mechanic. Over two years he saved up and bought the site for £180. He then put up a notice inviting builders to dump their rubble there for a pound a load. When the hole filled up, he levelled it off and sold the land to a developer for £2,000.

'The locals passed that hole every day and hardly noticed,' he said. 'But I came with a fresh eye and wondered what the hell it was doing there and why nobody did anything about it.'

I found surprisingly few examples of failure, perhaps because such people were reluctant to come forward. There were some success stories like the man who bought the hole but what struck me was the way in which the ordinary migrant had settled quite happily for doing much the same job as back home. I found one of my fellow passengers on the *Otranto* who had been a petrol pump attendant in Newcastle manning the pumps at a garage in Rockhampton, Queensland. When I asked him if this was why he had pulled up his roots and travelled 12,000 miles he replied, 'I like the job. Always have. But I couldn't stand the climate back home. Here you've always got the sun on your back.'

Cairns in northern Queensland was then a small town on the Great Barrier Reef with a fruit market, one main street and one motel – thirty years later the small town had become a prosperous resort and I heard it described as 'an island surrounded by motels'. I certainly did not expect this sleepy little place to come up with any surprises but I was proved wrong, not once but three times.

The first surprise came as I waited outside the motel for a car to take me to the local radio station. A man paused as he went to walk past and then greeted me. To my astonishment, I saw before me a friend with whom I had played tennis in Orpington, Kent, just three or four months earlier. A bank manager, he had retired and come out to Australia to see a married daughter.

I had scarcely recovered from this coincidence when, after my radio interview, the receptionist told me that I was wanted on the telephone. A deep Aussie voice introduced itself as George Snow and followed this up with a remarkable statement.

'Heard you on the radio. I reckon I'm your cousin.'

Over a drink at the motel he proved his point. An ex-Royal Navy man, he had elected at the end of the war to take his discharge in Australia and had set up in business diving for pearl-shell off the Great Barrier Reef. Scarcely any trace of Englishness remained – this big brawny man was as Australian as gum trees or Ayers Rock.

He named several relatives we had in common and we cemented our kinship over a drink or two. In his job he came across the occasional pearl and producing one from the pocket of his shorts he asked me to present it to Audrey. I did so when I got home but I am ashamed to say that, with her usual caution, she put it away somewhere safe and it has not been seen since.

The third Cairns surprise came one evening in a rather nondescript café. The menu was chalked on a blackboard attached to the wall and it offered an enterprising selection of dishes:

> Steak and one egg
> Steak and two eggs
> Steak and chips
> Steak, egg and chips
> Steak, two eggs and chips
> Lamb's fry
> Carpetbag steak

As you can see, it wasn't too easy to make a choice and, as I wrestled with the problem, I became aware of a woman weeping. Looking round I saw a girl in a seat by the window, a girl whose face seemed vaguely familiar. We were the only two customers in the café and, as her tears turned to sobs, I went across and asked politely if there was anything I could do to help. As she looked up I saw her more clearly and recognition was instant.

That young woman was Elaine Fifield, a leading ballerina from the Sadler's Wells company. Her talent was such that many experts in ballet considered her to be the natural heir to the crown of Margot Fonteyn. Relieved to meet a fellow countryman she gradually unwound and explained why she came to be sitting in an unprepossessing café in Cairns, 12,000 miles from home. About two years before, she had met and fallen passionately in love with an Australian who owned and ran a plantation in New Guinea. Romantically, if not wisely, Elaine married him, abandoned London and her burgeoning career and became a planter's wife.

The idyll had prospered at first but in recent weeks it had been fractured by quarrels. She had fled to Cairns from Port Moresby after a particularly strong difference of opinion and was uncertain whether to go on to Sydney where she could seek out her former colleague Robert Helpmann or to go back to her plantation home. I offered to help either way and we agreed to meet the next morning but she did not turn up for breakfast as arranged and it came as no surprise to

learn that she was on her way back to her husband. I did
not hear of her again and I hope it worked out for she was
a lovely lass.

So much for Cairns and its surprises. However, Queensland
had not yet finished with me. We had driven up to the Atherton
Tablelands, a fertile plateau that lies inland from Cairns, and
pulled up for the night at a small pub in a place called Malanda.
During the course of the evening we relaxed in the bar which
possessed an old upright piano and a fairly upright pianist
who, at one point, struck up the unofficial national anthem,
Waltzing Matilda.

Now, it is not generally known that this evocative piece
started life in the late seventeenth century as an English
marching song. Exported to Australia by the early settlers,
it was taken over by Banjo Paterson, who kept the tune
and added a new version of the lyrics. The original goes as
follows:

> Once a bold fusilier
> Was marching through Rochester
> Bound for the wars in High Germany
> And he sang as he marched
> Through the good old streets of Rochester,
> Who'll come a-fighting for Marlborough with me?
>
> Who'll come a-fighting?
> Who'll come a-fighting?
> Who'll come a-fighting for Marlborough with me?
> And he sang as he marched
> Through the good old streets of Rochester,
> Who'll come a-fighting for Marlborough with me?

I am not sure what fit of madness possessed me but I began
lustily to sing these ancient words until I became aware that
the pianist had stopped playing and a graveyard silence had
descended on the bar. The pianist, who stood well over six feet
in his thongs and had the muscles of a cane-cutter, dropped
a hostile hand on my shoulder.

'That's our bloody song!' he growled.

I have an intense dislike of physical violence especially if
I am the smaller man and with instant diplomacy I replied,
'Yes, of course. And I like your words better.'

His grip tightened to a point where it threatened to splinter my shoulder blade. 'Then bloody sing 'em,' he said firmly.

So I did.

5

The fates seemed to conspire to delay my departure from Australia. A lunch-time drink at the Standard Hotel in Orange, New South Wales, developed into a two-day stop-over due to the generous hospitality of the publican, a well-known local character named Maxie Foulds. Senator Doug McClelland, who later became High Commissioner in London, was equally hospitable and my visit to Canberra extended itself effortlessly from two days to four.

On the night of my departure on a BOAC Britannia my new Australian friends entertained me to such good effect in the Journalists' Club that I almost missed the flight. And then when I did arrive at the airport to be told that the plane would be delayed for two hours while the engineers corrected an electrical fault, the revelries continued until, at close to midnight, I staggered aboard and we took off.

It soon became clear that the aeroplane had the temperament of a prima donna. We made a diversion to Jakarta in Indonesia for repairs and were held up there for something like eighteen hours. Another delay at Bahrain lasted even longer. A journey that should have taken two days at most stretched to four and when we did at last put down in London, I felt as if I had been done like a dinner. For poor Audrey and the children, this was the fourth attempt to meet me and they were beginning to think of the airport as a second home. True to character, John wept when I appeared at last, Sally giggled and Audrey wore a smile which was a blend of welcome and resignation.

Associated British had arranged for the press to be there and we had to go through the rigmarole of photographs and interviews before I could be released. Then it was home to a hot bath, the distribution of presents, to sleep – home, as I realised when I studied the neat piles of letters and papers which Audrey had carefully arranged on my desk, home to work.

Dougie Moodie was anxious about the supply of scripts for *Dixon of Dock Green*. Could I let him have some more as soon as possible?

6

With the rapid growth of television and the consequent demand for scripts to feed it, I became conscious of the need to organise writers. The Screenwriters' Association, founded by director-writer Frank Launder, was a useful professional association which had done much to secure recognition of the writer but it concentrated attention mainly on film and, in any case, did not concern itself with fees. The Radio Writers' Association, part of the Society of Authors, was similarly concerned only with the problems of radio writers.

I talked with Leigh Vance of the Screenwriters' Guild and others and together we dreamed up a plan for a writers' trade union, an organisation which could unite the increasing number of television writers. Not without difficulty, we persuaded the Screenwriters and the Radio Writers to merge and form a new Guild and I became the first chairman with Leigh as my deputy and Bryan Forbes as treasurer. We elected a formidable council, with distinguished writers like Denis Norden, Alan Simpson, Philip Mackie, Alun Owen, John Lemont, Alexander MacKendrick, Larry Forrester, Dick Sharples, Gerald Kelsey, Edward J. Mason, Allen Prior, Eric Paice and the noted Australian author, Peter Yeldham. We needed them, for often in the first two years we had to have a whip-round to collect money to pay the staff wages.

Most of the leading members of the Guild were already successful and established writers who really did not need the protection and services a union could offer. They joined out of a deep conviction that the standards of television and film could only be improved if all writers were paid fairly and treated with dignity. Sadly, there were – and still are – a few fat cats, talented and wealthy authors who seldom raised a finger to help their fellow professionals. They, no doubt, believe that their creative work is too important to humanity to be interrupted by such trivialities.

I little knew when I agreed to take the chair what inroads

the new Guild would make on my time. For the first three or four years we had to battle constantly with the ITV companies and the BBC for recognition and, on occasion, with impatient writers in our own ranks who felt that we were going too slowly. Long days and longer evenings were spent in negotiation and debate. But slowly we hammered the Guild into shape and made it a force to be reckoned with. One of the proudest moments of my life came when, together with Kim Honess, our general secretary, I signed our first agreement, laying down basic fees for television drama. This represented the crucial breakthrough: other agreements followed, covering every area of film and television. The film and television writers of today owe more than they realise to those early pioneers.

The Writers' Guild will always occupy a special place in my heart: I spent five hectic years as the first chairman and a further five as president, years in which I had more headaches and problems than you could count but wonderful years also in which I forged friendships which lasted to this day. I got more from the Guild than I ever put in.

A meeting with Lew Grade much later in our history illustrates our approach to the fight to achieve full recognition for writers. We had been pressing for some time for a pension scheme for free-lance television writers without the least success. We had at least a half-dozen elderly members of the old Screenwriters' Association – successful writers in their day – who were living in poverty and relying on benevolent handouts. The problem was very much on my mind and when I went to see Lew on another matter I raised the issue. His reply came in the usual robust manner. The idea was a non-runner: free-lances were well paid, they should save for their old age like other people. I decided to try a frontal assault.

'Lew,' I asked, 'who has made the greatest contribution to British television – you or me?'

For a moment, unusually, he was lost for words, so I pressed on. 'You have run a major TV company and made a success of it. But you could not have achieved that success without the plays and series which I and other writers have brought to you. When you retire you will have a fine company pension to take with you. Yet despite all the work I have done for television I shall not have one penny pension when I retire. Do you think this is fair?'

His eyes twinkled. 'Ah, but I shall never retire.'

'That's not the point. You could if you wished to. I don't have that choice.'

He held out a hand. 'All right,' he said, 'you've got your pensions.'

A lot of hard talking had still to be done with other ITV companies and the BBC but this meeting with Lew gave us the breakthrough we had been seeking. The pension scheme, alas, came too late for me but at least I knew that when Guild members reached the end of their careers they would get something from the industry they had served.

One strange and rather amusing spin-off from my role as Writers' Guild negotiator was that I inadvertently became involved in the gold-mining business. What happened was this.

A television executive whom I had often faced across the table when debating contracts went to Canada on business for his company. During his stay he was approached by a friend who asked if he would be willing, for a fee, to negotiate a settlement in a dispute between two companies who owned adjoining properties in the Val d'Or in Quebec. A rich seam of gold-bearing ore ran from one company site into the other and the argument centred around the location of the border.

The television executive had to decline the offer for he was wanted back home but he recommended that they should contact me, adding that in his view I was one of the best negotiators in the business. As a result, some weeks later I found myself installed in a luxurious suite in the York Hotel in Toronto trying to reconcile what seemed to be the irreconcilable.

The problem soon became clear. The respective heads of the two companies were former prospectors, tough and granite-like in their obstinacy, and they had locked horns over the issue like two warring rhinos. It took me a week to talk some sort of sense into them but in the end they backed off and agreed the very reasonable deal that I had worked out. Since my knowledge of gold is more or less confined to Audrey's wedding-ring I consider this a pretty fair achievement.

Another excursion into business some years later led me briefly into the position of chairman of a property company in Sydney, Australia. The men who persuaded me to undertake this unusual role were old friends, Jack Wayland and his son John, who refused to listen when I protested that I was to property-development what Jack the Ripper was to the sanctity of womanhood.

I spent about two years at this game, flying out to Australia at regular intervals, negotiating with government departments in Canberra, with builders, unions and banks. This was not really my scene and I wasn't sorry to get out. However, there remains one enduring monument to my spell of office: the building in Philip Street in which the Australian prime minister has a suite of offices was built by our company.

Chapter Fourteen

1

There were at least two millionaires in the top echelon of Associated British and neither looked or behaved remotely like any film people I had ever met. Eric Fletcher – later Lord Fletcher – a solicitor, was deputy chairman and, improbably, a Labour MP who became a junior minister in the first Harold Wilson government. Fletcher represented the tough working-class area of East Islington and, so it was said, kept an old banger of a car for use in the constituency and thoughtfully left the Rolls-Royce at home. I was never able to confirm this story but, if it were true, he certainly would not have been the first politician to indulge in shabby masquerade.

Robert Clark, the managing director and executive in charge of production, was a dour Scottish accountant who, as a partner in a major London property company, had piled up a fair old fortune. His caution with money became a legend in the business. Described as a man with short arms and long pockets who put more thought into signing a cheque than reading a script, he husbanded the film companies' money and his own as if it were water in the desert.

All the same, I grew to like Robert and, apart from the inevitable differences over fees, we got on well. He once said that he liked me because I was one of the few people around him who knew the word 'No'. And he had a pretty decent track record, with films like *The Dam Busters*, *Angels One-Five*, *The Hasty Heart*, *Ice Cold in Alex* and *Woman in a Dressing Gown* all of which were part of the studio output under his regime. Basically a shy man who carefully avoided the extravagances of the film world, he had in May, his down-to-earth wife, someone who smiled on his

164

foibles and placidly provided him with a good Scots home life.

Robert's enthusiasms seldom showed above the surface but he was clearly interested when I described my Australian experiences and commissioned me to proceed to the next stage, the writing of a screenplay for the film, to which I had given the working title of *The Wide Brown Land*. At the same time, I put forward a proposal for another project. I had seen something of the Flying Doctor Service at work in the outback and I believed this could provide an exciting background for a major international television series.

Within a week the idea received approval and since I had my hands full with other work we cabled a young Australian writer I had met in Sydney and offered him a contract to develop the series. Michael Noonan arrived on a six-month deal a few weeks later and stayed in Britain for over twenty years. He became almost a part of my family, spending Christmas after Christmas in our company.

Mike wrote a half-dozen fine scripts and all looked set fair for *The Flying Doctor*. Then the roof fell in and our intended epic turned into disaster. An American company heard about the project and offered to put in finance and what they called 'production know-how'. Robert Clark, who never turned away money on principle, promptly accepted and the studios were invaded by an American producer, of whom I had never heard, and his assistant.

I became immediately suspicious when the assistant began to refer to his boss as 'Coach', and these suspicions were confirmed when, within weeks, the pair of them performed the reverse of the old alchemist's trick and transmuted the gold of Mike Noonan's scripts into base mid-Atlantic metal. The series, they insisted, had to have an American star in the central part and Coach knew just how this could be achieved. Here, in synopsis form, is the plot he provided for the first episode.

John, a young American doctor, is on holiday in the outback staying with his father's old friend Dr Lewis, who naturally has a beautiful daughter. A call comes for Lewis to fly out to a cattle station to check on a very sick patient. However, just as he prepares to go Lewis loses his sight. I will repeat that – Dr Lewis goes blind. John bravely sets out in his place, only to discover when he sees the patient that he must operate on the spot to save his life. Not knowing how to do this he gets on the radio to the blind doctor who gives him blow-by-blow instructions. The patient is saved. John, partly persuaded by the presence of the beautiful daughter, agrees to stay on in the Flying Doctor Service as a replacement for poor Dr Lewis.

This garbage was actually filmed, with a fading American B-feature actor in the lead. The lines were bad enough but he delivered them with all the emotional intensity of a turnip. The series, of course, was a massive failure. The Australians, incensed by what they saw as an insult to their magnificent Flying Doctors, refused to take the programme and it died the death here and in America. Long before this, Mike and I had quit the project in disgust.

I completed the screenplay of *The Wide Brown Land* to my own and Robert Clark's satisfaction. Lee Thompson was nominated as director and then, with the pre-production stage well advanced, a palace revolution swept through the studio. The American owners sold out and heads began to roll, Robert Clark's among them. The new bosses had their own ideas about what films should be made and mine was not among them.

The Wide Brown Land never reached the screen.

2

One of the most extraordinary and popular characters among London's theatre producers was a man named Henry Sherek. Hugely fat, a natural *bon viveur*, he embraced life with a vivacity that was infectious: it was said of Henry that his day began with a champagne breakfast that lasted until bedtime. He adored the theatre, had a shrewd eye for a play and brought good taste and the highest standards to his productions.

When he asked me out to lunch I was intrigued and when he told me the reason I was flattered. He had recently seen the film of *Woman in a Dressing Gown* for the third time. Would it be possible to turn it into a stage play? He had, he said, already formed a plan. If she liked the part he would ask Googie Withers to play the lead and open the production in Australia before bringing it to London. I agreed without hesitation with the result that I found myself *en route* for Australia once more, this time by air.

The flight arrived way behind schedule and I rushed straight from the airport to the theatre in Melbourne, getting there just as the curtain fell on the first act. There was an ominous silence as the lights went up and then a sudden wild outburst of applause. Women around me wept openly – and when the second act got under way I understood why. Googie's performance was magnificent, breathtaking: Joan Miller had been superb in the television version, Yvonne Mitchell had earned awards for her performance in the film but Googie outshone them. I have seen a dozen or more actresses in the role since then, most of them excellent, but none has matched Googie. The play ran for over nine months all over Australia and New Zealand, a phenomenal run for countries that then had a combined population of about fifteen million people.

We parted on the understanding that Googie would come over the following year to do the play for Henry Sherek and on my way home I called in at Perth to see a sister, Nancy, who had settled there with her family, and a well-known Australian author named Helen Wilson. I'd become interested in one of Helen's short stories and she agreed to sell me the film rights. I put the story away in my case to await its turn, little realising that one day it would open another improbable chapter in my life.

I arrived home to receive the devastating news that Henry Sherek had died. In the short time I'd known him he had become a good friend and, with hundreds of others in the theatre, I bitterly mourned his passing.

3

They had assured me that there was not a spare seat in the house but as I entered the theatre foyer I was struck by the silence. There was none of the usual rustling and chattering which goes on among a waiting audience. The producer ushered me into a box which had been so heartily decorated with flowers that it smelt like a florist's shop and, stepping forward, made a signal with his hands. Immediately, the strains of 'God Save The Queen' came blasting out of the speakers and, looking down, I saw a full house standing to attention, their smiling faces turned towards me. When the music ended they broke into applause, giving me the sort of standing ovation which would have cheered the heart of a party conference warm-up man.

The year was 1962, the city Buenos Aires. I had decided to mix business with pleasure and go to Argentina to see the opening of *Woman in a Dressing Gown*, then fly on to Chile where another sort of drama, the World Cup, was reaching its final stages. I'm afraid that I had not reckoned with the hospitality and enthusiasm of the Argentinians.

When the curtain did at last go up on that first night, there was an instant round of applause for the setting. When Rosa Rosen, the star, made her entrance, more frenzied applause followed – so much so that she came down to the footlights to acknowledge it, bowed to me, and then went off to make the entrance all over again. The entire performance was punctuated by such interruptions: when Rosa delivered a particularly moving speech, the audience rose to her and she responded by reprising it. In this way, a play that should have run for just over two hours stretched to three. The performances and the production looked excellent to me and the evident enthusiasm of the audience was exhilarating, but I cannot deny that I found it all a little bewildering.

Nor was it over when the curtain came down. I was taken on stage to make my bows with the company, presented with more flowers and kissed by various ladies and gentlemen. To my horror, I discovered later that some of these gentlemen were theatre critics: I can only claim in my defence that I did not know this at the time. When I confessed this misdemeanour to J. B. Priestley a year or so later, he gave me a look in which contempt and astonishment vied with each other and said curtly, 'Ignorance is no excuse. Surely you could tell!'

I stayed until the early hours of the morning at the backstage party that followed the performance but jet lag and excessive hospitality combined to make me bid farewell to festivities which, it seemed, were just getting into their stride. The producer offered to walk me to my hotel which was only

a few hundred yards away, and as we left a beautiful girl
with long black hair that shone like anthracite fell into step
beside us.

I had noticed this lovely creature at the party – indeed
I would have been hard put not to do so since she was
seldom far from my elbow, smiling demurely whenever I
caught her eye. She did not speak English and I had no
Spanish so we did not get beyond the smiles. All the same, I
was puzzled by her presence and I asked the producer, who
also acted as interpreter, if she was his girlfriend. He shook
his head and gave me a sly grin. 'No, no,' he said. 'She is
yours.'

'Mine?'

'For you. She likes you. Very nice girl. Her name is
Maria.'

'But this is impossible,' I stammered.

He squeezed my arm. 'Please, we wish you to be happy.
Think of her as an extra blanket.'

4

Towards the end of a hectic week of lunches and dinners,
a barbecue at a large ranch at which our host roasted an
entire ox, several personal appearances and interviews and
a one-hour radio show put on in my honour, my thoughts
began to turn to Chile and the World Cup. Unfortunately,
England had already been eliminated but I had a ticket for the
final, which promised to be an exciting match and, anyway,
I wanted to take a look at the country.

On the evening before my departure I had started to pack
my bags when a call came from reception to say that a group
of young people had arrived to see me. I told the clerk to send
them up and braced myself for another interview. There were
three of them, two young men and a girl, and I was rather
taken aback when the girl, who spoke good English, explained
that they had travelled from the town of Rosario, a distance of
some 250 miles, to ask me a small favour. Why did I find these
young strangers familiar?

'You see,' she told me, 'it is an amazing coincidence that
you should be here in Argentina. When we heard you on the

national radio we could hardly believe it. We are members of a
theatre group in Rosario and we have just built our own theatre
out of what was formerly a warehouse. We open for the first
time in two days.'

Of course! I understood then: these youngsters, with their
eager enthusiasm, reminded me of my friends at Unity Theatre,
of the days when they had transformed an old chapel into one
of London's most exciting playhouses. But what, I asked, had
she meant by a coincidence? Why had they come to see me?

'Don't you know?' the girl, Dolores, asked in some surprise.
'Your play, *Hot Summer Night*, is to be our first production in
the new theatre. Were you not told?'

I knew nothing of this and said so, adding how pleased
and flattered I felt by their choice. Dolores then produced a
small tape-recorder. 'We realise you are very busy,' she said.
'We heard you on the radio and know that you have plans to go
to Chile. We would like you to come and see our little theatre
but we know that will not be possible. But perhaps you will be
kind enough to record a message of greeting which we can
play to the audience on our first night?'

Whether it was the gentle, almost humble way in which
she had spoken or the sentimental memories of Unity their
appearance had evoked or a combination of both, I don't
know, but I reacted impulsively.

'I'll do better than that,' I said. 'I'll come to Rosario for
the opening.'

'But what about your visit to Chile?'

With a conviction I did not feel I replied, 'I can always see
a football match but it is not every day that I can see one of
my plays in a brand new theatre.'

As Dolores embraced and kissed me and the others pumped
my hand, I remember thinking, 'Greater love hath no man than
this that he gives up a World Cup Final for his friends.'

But the sacrifice was more than worthwhile. Dolores and
her colleagues had pulled out all the stops for at the moment
of arrival they whisked me off to a civic reception in the
grounds of the Mayor's house. A banner, inscribed with the
message, WELCOME TO SEÑOR TED WILLIS, had been strung
above the platform and a brass band struck up 'God Save
the Queen' as I took my place. The Mayor then proceeded to
welcome me to his suburb, a speech which with translation

into English took forty minutes. The temperature had hit 32 degrees centigrade, the platform had no protecting cover and by the time His Worship finished, I was in danger of dissolving into a grease ball. They seemed disappointed when I replied in three minutes flat.

The theatre lived up to all my hopes. Neat and functional with seating for 150 people, it bore eloquent testimony to the hard work and dedication that the group had put into it. And the production, I have to say, was absolutely first class with none of the extravagances I had seen in Buenos Aires.

I stayed for three days in Rosario and left Dolores and her friends with a certain sadness. They were the stuff the theatre is made of, lovely, intelligent, vital people to whom an obstacle was merely something to be overcome. Hanging in my office I have, as a memento of my visit, a beautifully designed scroll signed by members of the group and inscribed, 'AL AMIGO TED WILLIS from his friends of TEATRO LA MASCARA'.

There are two other memories of Argentina which come back to me. In Buenos Aires I was invited to the sumptuous headquarters of the Writers' Society, a place so big and so expensively furnished that, with the poverty of our own Writers' Guild in mind, I could not help wondering where they found the money to maintain it. The answer came when they introduced me to a huge ledger, showed me an entry in my name, and invited me to draw royalties from the production of *Woman in a Dressing Gown* in cash.

No fools these Argentinian writers! They employed inspectors who called on the box office of every professional theatre in the country each night to collect the author's royalties! I drew some of what was due; not much because by the time the Writers' Society had taken 20 per cent, the government their 15 per cent, and my South American agent, Catarina de Wulff, had received her rightful 10 per cent, there was not a lot left for me. Still, it was fun.

The other incident was a little more serious. Argentina was then undergoing one of its periodic bouts of military dictatorship and all opposition had been suppressed ruthlessly. The daughter of my agent asked if she could bring someone to see me and, at a small flat in Buenos Aires, I met a striking young man who was a member of the underground democratic resistance. Aged twenty-seven, he had already served two jail sentences and had a scar over his left eye and a permanent limp to show for it.

He began by thanking me for a broadcast I had made two days before and for what he called my 'brave words'. I had no idea what he meant – my recollection of the broadcast was simply that I had talked in general terms about the importance of freedom and democracy, nothing very special. But apparently it had been special to him and his comrades and he went on to warn me that the authorities had put a watch on my movements.

He gave me a dossier, written in English, which he asked me to take home and send out to the newspapers. It gave a detailed account of certain atrocities which had been perpetrated by the military government and called upon the international community to protest. He then presented me with a beautifully decorated leather brief-case which, he said, his comrades wanted me to accept as a token of their gratitude for all I had done.

I am glad to say that I did manage to get some coverage of the problems in the more serious English papers. The brief-case is now in the possession of my son, John, who carries it with pride.

In addition to South America, *Woman in a Dressing Gown* enjoyed considerable success in a dozen other countries. The play eventually opened in London at the Vaudeville Theatre under the management of Bob Swash with Brenda Bruce in the lead. It ran for almost three years in Germany with the celebrated actress Inge Meysel as the star and had long runs elsewhere. There must be something in it to which people of different nationalities can relate for even in Japan, where the action had been transferred from London to Tokyo, the audiences responded enthusiastically and the critics were more than kind.

5

Looking back on this period, it seems as if I never stopped travelling. One trip took me to Czechoslovakia to research a film about Lidice, the village that the Nazis murdered in revenge for the assassination of Reinhard Heydrich, the SS leader. Alas, when I returned and wrote the script I discovered that an American company had just completed a film on the same theme and the studio cancelled the project.

My next destination was a small town in Austria named Bad Aussee, near Lake Toplitz. The Nazi leaders had chosen this area as a sort of redoubt in which they would make their last stand against the Allied armies. No such stand took place but recently there had been stories in the press which told of boxes of American dollar notes floating to the surface of the lake.

I sold the idea of a six-part series based on these events to the BBC and persuaded Edward J. Mason, one of the originators of *The Archers*, *My Word* and *My Music*, to join in as co-writer: out of this collaboration emerged a highly popular series starring William Lucas called *Flower of Evil*. The BBC came back for more and we did two further series with the same central character, *Days of Vengeance* and *Outbreak of Murder*.

In Bad Aussee I had one of the most shattering experiences of my life. The Nazis had brought hundreds of thousands of slave workers to the area to burrow into the mountains and construct vast underground workshops in which they hoped their scientists would be able to develop the ultimate atomic weapon and so turn the tide against the Allies. Ted Mason and I visited the site of the concentration camp where the slave workers were kept and we were stunned to silence by what we saw.

An area about the size of a football pitch had been cleared and grassed over. A tall, simple, wooden cross stood at one end and beneath it a stone slab inscribed to the memory of the hundreds of thousands of people of many nationalities who had perished in those deadly tunnels. In a nearby hut, pathetic souvenirs lay in glass-fronted boxes – faded photographs, children's shoes, name tags, wooden spoons.

Private houses and apartments overlooked this memorial on two sides. I wondered if, when these residents opened their windows, they saw ghosts in striped uniforms or heard screams.

That evening back at our hotel we fell into conversation with a member of the local council, a jovial man who walked with a pronounced limp. This, he told us proudly, was the result of a wound he had received on the Russian front.

'Ah, those Russians,' he continued. 'They were swine! My

regiment was just outside Moscow, freezing in the trenches. They had bandits behind our lines who would steal up in the snow, camouflaged in white sheets, and murder our soldiers. I had one comrade who died like that – one moment I was talking to him, the next he was dead with a knife in his back. They were murderers those Russkies, not soldiers.'

With the memory of the campsite I had seen that afternoon still sharp in my mind I said, 'What were you doing there?'

'I don't understand?'

'What were you doing in Russia? Did the Russian people invite you to go? Or perhaps you were on holiday?'

He looked blank for a moment, then clapped me on the shoulder and laughed. 'Ah,' he cried, 'English humour. Very funny.'

Ted and I looked at each other in disgust and disbelief and decided to leave.

6

I wrote one screenplay in 1963 the research for which took me no further than Bolton in Lancashire. It was inspired by a true incident in which a school had gone on strike to demand the reinstatement of a music master who had been dismissed.

This was my first attempt at a musical and it worked out very well. Called *It's Great to be Young*, the film starred John Mills and featured a young boy, Richard O'Sullivan, who went on to become a star. I worked for a decent fee plus a tiny percentage of the producer's profits but, despite being a smash hit at the box office, I never saw a penny of the percentage. The old, old story – expenses and overheads had swallowed up the profits though, strangely, the producer retired to live comfortably in the country a couple of years after the film's release.

Associated British asked me for another musical and I devised a story in which a group of youngsters went to France in an old double-decker bus to take part in a song contest. The finished script, called *Six Men and a Nightingale*, duly went to the studio but the film was never made, although some time later a very similar story called *Summer Holiday* starring Cliff Richard went into production.

Another screenplay that never reached the screen was *Iron Road Ahead*, a story centred around the lives of railwaymen. I did, however, get to ride on the footplate with the driver and fireman on a journey from London to Carlisle, an experience that instilled in me a lasting respect for railway workers.

Then, towards the end of 1963, I received a telephone call which, literally, was to give my life a new direction.

Chapter Fifteen

1

'I have been asked by the Prime Minister to recommend six people for life peerages. I'd like you to be one of them.'

The place was the office of the Leader of Her Majesty's Opposition in the House of Commons, the time early November 1963, the speaker the Right Honourable Harold Wilson, MP. The phone call from his secretary had given no inkling of why Harold wished to see me and, since the British film industry was staggering towards yet another crisis, I had assumed that this was what he wished to discuss. I must have looked poleaxed by his opening statement for he went on, 'You've done a fair bit for writers – that ought to be recognised. And the Labour people in the House of Lords are getting thin on the ground. We need some younger blood there.'

I think I managed to murmur some trite words about being honoured and similar claptrap while my mind, whirring like a top, tried to take in all the implications.

'Will you do it?' Harold asked. 'You'll be in some very distinguished company.'

'When do you need to know?' I asked.

'I want to give the list to the Prime Minister this afternoon. It will then go to the Queen for approval.'

I told him that I would be delighted to accept but would like to consult Audrey before making a final decision. Not wishing to make the call from his office, I went across Westminster Bridge to a telephone box just outside County Hall and rang my unsuspecting wife.

Her first reaction was that this must be one of my stupid jokes; her second was to laugh. 'You a lord,' she said. 'Now I've heard everything.'

'You'll be a lady,' I reminded her.

'Oh, no,' she said firmly. 'They can call you what they like but if anyone calls me Lady they'll get the rough edge of my tongue!'

And so began a very long six weeks.

2

A letter duly came from Sir Alec Douglas-Home, the Prime Minister, to say that he had it in mind to put my name forward for a life peerage and would I kindly and promptly let him know if I agreed. I was warned that I must keep absolutely silent on the matter.

Up to this time I had thought very little about the House of Lords but, in the next weeks, I swear that the place seemed to come up in almost every conversation. Perhaps, nursing my secret, I simply felt more aware of it. At dinner one evening I faced a friend, someone quite well known, who bluntly told me that he would like a peerage and asked if I had any influence with the relevant authorities. I had to say no, but I couldn't help wondering what he would think when he heard that I had been sent upstairs.

I learned that the announcement would be made on Christmas Eve and Audrey and I decided to make a bolt for it and go to Devon for the holiday. We also decided that my mother, who knew nothing of what was afoot, should come with us. On the eve of our departure we took John and Sally into our confidence, swearing them to secrecy. They accepted this interesting piece of information with a certain irreverent hilarity, finding it hard, no doubt, to picture their daft father sitting in Parliament with a bunch of dukes and earls.

At one o'clock the next day, we were well on our way to Torquay when Audrey decided to switch on the car radio. The announcement came at the top of the news giving the full list which included Gerald Gardiner, QC, and Hugh Gaitskell's widow, Dora. There followed a great deal of guff about my background in show business and the possibility that I might take the title Lord Willis of Dock Green.

When I thought we had heard enough I switched off. My

mother sat in ominous silence, then she said, 'Does that mean you're a lord?'

'That's right, Mum,' I replied uneasily.

'Stone the bloody crows,' she said. 'If you're a lord, I must be a bleeding duchess!'

Strange how a man never gets from his nearest and dearest the respect he feels to be his due!

The press had tracked us down to the hotel and the street outside resembled sales day at Selfridges. When the manager opened the car door and said, 'Welcome to the Torbay Hotel, my lord,' it took me a full twenty seconds before I realised that he was addressing me. We eventually shook ourselves free and, in our room, started to go through the telegrams and messages which were arriving from friends and colleagues by the minute.

After about an hour I went in search of my mother, eventually running her to ground in the lounge where she was holding a press conference. Surrounded by a circle of delighted reporters, this tough old Cockney lady, her grey-black hair pinned in a bun, arms confidently folded over a large bosom, fielded questions with all the aplomb of a seasoned politician though, perhaps, with more directness.

'What was your son like as a boy?' asked one young lady.

'He was forever making up stories,' replied my dear mother. 'In fact he was the biggest bloody liar this side of the Old Kent Road. He could lie quicker than a cat can lick milk.'

At this point I thought it expedient to leave.

3

I very nearly failed to take my seat in the House of Lords. For some months I had been working on an idea for a film set around the Monte Carlo rally and, shortly after my meeting with Harold Wilson, I was given the opportunity to join one of the participating cars. They classified me as navigator which, since my knowledge of map-reading is only marginally better than my understanding of nuclear physics, was rather dangerous.

Fortunately I had two drivers who knew the way and my services were rarely called on. The first driver, Philip, was an old China hand who had formerly raced at Brooklands. His driving technique had a strong authoritative edge to it – from the moment he took the wheel the car could have no illusions about who was in charge. By contrast, David, the co-driver, almost made love to the car, caressing the clutch as though it were a girl's knee and murmuring endearments to the engine.

Each in his own way was a superb driver, true professionals whose skill served to emphasise my amateur status. They, and the other car crews whom we met *en route*, lived in a world entirely new to me, a world in which the vocabulary had a distinct flavour of the internal combustion engine. A man did not simply fancy a woman; his 'big end was knocking', or he was 'revving on all cylinders'. When you were tired you had 'run out of juice' and you took a 'zizz'. A bald-headed man was 'in need of a retread', a shapely female had 'decent lines' and 'a lot of power under her bonnet' and if she seemed interested in you then it was time to 'take the hand-brake off and put your foot down'.

We set off from Scotland in late January and by evening we reached an official checkpoint on the road to Dover only a mile or so from my Chislehurst home. Forewarned, Audrey brought John and Sally along to see their father and, just before we sped off again, she whispered, 'Do you have to do this sort of thing?'

Her question came home to me with full force in France, just outside Chambéry. Up to this point we had made good time and were well up with the leaders, but on a mountain road we struck black ice. David was at the wheel with me beside him, while the unsuspecting Philip had a zizz in the back. The car went crazy, lurching and spinning across the narrow track like a drunken skater as David fought to bring it under control. To my left I could see a terrifying drop into the valley below, to my right a solid wall of mountain and then, as the car twisted, these views reversed themselves. We hit the impassive mountain once, twice, three times and skidded over to within inches of the edge. Only the skill and strength of the driver saved us from a very long drop.

When the car at last came to a halt under the overhang of the mountain, we climbed out to inspect the damage. The front wheels were buckled, the body, crushed inwards, had taken on the shape of an egg-timer. Another car pulled up briefly and the driver asked if we wanted any help.

'Well,' Philip said, 'do you know anyone who would like to buy a long, thin car?'

Miraculously, they managed to get us back on the road and we limped into Monte Carlo late that night, some twelve hours behind schedule. I was ready to head for bed but both Philip and David counselled against it; their experience suggested that it would be best to unwind slowly, that a leisurely meal in a good restaurant would properly relax me.

I allowed myself to be led off to a sort of night club where, it seemed, most of the rally crews had gathered. Several semi-nude ladies of buxom appearance mingled happily with the crowd and the noise, which was pretty deafening, rose a decibel or two at intervals as heavy hands slapped their quivering bottoms.

It was all a bit hearty for me and I slipped away. I rang Audrey from my hotel room to find her in a state of some distress. The BBC had reported our crash in their early evening bulletin but my poor wife had been unable to get any further news. Not unnaturally her imagination had been working overtime as she considered my possible fate and when she heard my voice she burst into tears. She had recovered by the next morning when I telephoned again and treated me to a long harangue about our new dog, Jasper, who had put down several deposits on the sitting-room carpet.

4

Harold Wilson was right about the need for new blood in the Lords. There were only about thirty Labour peers at the time, average age seventy, led in sprightly style by the eighty-one-year old Viscount A.V. Alexander, a former Cabinet minister. My formal introduction took place in February 1964, an occasion which reminded me of a couple of lines from Tennyson's poem, 'The Lotus-Eaters':

> In the afternoon they came unto a land
> In which it seem-ed always afternoon.

Certainly, the old place had a languid air in those days. We sat for three afternoons a week and usually rose at about seven in the evening– any later and their lordships threatened revolt. But within a year a Labour government took office and Wilson began to stock up the empty benches with life peers who rapidly changed the habits of the House. Today we meet four or five days a week and consider ourselves lucky if we can leave by 10 p.m.

My maiden speech on the Police Bill drew a great deal of media attention, mainly because of my connection with *Dixon of Dock Green*. Thereafter, until Wilson sent in the reinforcements, I spoke frequently on a broad range of issues and played an active part in the affairs of the House.

More media attention came my way when I made a speech attacking pop music in general and the Beatles in particular. It was a rather priggish contribution in which I referred to pop as carbohydrate and suggested that young people needed to balance their musical diet with some protein, to take in Beethoven as well as the Beatles.

The pop world gave me a prompt and noisy answer the following Sunday when a group called the Yardbirds, led by Eric Clapton, turned up at Chislehurst and demanded to be heard. They plugged into my electricity supply, arranged themselves on the garden terrace and for three hours rocked the neighbourhood with a selection of numbers. John and Sally loved every minute of it and the music drew in most of the local youngsters. Eric Clapton had taken care to warn the newspapers and the exploit garnered headlines the next day. 'POP IMPRESSES PEER' was a fairly typical example and most of the stories were illustrated by photographs of a suitably humbled Lord Willis shaking hands with the triumphant members of the group.

I trod on safer ground some time later when I introduced a debate on poets and poetry. This, I believe, was the first time that Parliament had ever discussed such a subject and it produced a lively and entertaining discussion enlivened by ample quotations. Even so I still came in for some punishment, for all the unpublished poets in Britain – or so it seemed – sent me samples of their work accompanied by anguished pleas for help.

On the whole, their lordships are a decent, friendly,

hard-working lot but one cannot say, hand on heart, that they are notable for their charisma. I suspect that is a word they would frown on, seeing it as a departure from the respectability which is as much a part of the place as the Lord Chancellor's wig and breeches.

There are, of course, exceptions, a few remarkable characters – one such was Lord 'Manny' Shinwell who not only reached the age of 101 but retained his physical and mental health almost to the end. We celebrated his hundredth birthday with a little party in the library at which the Leader of the House unveiled a plaque commemorating the occasion. A young photographer took a shot of Manny and then asked good-humouredly if he could come back in fifty years and take another one.

Without a moment of hesitation the old man replied, 'I don't see why not. You look pretty fit to me.'

And there was an occasion when a London pigeon somehow invaded the Chamber. Their lordships watched in fascination as the intruder flapped and swooped around until it finally came to rest on the Woolsack. The then Lord Chancellor, Lord Hailsham, eyed the pigeon for a long moment and then in his best legal voice said, 'Any messages?'

Sometimes the House of Lords assumes a kind of ghostly quality, its corridors stalked by faded faces that one seems to have seen in a previous incarnation. When I first arrived there was Attlee, former Prime Minister, a little hunched walnut of a man who wore the resigned look of someone who knew that what went on in the House of Lords was largely shadow-boxing, politics at second hand; Herbert Morrison, forever turning his head as if suspecting that someone was about to creep up behind him with a knife, a spiky humourless man, still embittered by his failure to become prime minister; and Edith Summerskill, tall and statuesque, a doughty fighter for women's rights. Edith had been one of the sponsors at my induction and, years before in Tottenham, our family doctor. She enjoyed telling their lordships that I was the only peer she had ever seen in the nude, omitting to add that I was eight years old at the time.

Bob Boothby was there, his voice still reverberating like an organ almost to the end, his sense of humour as wicked as ever. One of my delights was to coax Bob into an anecdotal mood and then to sit and listen while the stories boomed out. One of the best, which he told against himself, concerned a train journey in which he found himself sharing a carriage with an attractive young lady. She cast several surreptitious glances in his direction and eventually asked, 'Excuse me, but are you Lord Boothby?'

'Yes, I am,' he replied, pleased to be recognised.

'Are you the Lord Boothby who appears in *Free Speech* on television and *Any Questions* on radio?'

'Yes. I do appear on those programmes.'

'Then you are *the* Lord Boothby!'

'You might say that.'

'Oh,' sighed the young lady, 'how very disappointing.'

5

Then there was George Brown. I had known George for a long time, first as a political opponent and then as a friend and, like most people, I knew his qualities and his frailties. By the time he came into the Lords he was largely burned out – there were a few familiar outbursts but as his health deteriorated the old fires sank lower.

Someone once said of George that he had the best untrained mind in the country. A former secretary at the Foreign Office told me that up until midday George was a brilliant Foreign Secretary, one of the best ministers he had ever worked for. Then he called for his first gin and tonic and after that the day went downhill. Alcohol acted like a poison on George though he obstinately refused to recognise it: one drink was a trip-wire which sent him stumbling, the second put him over the edge. There were two distinct phases to his drunkenness: at first he became bullying and aggressive, then the mood descended into maudlin sentimentality. I much preferred the aggression.

Once, when he was still Foreign Secretary, I was invited to the Yugoslav Embassy to meet a young film director and to see his latest film. As Audrey and I stood talking to the Ambassador and the director we heard a commotion at the door and in the next moments George came weaving uncertainly towards us trailing a wake of officials, secretaries and detectives. Ignoring the politely smiling Ambassador he embraced and kissed Audrey in his customary lusty manner then turned on me and boomed, 'What the devil are you doing here?'

Ever the diplomat I replied that I had come to see this new film and how much I was looking forward to the experience.

Her Majesty's Foreign Secretary brushed this aside impatiently. 'You don't want to waste your time with that bloody rubbish. Come on, we'll go and have a meal.' Then, turning to the Ambassador he added, 'What's the matter here? Have you run out of drink?'

George was eventually hustled out gently, still protesting, and we stayed to see the film. He had been right about that, anyway – it was awful.

Audrey and I were with George and his long-suffering wife Sophie at the Foreign Secretary's official residence in Carlton House Terrace on the night he resigned from the government. He paced from the bedroom to the sitting-room and back again, getting steadily more drunk and railing bitterly against the Prime Minister, Harold Wilson. George fully expected Harold to telephone to refuse the resignation but no call came. This happened to be the third or fourth time George had offered to quit and Harold had decided that enough was enough. As the evening wore on the maudlin phase took over with George embracing Audrey, declaring that we were his only true friends and much rubbish of that sort.

Another incident almost ended in tragedy. Shortly after his resignation I took George and Sophie out to dinner with a television producer to float the suggestion that George should do a series of interviews with world leaders. In the event, George got so drunk and offensive that the producer left early making it clear that the project was a dead duck. There remained the problem of getting George home.

He vigorously refused all offers of help, insisted that he was quite able to drive and set off to locate his car. Sophie rightly refused to go with him. Luckily I had my car outside and we trailed George as he wove his way, head down, to a car park at the back of Leicester Square. He came out a few minutes later in his car and we followed. Somehow or other he got to Haymarket, a one-way street, and turned the wrong way. Traffic squealed to a halt, horns protested and George pulled up facing the hostile motorists. I stopped in the side street in time to see two young policemen approach George with ominous tread. I ran towards them.

'Officers,' I said gravely, 'that is George Brown, the Foreign Secretary. He has accidentally made the wrong turn. If you will hold up the traffic, I will straighten things out.'

To my intense relief they swallowed this lie. I shoved George into the passenger seat, manoeuvred the car into the right track and, leaving Sophie to bring my vehicle, drove to their flat near Marble Arch. As we left Haymarket the two policemen saluted but George was then too far gone to notice.

On the evening of the day on which Kennedy was assassinated George was located at a dinner by the television producer Jeremy Isaacs – later Head of Channel 4 – and hurried off to the studio to participate in a tribute to the late President. He had already taken a fair amount of drink on board and the producer made the fatal error of settling him in the hospitality suite where more liquid dynamite was freely available.

A number of other personalities had been roped in for the programme, among them Eli Wallach, the American actor and film star. Milton Shulman, the distinguished drama critic who was involved with the programme described what happened when Brown met Wallach in an article for the London *Evening Standard*:

When Wallach arrived he was clearly upset about the news and was in no mood for small talk.

He was introduced to George Brown, who immediately told Wallach how he admired the actor's work. Wallach accepted Brown's compliments with good grace but was not anxious to chat about himself.

Brown, however, persisted in trying to steer the conversation in that direction. And when Wallach did not respond, Brown loudly asked why actors were so conceited. Someone like Wallach, said Brown, always carried a newspaper in his pocket with his name in prominent headlines.

On the contrary, Wallach was finally stung to reply, he was always meeting people who said they recognised his face but could not place his name. It was all meant to be light-hearted banter. But Wallach, emotionally upset by the President's death, clearly wanted none of it.

'Have you ever been in a play by Ted Willis?' asked Brown.

'No,' said Wallach. 'Who's Ted Willis?'

Wallach's curt denial of any knowledge of Ted Willis annoyed Brown.

Wallach, in an effort to break off this pointless conversation, walked off.

This did not stop Brown. The American actor returned to his seat and said nothing, while Brown continued to mutter about the conceit of American actors. Suddenly Wallach lost his temper. He rose from the sofa, pointed at the Deputy Labour Leader and shouted, 'I didn't come here to be insulted. Is this bastard interviewing me on the programme? If so, I'm leaving now.'

Brown said something deprecating which infuriated Wallach even more. Wallach began to strip off his jacket. 'Come outside!' he said to Brown, who was sitting on a low chair looking up at him. 'Come outside and I'll knock you off your can!'

Undeterred, Brown shrugged the threat away and told Wallach to shut up and sit down.

The American actor rushed forward as I leaped between them and pushed Wallach back onto the sofa.

At that moment Carl Foreman arrived to see me wrestling with Wallach.

Although he had no idea what it was all about, Foreman joined me in restraining Wallach.

'He's not going to interview you on the programme,' I hissed at Wallach. 'He's one of the guests.'

'Well, who is he?' Wallach kept asking.

Although there had been formal introductions when he arrived, Wallach had obviously not worked out who everyone was.

'He's George Brown. He's Deputy Leader of the Labour Party,' I whispered.

'I don't care who he is,' said Wallach. 'I'll still knock the shit out of him.'

By now George Brown was reduced to silence.

We then asked the three Americans – Wallach, Foreman and Crosby – to go downstairs to the studio.

As they rose to leave, Brown got up from his chair and extended his hand to Wallach.

'Brother, brother,' he said. 'I don't think we should go into the same studio feeling this way. Let's shake hands.'

Wallach shook Brown's hand, they exchanged a few terse words and I thought that was the end of the matter.

I was wrong.

Just as Wallach was leaving the room Brown could not resist one final word.

'And now you'll know who Ted Willis is,' he shouted after the retreating figure of the actor.

Towards the end George became a sad, deflated figure. The few directorships had dried up, he was short of money and he left Sophie to live with a young secretary. It was a rotten end to a marriage that had survived more ups and downs than your average lift: Sophie had endured his drinking, his volatile temperament, the selfishness that every ambitious politician carries in his knapsack, and stood faithfully by him in the darkest moments of his career. Not surprisingly she died a bitter woman. To be fair, the young secretary cared for George in his last two years and nursed him lovingly to the end.

I loved him too. He had massive faults and equally massive abilities, and he could be touchingly generous and thoughtful and genuinely funny. It was his misfortune to be born with a self-destruct mechanism.

6

This is not the place to argue the pros and cons of the House of Lords. All I will say here is that it does a hell of a lot of useful work on government bills and if, one day, the Other Place decides to abolish us they will have to think up something to put in place of the Lords pretty damn fast or the legislative process will bump to a halt.

Apart from the revising function, the House of Lords is a good test-bed where new ideas for legislation can be tried out and put before the public for debate. I have found it useful on such disparate subjects as broadcasting, the arts,

revision of the Sunday trading laws, copyright law, abolition
of the law of blasphemy, the improvement of the law on rape,
Iceland's fishing limits and, above all, on public lending right
for authors. This latter campaign, brilliantly spearheaded by
Brigid Brophy and Maureen Duffy, was debated in the Lords
three or four times and the huge majority my bill won there
finally forced the government to concede the case.

I am no longer as active in the House as I once was,
although I still attend and vote as often as possible and speak
when I can. I have made some good friends there among both
peers and staff and – dare I say it? – if they do decide to do
away with the old place I shall miss it. The old cliché is true:
the House of Lords is the best club in London.

As for the Commons I have come round to the view
that it takes itself much too seriously. There is far too much
legislation, the country is grossly over-governed. MPs don't
solve problems, they either create or compound them. It goes
against their nature to leave well alone so just because they
happen to be there, just because they are called legislators and
feel that they must make a show of actually doing something,
our MPs keep dreaming up one daft law after another. Or, to
be exact, a minority of MPs, for most of this parliamentary
lunacy stems from a small select company. This group calls
itself the government.

It is one of the sadder facts of life at Westminster that
when MPs are appointed to government they take it seriously.
They are at once overcome with an irresistible urge to govern
which, in plain words, means to meddle with matters about
which they know little or nothing. Possession of a red box
seems to turn them into legislative Rottweilers.

As for the backbenchers, a great many have digested the
bitter fact that being an MP is only marginally better than
being a dog warden and they have had the good sense to find
themselves something useful and remunerative to do outside
the House. Others protect their sanity, if not their livers, by
travelling the world on what are laughingly called fact-finding
tours. The rest drag themselves to Westminster, using it either
as a club or a rest-home and satisfy their consciences by draft-
ing Private Members' Bills which propose such vital measures
as a ban on ring-top drink cans or preparing speeches which
will never be delivered. For these, the only excitement in a

dull life is when they participate in an ancient ritual called 'Catching the Speaker's Eye' which demands that they jump up and down in the manner of a fat lady who is trying to dislodge an unwelcome spider from her knickers.

No, I have long held the view that the whole country would benefit from a moratorium on new legislation for at least two years. The hard-pressed electorate would get a much-needed breathing space, MPs would have time to do some useful community service in their constituencies and the House of Lords could make a welcome return to the more leisurely days of the past.

Chapter Sixteen

1

One of the least pleasant aspects of my nomination to the House of Lords was that the supply of film and television commissions began to dry up. Normally, the telephone would ring about twice a month with an offer of some sort but now the producers fell strangely silent. My last two films were *The Horsemasters*, a story set in the world of showjumping for the Walt Disney Organisation, and *Bitter Harvest* for Rank, an adaptation of a novel by Patrick Hamilton. My most recent television series had been *Taxi* for the BBC, starring the marvellous Sid James.

The curtain fell so abruptly that I began to wonder, as all writers do at such times, if I had run out of road. Was the entertainment business pointedly showing me the exit? Had I burned myself out? Determined not to go down without a fight I sat down and wrote a new stage play, *A Slow Roll of Drums*, about a young man in revolt against society, a sort of rebel without a cause, which we tried out at my local theatre in Bromley. It proved to be an effective piece, made the more so by an electrifying performance from the leading actor, David Hemmings. However, no London theatre management would take it on and the play went no further. Oddly enough, the following year it became a smash-hit in Poland.

A clue as to why the film and television offers had stopped came my way at lunch in a restaurant. An old friend, Joe Janni, a producer for whom I'd done some work, came to my table as he was leaving and dropped a hand on my shoulder.

'It's a pity that you've retired, Ted. I could have done with your help on a script.'

I assured him hastily that reports of my retirement were not only premature but exaggerated. He was not convinced. Shaking his head, he said, 'But you're a lord now, aren't you?' And he went on his way, leaving me with the uncomfortable thought that being a member of the Upper House somehow disqualified me as a writer.

I brooded over this encounter for some time. If this was the general attitude of the producers out there, then I really was finished. What could be done? I decided to take a gamble and write a screenplay on a speculative basis, that is to say without being paid money up front by a producer, which had been my usual practice.

The short story, 'The Skedule' by Helen Wilson, which I had bought on my last visit to Australia, came at once to mind. The central idea was a good one, a sort of boy-meets-girl, boy-loses-girl, boy-gets-girl theme set against the rugged background of Australia's Northern Territory, but it was a little too thin for a film.

I had always been fascinated by the Birdsville Track, the old cattle trail that links Birdsville in Queensland with Maree in South Australia, and I saw this as the ideal background and starting point.

Within a month I went off yet again to Australia to do the fieldwork.

2

Maree is where the railway line from Adelaide and a lot of other things run out. I'd been informed at Australia House in London that a truck shuttled up and down the Birdsville Track at regular intervals. The truck carried supplies for the hardy farmers who lived along the trail – with luck, and for a fee, the driver might take a passenger.

The little bush town, baked hard and dry by a relentless sun, had the friendly openness I had learned to expect in the outback. If the natives thought it odd that a Pom should descend upon them and ask for a lift to Birdsville they did not show it. The cheerful man in charge at the railway station not only pointed me in the direction of the hotel but took me across personally. I booked a room, had the customary beer with my new friend Ken and then he took me to meet Stu.

An old truck, with corrugated iron sheeting lashed to its side, stood under the shade of an awning outside a ramshackle shed. A middle-aged Aboriginal loaded supplies while Stu sweated under the open bonnet. The condition of the truck and Stu's curses did not hold out a lot of promise: I had the impression that this old crate would find it difficult to make it to the end of the street, let alone weather the three- or four-day journey to Birdsville.

Stu was a tall, lean, laconic Queenslander of about fifty with keen humorous blue eyes set in a crinkled sunburned face. The Australians have a knack of clipping the end from names and I assumed, correctly as it happened, that his full first name must be Stuart. He did not believe in wasting words. When I explained what I wanted he said, 'Fifty quid?'

He transferred a splodge of engine oil to my hand as we shook on the deal.

'Would you like me to pay you now?' I asked.

Stu did not believe in exerting himself too much either – a sensible precaution in that heat – and the shake of his head was barely perceptible.

'Nope. Settle up at the other end.'

He then introduced me to his Aboriginal helper whom he called Suit-Yourself. I never did learn his real name but the reason for this odd title soon became apparent – he answered almost every question or instruction with a grin, a shrug and those very words – suit yourself. An amiable man with the broad coal-black features of his people, he had that slow deliberation of movement that seems to come naturally to those who live and work in tropical temperatures. Although he clearly respected Stu and called him Boss, there was a relationship of complete equality between the two and they habitually traded genial insults in the approved Australian manner.

I spent a very long evening with Stu, Ken and a few of their mates in the pub bar during which Stu proved beyond doubt that he had hollow legs. Schooner after schooner of Toohey's beer disappeared without trace and without any apparent effect. They remained politely incurious about me or my background but I realised after a while that they were quietly testing me, making certain that I matched them glass for glass. I just about came through this ordeal by liquid and by the finish I had been accepted into the great Australian institution of mateship.

An old man, who seemed to be welded into a corner seat, told me of the time when the Birdsville Track used to be crossed by camel trains. 'Jesus,' he said, 'they had a bloody great Afghan camp here. Thousands of camels and their owners. Then the trucks came and nobody wanted the bloody animals. Most of the poor bastards were shot but there's still some out there, running wild.'

And then as if to prepare me for the journey he said, 'The Track? That's a real bastard. Hot as hell. And full of bloody mirages. Do you want to know what they used to call some of the places around here? Illusion Plains, Mount Delusion, Decoy Hill.' He cackled as he added, 'A lot of good blokes have done a perish on the Track, done a real perish.'

The next morning I felt like something brought in by the cat but Stu appeared totally untouched by the previous evening's excess. I climbed into the truck beside him, Suit-Yourself perched himself on the load of supplies in the back and by eight o'clock we were heading out of town towards Birdsville.

The outback that I had seen further south in West Australia and New South Wales had only partly prepared me for the scenery that opened up like a film in glorious Cinemascope. I could see what the old man had meant by mirages. There was no sense of perspective: perhaps because of the pure translucency of the light, the town that we had left seemed to be no further away and I could see the outline of the buildings even more clearly than I had an hour before. Ahead, a frieze on the skyline, I could see trees yet although we were travelling towards them they seemed to get no nearer. At times I thought I saw wide pools of blue water and even mountains, only to find as we drew nearer that the pools were dry salt-pans and the mountains mere sand-hills. I began to understand why this region is called the Never-Never Land.

At first the landscape appeared flat, featureless and stark, an endless plain dominated by a vast dome of indigo sky and a huge brick-coloured sun. Then gradually my eye tuned into the boldness, the larger than life beauty of it all – the red gibber plains glittering and gleaming like a carpet of rubies, the smooth patches of green mulga, the gentle pastel of the salt-bush, the distant sand-hills that changed colour as the track twisted, one moment ablaze with crimson, the next saffron-coloured or as white as alabaster. Then, at times, as if the land were afraid that it had revealed too much, the colours seemed to fade and brown became dominant: yet, after a while, the eye picked up not one brown but many, a variety of shades that ranged from copper to auburn, from fawn to russet.

We drove on in silence for a long time although I could feel that Stu was observing my reaction. From time to time he cast a brief look in my direction. At length he said, 'Well, what d'you reckon?'

'It's incredible!' I replied. 'The colours. And the light. I've never seen such pure light.'

'Yeh,' he said cryptically, dismissing my romanticism. 'A man could chase a flea all over this bloody country and never lose sight of it.'

3

It did not take long for me to find out what the sheets of corrugated iron attached to the truck were for. Stu put the truck into second gear when faced with a steep sand-hill and accelerated to the top only to find an unexpectedly deep drop on the other side. The truck bucked at this descent and we finished up in a drift with the wheels churning the sand uselessly.

'Bugger it!' said Stu and shouted, 'Everybody out.'

There was no question of my being a fare-paying passenger. I spent the next forty minutes with the others digging the wheels clear and laying down the plating until the wheels had a proper purchase and we could move on.

We left the track at intervals to deliver supplies to isolated homesteads and for Stu to take note of new orders. These tough outback people, true to the old frontier tradition, were warm with their hospitality and Stu never seemed to be in any hurry.

I cannot deny that I appreciated the breaks from the ceaseless bumping of the truck and that I learned the value of cold beer as an antidote to heat and dust.

Towards evening on the first day, a girl came galloping towards us on a big-boned, chestnut horse. Stu pulled to a halt and Suit-Yourself handed the girl, whose name was Marion, two or three packages.

Perhaps it was yet another trick of that damned light but she seemed to bear a striking resemblance to Vivien Leigh, even to her voice which had a markedly English middle-class accent. Marion became intrigued when she learned that I came from England and revealed that she had just returned from a five-year stint at a college in Cheltenham, which explained the accent. What was more she had the perception to ask if I was the Ted Willis who wrote *Dixon of Dock Green*, and looked at me with a new respect when I admitted the fact.

'I used to watch the programme every Saturday night,' she told me.

I was rather proud to know that I had a fan who lived along the Birdsville Track. She gave Stu a couple of bottles of beer and some fresh steaks and, smiling at me, said, 'Evening all,' and rode away.

Stu decided that we had done enough for one day and that anyway it would be best to drink the beer before it got warm and eat the steaks while they were still fresh. He drove on for about a mile and drew up outside the ruins of an old hut that was almost encircled by coolabah trees and tall green rushes. The area was in fact a man-made oasis; water from an artesian bore, bubbling up from beneath the earth, flowed down a gully into a small, beautiful blue lagoon. The site, once used as a staging-post by drovers taking cattle south to the rail-head at Maree, had long been abandoned but what the hut lacked by way of roofing was more than compensated for by the bathing facilities provided by the lagoon.

Suit-Yourself lit a fire and cooked the two steaks which were then shared between the three of us and Stu passed round the beer. We unrolled our swags and sat yarning for an hour or so as a copper sun slipped below the rim of a horizon that flared with great brushstrokes of crimson and purple.

A crescent moon took over the night-shift, the sky glittered with stars and as the temperature dropped like a stone we slid under our blankets and slept.

4

Early the next day we reached the Clayton river, another man-made oasis. Once again, the engineers of long ago had struck water deep underground and arranged matters so that the flow would run from the borehead into what would otherwise have been a dry river bed. All the birds of Australia seemed to have gathered here for a jamboree – flights of cockatoos, crested pigeons, galahs, finches and hawks made patterns of vivid colour above our heads.

Here Suit-Yourself caught some plump fish which were reserved for lunch. When the time came he cooked them in the way I'd seen gypsies do in England: wrapped in a thick layer of paper they were then placed in the glowing ashes of a fire and within ten minutes or so the fish were cooked to perfection. Later in the day he killed a sand-hill rabbit, throwing a stone at it with incredible accuracy, and this delicacy – more tender and flavoursome than the best free-range chicken – he cooked over an improvised spit.

This second day passed much as the first. The truck ploughed on over the glittering gibber plain and the red sand-hills, diverting here and there to make deliveries and to sample the hospitality of the outback. Once we found a steer that had trapped itself in a sand-pit. This was something like a marsh except that instead of being wet it was utterly dry, filled with a drift of greyish sand in which the poor animal thrashed helplessly. Stu simply lassoed the steer, tied the rope to the truck and winched it out.

Towards evening the Track began to change, to become less harsh. The sand-hills had a covering of green: wattle blossom waved on the plain, there were patches of feed on which cattle grazed. Silhouetted against the sky on the crest of a sand ridge a small herd of wild camel, descendants of the teams that had once hauled wagons and buggies over the Track, watched our progress.

We crossed the Cooper river near a place called Kopper-amanna without too much difficulty for the cracked river bed had not seen water for years. It is only when the heavy rains come down from Queensland that the Cooper becomes a real river and then, Stu told me, the force of the flood can be fearful. He pointed to some trees: caught in the top branches, like eerie decorations, I could see the bleached bones and grinning skulls of cattle.

'When the river's in full spate the water covers those trees,' he explained. 'Those poor bloody cattle were caught on the river bed and washed into the branches.'

We ended the day at a large homestead, the centre of a cattle station which covered an area bigger than Wales. The place had an airstrip and the woman of the house flew down to Adelaide in a private plane each month to do the household shopping. More hospitality here including an invitation to take a shower.

I stripped off with some relief and had just turned on the water when I saw what seemed to be a dozen or so bars of soap lying on the floor of the shower. But soap does not move of its own volition and these things, green and slimy, were clambering over each other. I let out an involuntary yell and our host's wife came charging in.

'It's those bloody frogs again!' she said and, ignoring my nakedness, scooped the creatures into a bucket. As she went out she gave me an appraising look, a smile that had a hint of pity, and threw me the customary Australian words of comfort.

'She'll be right.'

I couldn't make up my mind whether she was referring to the shower or to something else.

The next day, the landscape began to change again as we reached a huge gorge called the Mungerannie Gap where the Track curled between great boulders, rocky ridges and brick-red cliffs. Then it was on to Goyder's Lagoon, which turned out to be nothing more than a swamp, though a pretty big one, for it was twenty-five miles across, wider than the English Channel. We crossed the dry bed of the great Diamantina river in late afternoon and by evening we were in Birdsville, at the end of the Track and the journey.

I managed to get the last seat on a bush plane the next

morning which, with one or two stops, would take me to Brisbane. When I said my farewells to Stu he asked me, 'Are you a real lord?'

I had not mentioned the peerage on the trip, referring to myself always as Ted or Mr Willis, and the question surprised me. 'How did you know?'

'Got a dekko of your passport when you were unpacking your gear.'

'I'm a sort of made-up lord,' I explained lamely.

'Had another lord out here once,' he said laconically. 'Owned a big spread West of the Track. Liked his whisky. Three bottle a day man. Got the screaming heebie-jeebies and died of the booze. Wasn't a bad bloke.'

5

I called the screenplay *Last Bus to Banjo Creek* and set the story along the Birdsville Track, making the central character a younger version of Stu and including an Aboriginal assistant called Suit-Yourself. Marion, the girl on horseback, gave me the inspiration for the female lead: I invented a cool, laid-back young English girl who goes to the outback to marry an Australian she had met in London the previous year. A mix-up in the dates prevents the boyfriend from meeting her at Maree so she sets off to his station in Stu's truck. Because of their differing backgrounds they quarrel violently at first but then come to respect each other and fall in love. In the end she has to choose between Stu and her boyfriend.

Yet again, research had paid off. The characters and the story came easily and I was pleased with the resulting screenplay which was full of incident. Now the only problem was to sell it, a task that I left to my agent.

In the meantime, some producers had at last got the message that I had not retired. Joe Janni called, invited me to lunch and asked me to write the script for a picture that he provisionally called *The Square Mile*. The idea was to write three or four stories of London life set within a square mile of Piccadilly Circus.

This meant more research though at least this time it was nearer home and I could sleep in my own bed. I spent a day with workers in the sewers under Piccadilly, a fascinating and sometimes frightening experience which convinced me that these unsung and underpaid men were worth a thousand pounds a week. If they were to quit or strike the consequences for London would be unimaginable.

For a week I worked as a commis waiter at the Piccadilly Hotel, a hectic dogsbody of a job that left me exhausted. A commis works as assistant to a waiter and is at his beck and call as well as the customers. I was left with the indelible impression that 25 per cent of people who dine out have no manners. I had one narrow squeak when a noble lord looked up from his menu into my face. He gave me a startled puzzled look and then, evidently deciding that I was simply a look-alike for the Lord Willis he had seen in the House of Lords, he smiled and the danger passed.

Harrods were kind enough to co-operate and I went to work in their garden accessories department for a few days. A pleasant and undemanding experience, enlivened by the appearance of an elderly lady one day who enquired whether we could supply a lawnmower with headlights. I assured her that Harrods could meet any demand but could not resist asking the reason for the headlights. She explained, somewhat impatiently, that her gardener who doubled as chauffeur was somewhat overworked and she needed the lights so that he could cut the lawn at night. The dear old thing added, 'I don't want him to run over the peacocks in the dark.'

Moving on, I arranged that Harry, a stallholder in the Rupert Street market, should employ me for a few days. A lovely assignment for there were some marvellous characters among the stallholders and a cheerful Cockney camaraderie that made the days fly past.

One afternoon Harry spotted two nuns moving towards the stall. To my astonishment he ran forward, embraced one and gave her a kiss for which the word passionate would be inadequate. When the nuns had passed on, I remarked on the incident, pointing out that although I was not particularly religious I held the view that one did not do that sort of thing with nuns.

'Oh, you don't want to worry, mate,' he replied cheerfully. 'She's my girlfriend. She's in the chorus of *The Sound of Music* up at the Palace Theatre.'

Again, I was pleased with the screenplay that resulted from this fieldwork and so was Joe Janni. He slated the film for production and began casting but then some problem with the backing forced him to postpone. After that, as so often happens in the picture business, the project went cold. For two or three years there was talk of putting it back into production but nothing came of these plans.

Some good cheer came from my agent, however. The Rank Organisation, in association with Universal, the Hollywood company, wanted to buy *The Last Bus to Banjo Creek* and had offered a very good deal. When could I go out to Los Angeles to discuss the project?

6

Towards the end of January 1965, my sister Peggy rang to say that my mother had been rushed to hospital following a serious heart attack. I hurried to see her, fearing the worst, only to find the indomitable old woman sitting up in bed knitting furiously.

'I'm not going yet,' she said firmly. 'I've only just bought the wool to make this bloody pullover and I am not going to waste it.'

She did finish the pullover but then another heart attack hit her and she died on 3 February. The grief was overwhelming. It was hard to believe that this woman, a fighter all her life, would no longer be there to nag or encourage me. Life had never given her a real chance. She had enough wit, native intelligence and drive to become a leader in one of at least a dozen fields but she was a prisoner of poverty and had been forced to fulfil herself at second hand, through her children.

I remember the first time she came to see our new home at Shepherds Green in Chislehurst when, to my astonishment, she burst into tears.

'Don't you like the house, Mum?' I asked.

'Oh, take no notice of me, son,' she said. 'I'm a silly old cow. It's lovely, I'm proud of you.'

'So – why the tears?'

'It took me back, that's all. I went to work as a skivvy in a house like this when I was twelve.'

Scarcely a day goes by without some thought of my mother, some mental picture, coming to mind. I tried to put the feeling into words some time later.

> Strange how you stir within my blood
> And – stranger with the passing years,
> How still the memories surge and flood
> And prick the eye with tears.

Chapter Seventeen

1

'Are you a regular member of the House of Lords, sir?' asked the polite lady at the American Embassy.

'Oh, yes,' I assured her, although I wasn't absolutely sure what she meant by the word regular.

'Then there will be no problem, sir. Just bring in your passport or mail it to us and we will deal with the matter immediately.'

I thanked her and put the telephone down. No problem! In the past ten years I had applied for a visa to enter the United States on at least three occasions and been turned down. As a result I had lost two opportunities to work in Hollywood. There could be no doubt about the reason: at each interview the officials consulted their records, asked searching questions, and the shadow of my left-wing past fell across the desk and darkened their faces. Now I was not even being asked to attend an interview! I posted the passport and it came back by return stamped with a visa for Multiple Entries – I could go to the States as often as I wished.

A strange but welcome bonus flowing from my peerage. Did they, I wondered, think that the acquisition of a title had changed my character and outlook overnight? Still, I was not going to argue or complain. Three weeks later I arrived in Los Angeles, checked in at the Beverly Hills Hotel, courtesy of Universal Pictures, and reported to the studios for work on *The Last Bus to Banjo Creek*.

It soon became clear that my new American friends, in spite of their country's sturdy democratic traditions, were intrigued by the peerage. I'd tried to keep the lord bit under wraps but a number of English writers out there had unthinkingly put the word around and I became the target of some curious questions. One producer and his wife assumed that I had aristocratic blood coursing through my veins and that I reigned over a castle and a vast country estate. They were quite disappointed when I disillusioned them. Others were plainly confused – they could not understand how I could be a lord and a working screenwriter at the same time. But like most Americans, at least in my experience, they were kind, generous and lavishly hospitable and we got on well.

There were times when the hospitality went over the top as, for example, when one of the producers at Universal told me that he wished to throw a small, a very small, dinner party in my honour. I accepted gratefully and he followed up by asking if I had brought a tuxedo with me. I had to reply in the negative.

'I'll organise that,' he said cheerfully. 'I'll have a car pick you up at your hotel at six o'clock that evening.'

The car arrived promptly on the appointed day and a polite gentleman whipped me off to his emporium, the Hollywood equivalent of Moss Bros. Within a half-hour he had kitted me out, from black tie and dinner-jacket down to shoes and socks. At just after seven the car deposited me in all my sartorial splendour at the imposing home of the producer.

I was slightly surprised when he greeted me for he had just come from the tennis-court and his white shorts and sweat-shirt made a strange contrast to my formal wear. He took me to his study, poured two large Scotch whiskies, and settled down to chat as if he had the whole evening free. His wife, also in tennis gear, came in to join us, and my glass was generously replenished.

This process went on for at least an hour during which time they left in turn to get changed, making certain before they did so that the Scotch in my glass stood at a respectable level. By eight thirty I could hear the regular drumbeat of car doors slamming and the sound of voices and merry laughter from below. Then, as my host rose to pour yet another liberal dose of whisky, the door opened, his wife appeared looking like a princess and hissed, 'Now!'

I rose unsteadily to my feet, advanced towards the top of the curving stairway and looked down, through what seemed to be a mist, on a swirling sea of upturned faces. Then I heard a series of small explosions and eventually traced them to a massive red-coated Master of Ceremonies who was beating hell out of a table with a gavel. His voice set up more reverberations in my poor head as he roared, 'Ladies and gentlemen. The Right Honourable, the Duke Willis of Chislehurst, England!'

The applause that followed was generous in the circumstances for I think they had expected to see someone with the noble look and stature of the Duke of Edinburgh or C. Aubrey Smith and not the short stubby wretch who clung desperately to the banister rail as he moved downwards to meet them.

There must have been a hundred or more people at this very small dinner party and it turned out to be a lively affair. At one point I got into a fairly heated argument with Burt Lancaster, an unwise move on my part since he stands at well over six feet in his socks and has muscles that a heavyweight champion might envy. I cannot be sure what the dispute was about but I have a faint recollection that he made some derogatory remarks about the British and that I reacted defensively. Apparently only the tactful intervention of my host stopped the argument from degenerating into something worse.

I had always admired Burt as an actor and I admired him even more as a man the next morning when he took the trouble to call at my hotel to apologise. In fact, we exchanged apologies and cemented the relationship over a meal and a visit to the theatre that evening.

Meanwhile, *The Last Bus to Banjo Creek* made slow, unspectacular progress. I am afraid that I could not get used to the working conditions or methods. There was nothing really wrong with the conditions for they supplied me with a sumptuous office and an equally sumptuous secretary but I missed the untidy comfort of my workroom back home and, as the weeks wore on, the homesickness got worse.

The working methods did not suit me either. On the first day they put me to work with a producer-cum-script editor called Ernie Nims, a pleasant, amiable fellow who informed me that our first job would be to cut thirty pages from the screenplay. We argued and tussled and in two weeks we managed to get out nine or ten pages. Ernie was not at all perturbed by this tortoise-like progression but it irritated me. This was the first time I had ever worked cheek to cheek, day after day with another person and I did not like it.

In the end, Universal agreed that I could go home, on the understanding that I would return when the film went into pre-production and make any further changes that were deemed to be necessary. In the meantime, the screenplay had gone to Robert Mitchum in the hope that he might agree to play the part of Stu.

The studio treated me very generously and I have no complaints. Over the years I have made many marvellous friends in the States, particularly among members of the Writers' Guild. Two who became very close were screenwriter James R. Webb and his wife Sue with whom I stayed on most of my subsequent visits. Jimmy Webb was the great Western expert, writer of such films as *How the West was Won* and *Vera Cruz*. He became the first president of the International Writers' Guild and I succeeded him two years later.

The day before I left for home Universal gave me a farewell lunch. Angela Lansbury was among the stars invited and we talked much about her late grandfather, George Lansbury, a former leader of the Labour Party. A leading television producer happened to be there also and I thought this might be a good opportunity to find out about the American market for television scripts.

'And what sort of new ideas are you looking for?' I asked naïvely.

He looked at me with some pity. 'We are not looking for new ideas,' he said gravely. 'We have recently carried out a marketing exercise and discovered that the public is not responsive to new ideas. What they want are familiar themes dressed up in a fresh and interesting way.'

The look on Audrey's face when she met me at the airport on my return was principally one of relief as if she were happy that I had escaped from America without being scalped by the Apache. I was reminded of the time when the novelist Scott Fitzgerald arrived back in New York after a working stint in Hollywood to be greeted by H. L. Mencken with the words, 'Thank God you have escaped alive. I was full of fears for you. If Los Angeles is not the one authentic rectum of civilisation, then I am no anatomist. Any time you want to go out again and burn it down, count me in.'

2

One would not think of the House of Lords as the ideal place
to pick up an idea for a television series but it did, in fact,
provide me with the theme for one of my most successful
programmes. One of the features of the wonderful library in
the Lords is a complete collection of *The Times* going right back
to the beginning of the newspaper. These have been bound into
heavy red volumes and a reading stand is provided to protect
elderly peers from the danger of hernia when handling these
massive books.

Walking past this stand one afternoon I saw a volume open
and stopped to glance at the contents. Here were copies of
The Times from the Victorian period and my eye immediately
caught an item reporting the creation of a Criminal Investigation Bureau at Scotland Yard. Within a few days I had
worked out the format for a series dealing with those early
Victorian detectives which I called *Sergeant Cork*.

I took the format to Lew Grade at Associated Television
(ATV) and, never a man for hesitation, he bought it in
about thirty seconds flat. Once again I struck lucky in
terms of chemistry. Jack Williams, an immensely experienced
producer and a genius at casting, took over the reins and
he signed the late John Barry to play the part of Sergeant
Cork, with a young William Gaunt as his assistant. I wrote
the first half-dozen scripts and then, as the series made its
mark, assembled a team of writers to provide more. Among
them were Bill Craig, Michael Pertwee, Julian Bond, Gerald
Kelsey and Eric Paice, the cream of British television writers
at that time.

Sergeant Cork remains one of my favourite series. It ran
for seven years and, because I liked it so much, I continued
to contribute episodes whenever I could. Thanks to Jack
Williams the programme had real quality in depth and was a
huge success with the public. Years later Granada Television
tried to camp out on similar territory with a series called
Sergeant Cribb.

I now began a very productive period in the field of tele-
vision writing. Most of the projects went to ATV and Lew
Grade although I did write one play for Sydney Newman at
Armchair Theatre, *The Scent of Fear*, which starred Anthony

Quayle. In fairly quick succession over the next few years I developed *The Sullavan Brothers*, the story of a family of solicitors, *Mrs Thursday*, *Knock On Any Door*, an anthology of single plays, *Crime of Passion*, *Virgin of the Secret Service*, a series about an Edwardian secret agent, and *Hunter's Walk*, a police programme.

Mrs Thursday developed on an early-morning journey. At the chill hour of seven o'clock I was driving up to town to see Lew Grade about a new programme idea on which I was not entirely confident. Going along Whitehall I saw a splendid Rolls-Royce in front of me and, standing at a bus-stop, a group of women. As the Rolls drew level with them, one of the women, a sturdy Mrs Mop character, lifted her skirt above one knee and jerked her thumb at the driver in the manner of someone hitching a lift. The Rolls glided on regardless and the woman, with a cheeky grin, gave the departing car a two-fingered salute.

By the time I reached Lew Grade's office I had worked out a mental story line about a Cockney charwoman's adventures when she unexpectedly finds that she has inherited a Rolls-Royce and a multi-million-pound business. I told Lew the idea, he gave me a cigar and a cup of coffee, and bought it.

I suspect that part of the reason for his speed in dealing with me was that he had little interest in home-grown studio television – his mind and his time were more fully occupied with transatlantic deals and filmed series like *The Saint*. He was content, I think, to leave the studio production to Bill Ward, his genial and experienced general manager at Elstree, and to Cecil Clarke, the head of drama. Indeed, in his recent autobiography, *Still Dancing*, Lew makes hardly any mention of the studio-based series which were the bread-and-butter of ATV's output and which brought the company considerable success.

Jack Williams showed his flair for casting yet again with *Mrs Thursday*, signing Kathleen Harrison for the lead with Hugh Manning as the butler she inherits along with the fortune. I recruited much the same team of writers to help provide the scripts. The first episode to be transmitted soared to number one in the ratings and thereafter was never out of the top ten. The series ran for four successful years. *Crime of Passion* was another notable success, notching up a seven-year run.

For *Knock On Any Door* I invited a dozen or so of the top television writers in the country each to write a one-hour play which would illustrate the theme 'the marvellous world of the ordinary'. The series went so well that Bill Ward asked me for more at very short notice and I rang around various agents asking if they had any plays that I might use. I bought one, I remember, from a young playwright named Tom Stoppard.

I tried an experiment with one of the two plays that I con-tributed to the anthology. I had been much taken some years before by a stage play called *Happy as Larry* which had been entirely written in rhyming couplets and I decided to attempt something similar. *The Ballad of Queenie Swan*, a light-hearted piece about the landlady of a London pub who is being pur-sued by three unlikely suitors, is, I believe, the only television play ever written in verse and I had some doubt about whether it would work on the small screen. In the event, with Billie Whitelaw and Fulton Mackay turning in superb performances, it was such a success that Bernard Delfont − now Lord Delfont − asked me to turn it into a musical for the theatre.

Directed by Arthur Lewis and with Vivienne Martin, Paul Eddington and Bill Owen in leading roles, my first musical played at the Yvonne Arnaud Theatre in Guildford to packed houses and then transferred to the Comedy Theatre in the West End where it died the death. The critics did not take kindly to two hours of Cockney doggerel and said so with painful bluntness. A pity, because I thought the piece had a certain originality and that there was an audience for it.

I received some consolation, however, when Noël Coward saw the show and courteously came backstage afterwards with congratulations and criticism. He thought also that two hours of dialogue in rhyme was a little too much for an audi-ence to take and that the music was not strong enough but he praised my lyrics and urged me to write more. Perhaps he was just being polite but there is pleasure in such politeness and to me it was more welcome than champagne.

3

Sydney Newman had now moved to the BBC as Head of Drama and, at a chance meeting, he asked me to write something for him. I had for some time been considering the idea of a quartet of plays based around the character of my

mother and some incidents in her life – not a biography as
such but a story about a working-class woman like her from
childhood to old age.

The Four Seasons of Rosie Carr, starring Jane Hylton and June
Barry and directed by Peter Graham Scott, was the result. It
is, I believe, one of the best things I have ever written and
the public seemed to share that opinion for over seventeen
million viewers tuned in to the first play and by the fourth
the figure had climbed even higher. Each of the four plays
reached number one in the ratings and the quartet was also
hugely popular abroad, especially in Australia and Japan.

In the meantime, *The Last Bus to Banjo Creek* had become
bogged down. There had been not one but two or three internal
shake-ups at Universal and although some feeble attempts to
cast it were still being made, I felt in my bones that this was yet
another screenplay that would not go before the cameras. In
the next ten years a half-dozen producers read it and became
keen but the project seemed to be jinxed for something always
intervened to stop further progress. *A Long Way to Shiloh*, which
I adapted from the novel by Lionel Davidson, was yet another
screenplay which was received with high praise but failed to
go into production.

After the burst of series for Lew Grade I developed *Black
Beauty* for Tony Gruner and Paul Talbot of Fremantle Productions and then I hit a mental roadblock. I had been working at a furious pace, writing late into the night, playing an
active part in the House of Lords and speaking at more dinners,
lunches and school speech days than you could shake a
stick at. So when the United Nations cultural organisation,
UNESCO, and the Australian government invited me to go
Down Under to study the film and television industries and
to make recommendations on how they could be developed,
I jumped at the opportunity. Once again I toured all the states,
meeting old friends and making new ones. My report proposed
the setting up of a National Film and Television Training
School, the creation of State Film Commissions to encourage
production and some financial pump priming by the federal
government – all measures which were carried into effect in
the next few years. I like to think that I played a small part in
the establishment of today's vigorous Australian film industry.

This change of scene recharged my batteries and I came

home to a fresh bout of work on my various series for ATV.
Then I was asked to lead a British delegation to the Moscow
Film Festival and it was pack-your-bags time again.

4

I arrived in Russia a day or so ahead of my colleagues to have
some discussions with the Soviet Writers' Union which had
become a member of the International Writers' Guild. They
checked me into the Moscva Hotel, which wasn't bad by
their hotel standards and not good by ours. My luck with
interpreters held out for I was allocated a lovely long-legged
blonde who as the festival official obligingly said, 'will be at
your disposal twenty-four hours a day'. My opinion of Russian
hospitality rose rapidly.

There is, of course, always a snag and this one lifted
a head over the horizon on the very first afternoon. At
about 3.30 p.m. I told Natasha that I wished to take a
nap and her face tightened. When I asked her to meet me
in the lobby at 5.30 p.m. it dropped again and her bottom
lip trembled. It took me a little time to find the reason for this
sea-change but eventually she confessed that she had a lover
who was a school-teacher and that they could only meet in
the afternoons between 4.00 and 6.00 p.m. She did not explain
the reason for this curious arrangement and I assumed that the
boyfriend must be married.

Magnanimously I sent her to the rendezvous and, when I
met her later, she seemed to be in high spirits. Thereafter, for
the remainder of my ten days in Moscow, she went off every
weekday afternoon to meet her *amour* with my blessing. I never
met the lover and for all I know she may have been an agent
reporting to her KGB chiefs each afternoon. If that were so, I
can only say that they had excellent taste for Natasha was the
nearest thing to Garbo that I have ever seen off-screen.

Breakfast presented a problem. I am a fairly early riser
and on the first morning I went to the dining-room to eat
before Natasha had arrived to help me with the menu. That
part need not have concerned me for menu there was none.
A middle-aged waitress, with the build of a Cossack warrior
and a face so stern and immobile that it looked as if it had just

returned from the Arctic, advanced on the table and thrust some black bread and a piece of cheese in my direction.

With a polite smile I waved this feast aside and asked for two boiled eggs. She stood staring at me. I then began an elaborate pantomime, shaping my hands around imaginary eggs, cracking imaginary eggs, even cluck-clucking like a chicken. Her features did not move so much as one millimetre. After a couple of minutes of this nonsense I jumped to my feet in exasperation, put my arms around her as far as they would reach, kissed her frozen face and cried, 'Look, darling, all I want are two bloody eggs and some white bread!'

Miraculously, the ice cracked. Her eyes came to life, her face broadened in a smile, and a great laugh came surging up from that sturdy body. She grabbed my hand and began to haul me away and, for one terrified moment, I thought that she may have taken my embrace too literally. But, no, she took me into the kitchen where I was able to point out some actual eggs and white bread and indicate my wishes.

Thereafter she became my friend and I had my boiled eggs each morning, served with a smile. When my fellow delegates arrived and were presented with black bread and cheese for breakfast they looked askance at my meal and asked how they could get the same.

'This is Russia,' I explained loftily. 'It is necessary to make love to the waitress.'

When I left I gave my new friend, Aksinia, a present and, with some shyness, she handed me a slim volume of poetry. Natasha explained that the poems were by Aksinia's son who also happened to be a colonel in the Red Army! A strange insight into this extraordinary country.

Grimmer insights came from various Soviet writers. From Alexei Kepler, for instance, who years before had the misfortune to fall in love with Svetlana, Stalin's daughter. For this crime they hauled him off to a labour camp for five years. On his release, he returned to Moscow. On the first evening, Svetlana telephoned to welcome him home, the call was intercepted by the KGB and the next day he found himself on the way back to the camp for another five years. Fortunately Stalin died and Alex was released and rehabilitated.

Two writers who worked in partnership were arrested in 1946 when they were still students and accused of plotting to

assassinate Stalin. They were sent to work in the coal-mines in
the far north, the tundra region, for ten years. At the end of
this period, they were released from the camp but instructed
to continue to live in the region and to work as 'free' miners.
They, too, were eventually rehabilitated and became successful screenwriters. They were kind, gentle people in whom I
found surprisingly little bitterness.

I remember one sunny afternoon at a *dacha* about a hundred
kilometres outside Moscow. From the garden one could look
down on a valley of lush meadows pierced by a gently winding
river. A Red Army soldier walked by the river with his girl,
playing an accordion. It seemed like a scene from a Soviet
film, a glimpse of the eternal Russia. The music, the sweet
scent of the garden flowers, the gliding river, combined to give
me an overwhelming sensation of peace. Alex Kepler stood at
my elbow and whispered, 'The Germans were here. On these
fields we fought one of the bloodiest battles of the war.'

5

At the beginning of 1972 I determined to keep a diary,
a resolution, I'm afraid, which lasted only a few months.
The very first entry records a landmark in the family, the
marriage of our son John to Janet at Gorleston, near Yarmouth.
I suppose I reacted like many parents at such occasions for I
wrote, 'Audrey is remarkably calm and controlled – I think she
is determined not to cry – but as John puts the ring on Janet's
finger I have to fight back my own tears. They both look so
young and vulnerable – God knows what kind of world they'll
have to fight their way through.'

Other entries suggest that I was doing far too much. I had
become chairman of Network, a consortium formed to bid for
a London commercial radio licence, an activity which took up
a great deal of time. In the event we narrowly lost out to Capital
Radio whose chairman was Sir Richard Attenborough. Dickie,
magnanimous in victory, generously accepted a suggestion
from Lord Aylestone, the then chairman of the Independent
Broadcasting Authority, and invited me to join the board of
Capital. I spent thirteen happy years as a director of what
turned out to be a highly successful company. In a certain

sense, my son John is now repeating the experience for, as deputy programme controller for Channel 4, he also serves under Attenborough, the company chairman.

I became heavily involved in the politics of the so-called Cod War with Iceland. Having been to Reykjavik to see a production of *Hot Summer Night* I had made many Icelandic friends and one of them, an author and Member of Parliament, came over to see me to plead his country's case. Convinced that Iceland was right on the issue, which revolved around a decision to extend the fishing limits to fifty miles, I raised a debate on the subject in the House of Lords. I'm afraid mine was almost a lone voice and, in the genteel manner of the Upper House, I was savaged by the government spokesman.

One result was that for a few weeks I became a national hero in Iceland and Audrey and I were invited there as guests of the government. Eventually Iceland won the fight for a fifty-mile limit and, within a few years, most other European countries followed its example.

The diary also records that I had been appointed a member of the Sports Council and of the National Film School and adds, wryly, 'more meetings'. Other activities that I listed for just one month include opening a Schools Careers Exhibition and a branch of the National Children's Home, attending the annual meeting of the Writers' Guild and board meetings of World-Wide Pictures, speaking at four luncheons and seven dinners, chairing a debate on racial discrimination, voting in the House of Lords on ten different days, television rehearsals and playing tennis.

I spent three years first as a member and then as chairman of the Script Development Fund, an offshoot of the National Film Finance Corporation, a job I enjoyed hugely because it involved handing out money to writers who had worthwhile script projects. The sums were relatively small but this seed money did yield a decent harvest of good screenplays.

And the writing? In the first six months of 1972, the period covered by the diary, I recorded that I worked on the television series *Hunter's Walk*, *Crime of Passion* and *Black Beauty*, wrote a four-part political romance for the magazine *Woman's Own* called *Arrows of Desire* and invented the original story for a film called *Our Miss Fred* starring Danny La Rue. Twice in those six months I disappeared into the country for twelve days at a time just to get away from the telephone. On these working stints I wrote for anything up to ten hours a day, ate only breakfast and came back exhausted and five or six pounds lighter!

It was a crazy, punishing schedule. The diary ends in July but in the second half of the year the pace began to slow a little and I was able to accept an invitation to visit Australia again. The request came from Senator Doug McClelland and a group of friends – a general election was coming up and they wanted me to act as a speech-writer for Gough Whitlam, the Labour leader, a job I had done briefly for Harold Wilson in 1964.

It would have made disastrous headlines if the Australian press had discovered that a Pommy peer had been pressed into service in this way, so I arranged with the *Evening Standard* to send back some articles on the campaign and travelled with Gough as a journalist.

Australian politics are a lot more robust than the English variety and I found the month spent on the campaign trail an exhilarating experience. At the finish Gough won a handsome victory and became prime minister and I came up with an idea that would change the direction of my writing career. Just before I returned to England, Gough and Margaret, his wife, invited me to spend a weekend with them at the PM's official residence, The Lodge, in Canberra. Somehow – who knows where ideas come from? – while walking in the grounds, I dreamed up a story about the kidnapping of a prime minister and began to plot it out in my head.

I had met and become friends with Elaine Greene, a leading literary agent, some time previously and she had consistently urged me to try my hand at a novel. So in 1973, as the television and film projects began to diminish, I did just that. I went back to Australia towards the end of that year to speak at a conference on the media and while I was there Elaine sent me a cable.

George Hardinge of Macmillan had accepted the book, *Death May Surprise Us*, and it would be published in the spring.

Chapter Eighteen

1

I had some luck with *Death May Surprise Us*. Published in 1974, the book was serialised in the *Evening News* and this gave the sales a useful kick-start. Subsequently it came out as a paper-back in America under the title *Westminster One*, in Germany as *Staccato*, and in Japan as something incomprehensible. My new career as a novelist was off to a good beginning, and it had come at exactly the right time for I had started to notice a slow but steady erosion of my work for television and film.

J. B. Priestley once told me that, with rare exceptions, the career of a professional writer might be measured in three decades: ten years of struggle on the way up, ten years at the top, ten years on the way down. Clearly he was one of the exceptions but for me the signs looked ominous – I had used up my thirty-year ration.

I soon worked out what was happening. Most of my contacts in the business, the producers, directors and script editors with whom I had developed a close and friendly relationship had also exhausted their thirty years and had either retired or moved on. The younger men and women who took their places turned, quite naturally, to writers from their own age group. Unlike the ancient priests, television treasures its virgins and sends its old writers to the sacrifice. Which, I suppose, is not a bad arrangement: television like everything else must constantly renew itself with fresh new blood.

I remembered my own hungry days as a young writer at Pinewood Studios, eager to prove myself, fervently ambitious. Then I used to look at the older established writers confidently lunching at the best tables and say to myself, 'I can write as well or even better than you. One day you will have to move over and make room for me.' The conceit of youth, perhaps, but no young man or woman would be worth a bent paper-clip without some such impulse.

Now it seemed that time had decided to pay me back in my own coin. The young Turks were moving in and shunting old Ted towards the sidelines. Not without success either for from 1975, with two minor exceptions, I have done no writing either for the BBC or Independent Television. The few approaches that were made concerned projects which did not interest me.

But I'd had a fair trot and I couldn't really complain. And, in any case, the success of my first novel had whetted my appetite and I wanted time to do more. Over the next ten years I managed to write a new book each year, all of which were published here and abroad in hardback and paperback, and enjoyed satisfactory sales. They were mainly adventure-thrillers, the exception being a trilogy in which I developed the Rosie Carr character I had used so successfully in the earlier quartet of television plays. I found it interesting that these three novels evolved on quite different lines from the plays and, apart from the central character, they bear no resemblance to each other.

One very satisfying aspect was that there were spin-offs from the books. Almost all of them found their way into newspapers or magazines as serials; three or four of them went into Book Club editions; one, *Man Eater* was bought by Warner Brothers and became a television movie; the rights of another, *The Left-Handed Sleeper*, went to a German company; I adapted three of the novels as serials for radio and there have been several film nibbles – but no firm bite – for what is probably the best of the lot, *The Buckingham Palace Connection*.

I owe a second vote of thanks to the House of Lords for this last novel. This time the idea was triggered at Question Time when the late Lady Ward asked the government 'whether there are any hitherto unpublished documents in the archives of the Foreign Office which relate to the murder of the Tsar and the Russian Imperial family by the Bolsheviks in 1917 . . . '

A polite but blank reply followed and, after a further exchange, Irene Ward asked if the government was absolutely satisfied that all the family were murdered and that none had escaped. The Minister replied, 'No, my Lords. Nor do I think that anybody can be absolutely satisfied on that point.'

That was enough for me. I began to do some digging into the subject and came up with a nugget of information which revealed that in 1917 a plan to rescue the Tsar had reached an advanced stage, only to be aborted first by King George V and then by Lloyd George. I tried to imagine what might have happened had the plan gone ahead and, at a stroke, I had the framework for the novel. Filling this in took another three or four months of research, including a second visit to the Soviet Union where, with some help from my old friend Alex Kepler, I booked on the Trans-Siberian railway.

Strangely, the journey turned out to be uneventful except for one incident. I'd been lucky enough to get a two-berth sleeping car to myself but on the second night, returning from the dining-car, I found that I had been joined by a female Red Army officer, a lady of such generous proportions that she made my waitress friend in Moscow look like Marilyn Monroe. Moreover, as I was shortly to discover, most of this formidable weight consisted of muscle.

We smiled amiably at each other, I uttered my three words of Russian and that effectively ended the dialogue. More from a sense of self-preservation than politeness I indicated by signs that she might take the lower bunk – I had no wish to have this colossus come crashing down on me during the night. I pulled down the little wash-basin attached to one wall and began to wash and clean my teeth, hoping that this would be sufficient hint for her to leave for a few minutes while I undressed for bed.

This manoeuvre had the opposite effect. To my alarm, humming happily she began to remove her uniform and I scrambled hastily up to my berth where I went through the difficult process of wriggling out of my clothes and into my pyjamas. When I looked again the lady, clad only in a bra and a pair of khaki bloomers the size of a bell-tent, was splashing water over every uncovered inch of flesh and still humming. She caught my eye in the mirror above the basin, gave me a beaming smile and said something which I did not understand. Hastily I turned my face to the wall. The night creaked and rumbled away. I found sleep at last and woke up to find the train at a station. To my relief, my Amazonian companion had gone.

Sverdlovsk, the new name for Ekaterinburg, depressed me. I went over the House of Special Purpose where the imperial family had been imprisoned with an interpreter who answered my questions parrot fashion with rehearsed answers liberally spliced with propaganda. There can be no doubt that the Tsar was a despot, albeit a weak and foolish one, but it was impossible not to feel his brooding presence in that grim place and to feel a surge of sympathy for the little man who had ridden so high and been brought so low.

2

Large ladies seem to crop up whenever I set out to research a project and a visit to the Windward Islands in the West Indies proved to be no exception. I had the outline for a novel about an extreme religious sect which virtually takes over one of the smaller islands and I needed to fill in the background. The title *The Most Beautiful Girl in the World* came later and has no connection with a certain lady whom I met one evening in circumstances that can only be described as painful.

Before leaving England I had arranged for some introductions to various people in the islands, mainly local politicians and one of these kindly invited me to dinner. About twenty of us gathered in the open air on a still warm evening and I found myself sitting next to a sister of our host, a genial perpetually smiling West Indian woman of considerable size with whom I chatted amiably enough. The meal went well, the wine flowed freely and I was enjoying myself until we reached the coffee stage and this massive hand dropped on my knee like a bird of prey.

I looked at her in some surprise, she gave me a coy sideways smile and started to attack the knee opening and closing her hand as if intent on strengthening the power of her fingers. My own view, admittedly biased, was that they were quite powerful enough.

'Where are you staying?' she asked. I told her and she added, 'Very nice hotel. Do you have a good room?' As she spoke her hand moved to my thigh and the kneading of the flesh grew more agitated and more agonising. Certain that this undercover activity would be noticed by the other guests, I turned to the lady on my other side and attempted to engage her in a discussion about the forthcoming marriage of Prince Charles and Lady Diana. This had no effect on the invading hand which now moved towards the centre and began to pump such essential if modest equipment that I possess with even greater vigour. The pain became excruciating and, stifling a yell, I made some excuse and headed for the toilet.

An inspection showed that I had suffered no permanent damage and when I returned the party was beginning to break up. My host gave me the look of someone about to confer a great favour and, pressing my arm in a significant gesture, said, 'My sister has very kindly offered to drive you back to your hotel.'

I could do no other than accept but on the short drive back I tried desperately to talk my way out of the trap. I had a headache, my stomach was upset, I needed sleep. The ploy failed utterly for she reached for my leg again and, with engaging bluntness, asked, 'Have you ever slept with a West Indian girl?'

'No,' I admitted.

'Then you have never had a real fuck, man.' Ominously she added, 'But it's not too late.'

As she drew up at the hotel I made a desperate bid for freedom. When she released my knee to engage the hand-brake I leaped from the car and ran like a hunted stag to my room where I bolted the door and poured myself a life-saving Scotch. Fortunately she did not pursue me and, after a restless hour or so, I was able to sleep.

No such adventure befell me during the research for *The Naked Sun*, a novel that is centred around an actual event – the mass break-out of Japanese prisoners from a camp in New South Wales. This fieldwork took me to Osaka in Japan where I met one of the ex-prisoners and to the bush town of Cowra, where the camp was sited. On this trip I met my old friends John McCallum and his wife Googie Withers, and John, who at that time was active in film production, expressed interest in the story.

When the book came out he bought the rights and the preparation of the screenplay took me back to Australia and Japan two or three times. We got very close to production on this one, even to scouting the locations but then the principal backer, a Japanese millionaire, got cold feet because of losses on another film and pulled the plug on the project.

This was 1982 and in something like eight years the only significant television work to come my way had been from Australian producers. For John McCallum I wrote the pilot script and one or two others for his highly successful series *Boney*, featuring a half-white, half-Aboriginal detective. And for Hector Crawford of Melbourne, arguably the father of Australian television series – *The Sullivans, The Flying Doctors, Matlock* and many others – I developed a story called *The Big Beat* about an English policeman who goes to work in the outback. Hector, incidentally, put on a very profitable theatre tour of my good old stand-by *Doctor in the House* in Australia.

It began to look as if the old war-horse was finished in terms of television but then, quite suddenly, another door opened. But first I must go back a little and pick up one or two bits and pieces.

3

The novels and the research involved had absorbed most of my time from 1973 on but I still managed to attend the House of Lords fairly regularly. The campaign for Public Lending Right, an issue which I had persistently raised in the Lords, finally triumphed over entrenched opposition and on 6 March 1979 the bill became law. I dubbed this date Bruffy Day after Brigid Brophy and Maureen Duffy who had led the assault so brilliantly. When authors receive their cheques each February they should raise a glass to this indomitable pair.

Hard on the heels of this success we formed the ALCS, a collecting society for authors. From small beginnings the ALCS has grown to a point where it collects and distributes hundreds of thousands of pounds on behalf of its members, money that they would be unable to claim individually.

During this period I made a couple of unsuccessful attempts to win a broadcasting franchise, as deputy chairman of a consortium which made a bid for the Midlands area and as chairman of a powerful group aiming for the Mid-Kent radio licence. Our failure to get the Midlands television franchise was perhaps understandable, although I thought it wrong and unfair that the experienced professionals on our team should have been sent away empty-handed. But with the bid for Mid-Kent radio our treatment by the Independent Broadcasting Authority (IBA) was scandalous.

We had assembled a formidable team, a near-perfect blend of financial know-how, professional radio experience and local knowledge led by Tim Blackmore, a top executive with Capital Radio. Indeed at one interview with the IBA panel, one member suggested that perhaps we were too good! In the event, they awarded the contract to a bunch of enthusiastic, well-meaning amateurs. Within months, having failed to come up with the necessary financial backing, this group virtually collapsed and, hiding its blushes, the IBA had to step in and save the situation by handing the franchise to Invicta, a company which had bid successfully for the other area of Kent.

This made me a three-time loser in the franchise stakes and I decided that since my face clearly did not fit with the IBA establishment I would try no more.

Television and radio appearances also claimed a good deal of my time. For ten or twelve years I was a frequent panellist on *Any Questions*; Roy Plomley interviewed me for *Desert Island Discs* and I turned up regularly on news and discussion programmes. Lew Grade and his company, ATV, generously recognised my work with a television programme called *Ted Willis: Tribute to a Writer*.

I have many pleasing memories of *Any Questions* but two incidents in particular take precedence and both concern that formidable figure Enoch Powell.

At a police club in Liverpool the panel had been invited to join members of the force in the restaurant after the show. I happened to be the first to go in and, to my astonishment, the assembled police officers rose to their feet and gave me a tumultuous ovation. I tried to look appropriately modest as some of them rushed towards me with outstretched hands – and then I came down to earth with the proverbial bang.

These eager enthusiasts swept past me as if I were no more than a table decoration and swooped on Enoch who had followed me in and was standing framed in the doorway. The cheers and the adulation were all for him. I was reminded of the time at a summer fête, when Jack Warner and I were persuaded to sell our autographs for charity at fifty pence a time. I sat in lone embarrassment at my table while a long queue formed before Jack. My daughter Sally took pity on me and, after borrowing fifty pence from her mother, presented me with my one and only sale of the afternoon. When it comes to public recognition authors cannot compete with television personalities, film stars or leading politicians and I have long since learned not to try.

The second Enoch Powell story concerns a moment at the end of one of the programmes when we were asked to name our favourite Shakespearean character. David Jacobs was in the chair and, together with Enoch and myself, the other panellists were Rosamund John, the actress, and Malcolm Muggeridge. David warned us that time was running out, that we should keep our answers brief, and turned expectantly to Enoch.

'Oh, Macbeth,' said Enoch.

Without a moment's hesitation, Muggeridge pounced, flinging in a quotation from one of Macbeth's speeches. 'Ah, very significant, Enoch,' he said. 'Vaulting ambition which o'erleaps itself and falls on the other side.'

It was not entirely accurate as a quotation but devastating in its effectiveness. With no time left for any more responses the programme ended there. Which was just as well for I had been about to say that my favourite character was Bottom in *A Midsummer Night's Dream* and I wonder what Muggeridge would have made of that!

4

I did very little work in the theatre during the seventies although I had a half-dozen plays, like *Woman in a Dressing Gown*, constantly in production somewhere, both at home and abroad. However, I had been associated with the local theatre in Bromley as a member of the governing trust for some years and when plans were made to pull down the old flea-pit which was our home and replace it with a new modern theatre, David

Poulson, the artistic director, asked me to write a play for the opening. Since the new playhouse was to be built more or less on a spot where the father of H. G. Wells had owned a sports shop and where the young Herbert had lived, it seemed appropriate to adapt a Wells novel and we chose *The History of Mr Polly*.

I approached Lady Churchill and asked if we might call the theatre *The Churchill*, in honour of Winston who had lived at nearby Westerham, and she kindly gave her consent. Prince Charles agreed to open the new building. Roy Castle read my script, liked it, and we signed him to play the lead.

So far so good. The nightmare came later. It was to be the new theatre's proud boast that it had the most modern stage machinery in the world and, indeed, on the plans the equipment at the command of the stage management looked amazing, even bewildering. Not one but two or three stages which moved up, down or sideways at the touch of a button, a double revolve, a computerised lighting system – almost everything within sight had been electrified, mechanised and rationalised. And, as is the way of these things, very little of it worked. To compound the problem, the engineering firm responsible for installing it went into liquidation a few days before the opening.

I had my problems also. Having written the book and lyrics, I recruited two promising but highly unprofessional composers to do the music. With a musical it is often necessary to write thirty songs of which only half might be chosen for the show. Above all, the composer should be present at rehearsals to make adjustments or even major changes. It is all part of the creative process. However, my two composers presented me with a score which was all right as far as it went – about 50 per cent of the way – announced that they considered their job complete and, after the first rehearsal, were not seen again.

We brought in another composer who worked night and day to put music to the new lyrics which I wrote as we went along. Then, some three days before the opening, we realised that the damned stage machinery would never be got to work in time and I had to go into overdrive to revise the script which had been specifically designed to reveal the wonders of that same machinery to the audience. All the quick changes from set to set, the use of the revolve

had to go and we were back to old-fashioned manual production.

Roy Castle and the director, Wallace Douglas, were marvellous, radiating patience and enthusiasm. By the opening,
we were all on our knees with exhaustion and so apprehensive
we could scarcely look at each other. But Roy, the sturdy professional, backed by a fine cast, saw us through and the show
went almost without a hitch. In terms of what I had aimed for,
Mr Polly remains a disappointment but at least the show went
on and drew appreciative audiences.

The moral of the story, in the theatre as in most things,
is to keep it simple.

Three other memories of this period of my life. A visit to
the Philippines on the inaugural flight of Philippine Airways,
where I was given an audience at midnight of Marcos and his
wife Imelda and presented with three weighty tomes two of
which were entitled *The Ideas of Imelda Marcos* and the third
The Democratic Revolution by Marcos himself. I wasn't game
to lug this heavy rubbish home with me and carefully left
the books behind in my room at the Manila hotel. No such
luck! In a few weeks they turned up in the post with a note
from the hotel manager to say that I had inadvertently left the
Philippines without these treasures.

I met another dictator in Romania whence I went as a
member of a delegation from the Inter-Parliamentary Union
(IPU) led by Fitzroy Maclean, the author and MP. One member of our group was a bluff old peer with sturdy Victorian
attitudes and a determination to speak his mind. On the last
day of the visit we were all taken to meet Ceaucescu. The
usual polite and meaningless exchanges took place until the
old peer who had some difficulty with his Rs broke in with,
'You have a jolly decent countwy here, Mr Pwesident. Jolly
decent. But I think I ought to tell you that I have no time for
Communism. I believe the world would be a better place if all
Communists were dwopped in the Atlantic Ocean.'

The startled interpreter hesitated at this, and I don't think
that Ceaucescu got the message for after the eventual translation he allowed himself a frosty smile.

On the way home, the old peer approached me and said,
'I understand that you do a bit of witing.'

'Yes,' I admitted.

'Make a bit of a living at it, do you?'

'A bit.'

He patted me on the shoulder. 'Jolly bwainy. Jolly bwainy.'

There was one delicious moment in Israel where I led a formidable delegation of writers – Iris Murdoch, John Bayley, Fay Weldon, Bernice Rubens, Melvyn Bragg, Beryl Bainbridge and William Trevor. Despite this full load of talent and artistic temperament all went well and I have seldom enjoyed a visit so much.

One day we had to travel from Tel Aviv to attend a reception of some kind and on the way I became separated from the others. I arrived late to find our host hopping from one leg to the other in agitation and my delegation standing behind him wreathed in broad smiles.

Later I asked Melvyn what had been so funny. 'Well,' he replied, 'we are in Jerusalem. Jerusalem of all places. And you are late. And the host keeps looking up to heaven and saying, "when is the Lord coming, when is the Lord coming."'

John Bayley, I think, had a fear of hunger for he prepared himself for the day – or the night – by stuffing his pockets with food. Once when I slipped and hurt my leg he came to me solicitously, produced a hard-boiled egg and said, 'Would this help?'

Alas, everything has a darker side. In 1981, my dear Jimmy Carr, founder of World-Wide Pictures, my friend and mentor died. In 1983 and 1984 two other close friends hung up their boots, Jack Wayland, my Australian mate, and Carl Foreman, writer and film producer.

Why do I feel a sense of guilt when a good friend dies? Is it because I keep so healthy and still work as furiously as I did fifty years ago?

5

The initiative came from Inge Meysel, the actress who had so movingly played *Woman in a Dressing Gown* many years before. A young German producer who had only recently started his own business had acquired the rights to some stories by Paul Gallico, stories which were set in London and described the adventures of an English charlady. Inge suggested that I might be interested in adapting one of these as a television movie, the producer, Hans Redlbach contacted Harvey Unna, my agent, and we were in business.

Thus I began yet another career in television and an association with Hans Redlbach and his company Phoenix Film Produktions of Berlin which has spread over eight years, still continues to this day and has kept me constantly busy. Berlin has become like a second home city to me. Sadly, Hans died suddenly in August 1990 at the ridiculously young age of forty-five and for me it was like losing a son. But he would be happy to know, I think, that his friends and partners, Karlheinz Brunnemann and Karl Schaper are continuing to run Phoenix as he would have wished.

I have now written five Mrs Harris films for Phoenix and am about to embark on my sixth. The books ran out some time ago and I have had to invent original stories. Inge Meysel is now eighty but shows no sign of flagging and her popularity is such that the films habitually soar to the top of the German ratings.

At the request of Hans Redlbach I devised and wrote a series for family viewing called in English *A Home for Animals*. This is now in its eighth year and a new series is in production. In addition, I adapted my book *The Left-Handed Sleeper* as a thriller series and wrote a mini-series called *The Valley of Kings*, based on the Tutankhamun story. A new series, *Rivals of the Racecourse*, became a huge hit and a second batch of programmes is in preparation. And I have devised four other series for Phoenix and another German producer which are awaiting production. Not too bad for a veteran, though I say it myself. I did think a couple of years back that I would retire and concentrate on novels and the occasional play but I have such a good and enjoyable working relationship and friendship with Phoenix that I am loath to leave it.

6

In-between the intensive bouts of work for German television I managed to block off enough time to do one or two other things. One of them was a major rewrite of the script of David

Puttnam's film *Defence of the Realm*. I put in a three-year stint as a book critic for the *Sunday Telegraph* and I produced two of my best stage plays.

The first, *Stardust*, was specially written for Googie Withers, a sophisticated comedy about an actress who finds it difficult to face the fact that she has reached her sixtieth birthday. Googie herself inspired the piece when I went to visit her in her home at Palm Beach near Sydney. At the time she happened to be 'resting' – a very rare occurrence in her career – and she was clearly bored out of her mind.

'It's terrible,' she complained. 'My life has gone full circle. When I was eighteen I used to sit and wait for the phone to ring. And now I'm waiting all over again.'

Duncan Weldon, the West End producer, bought the play, and with Googie and John McCallum in the lead it had a long and successful tour. We missed going into London by a whisker but, under the management of Lionel Abrahams, *Stardust* toured Australia and repeated its original success. Later the play opened in Düsseldorf, went on a long tour of German cities and proved as popular with German audiences as with the British.

Tommy Boy, the second play, opened at the Malvern Festival Theatre in May 1988, with Peter Howitt – then star of the television series *Bread* – George Sewell and a lovely young actress, Louise English, in the leads. Specially commissioned by Kevin Wood, the producer, it told a story of life at home and in the trenches during the First World War and it was one of the most satisfying things I have ever done.

The chemistry proved to be exactly right, the ensemble playing, as orchestrated by Warren Hooper, the director, came as near to perfection as one could wish, and the audiences loved it. The tragedy is that the West End managements, frightened I think by the failure of a recent revival of *Journey's End*, declined to bring the play to London. I believe that they missed an opportunity.

In 1989 I completed the trilogy of novels on the life of Rosie Carr with *The Bells of Autumn* and wrote a thriller for the stage called *Intent to Kill*. Starring Richard Todd, this went on a long tour of the country under the management of Bill Kenwright

who, though a decent enough fellow, has the misfortune to
be an Everton supporter.

<h1 style="text-align:center">7</h1>

And what of my family? Sally fulfilled a long-term ambition in
1974 by marrying Robin and changing her name to Murray. My
lovely daughter, though she is bright as a button, had never
shown much interest in a career – she worked briefly in an
office and as a social worker but really her heart was set on
the hardest job of all, that of running a home and a family,
which, incidentally, she does damn well. I wept when she
left because I thought I had lost her but, of course, that was
nonsense. We are as close as ever – perhaps closer because
she has presented Audrey and me with three grandchildren.

John and Janet are one behind, having only two children,
and it is likely to stay that way. Having started in the business
as a researcher and then made his mark as producer and
director of some outstanding documentary films, John has
progressed to a top executive position at Channel 4. In the
process he won more awards in ten years than I have in fifty,
damn him! Now, at television functions, people come to me
and ask, 'You're John's father, aren't you?'

And Audrey? Twenty-four years ago, fearful that, with John
at university and Sally rapidly growing up, my dear wife, for
lack of something better to do, would start mothering me, I sat
her down and urged her to find some useful outside interests.
She lacked confidence and was reluctant to take such a step
but eventually she joined the S E Regional Hospital Board on
which she has served for twenty-three years. In all that time
she has missed only one meeting and regularly devotes two or
three days a week to this voluntary service.

Some years ago she was also appointed a Justice of the
Peace. I well remember the day she set off for her first court
sitting.

'Goodbye, dear,' she said sweetly, 'I'm off to send a few
husbands to prison.'

In 1984 I tried to thank Audrey for her patience and
stamina by arranging a surprise party to mark our fortieth
wedding anniversary. About 150 guests turned up and the

surprise worked. She hadn't an inkling of what was going on. In typical fashion, on the way home, she said, 'You bloody fool. That must have cost a fortune.'

Dear Audrey. I have had a great deal of luck in my life but the luckiest moment of all was when I walked into Unity Theatre and fell in love first with your legs, then your face, and then you.

Epilogue

The scene is a crematorium near Guildford some months ago. Audrey and I were there for the funeral of an old friend. As we waited outside the chapel I struck up a conversation with a gentleman who, in his military-style greatcoat, looked like a retired army officer. Dignified, rather reticent of manner, I judged him to be about my own age.

He sat next to me in the chapel and sang the hymns lustily. We filed out at the end, said the usual awkward words of condolence to the widow and were invited by her son to go back to the family home for a drink and some funeral meats. I offered to give the military gentleman a lift and he accepted with a courteous smile.

Back at the house, where he tucked into the food and wine with a will, I ventured to ask him how well he had known the deceased. To my surprise he replied, 'Not at all, I'm afraid.'

'But you were at the crematorium, at the service,' I said.

'I go every weekday,' he said calmly. 'I live alone, you see. I go for the company. It's warm there too and I enjoy singing the hymns.'

'And how often do you get invited to take a drink afterwards?'

'Oh, about fifty per cent of the time,' he replied.

His confession both amused and saddened me. What a strange sad way to spend one's last years. The incident reminded me with some force of my own good fortune – to be surrounded by a mischievous, loving family and caring friends and still to be working with undiminished energy at the job I love.

Age raises the inevitable question of regrets. Would I, for instance, have been a better writer had I done less, had I concentrated on the theatre or on novels? The answer is that I don't know. I have been called 'the Paddy Chayefsky of Chislehurst' and a 'Katherine Mansfield in shirt-sleeves'. Flattering, but I am not sure that I am either of these. Writers are like fingerprints: no two are alike. What I do know is that I am what I am, a compulsive story-teller always bristling with ideas, and that given the opportunity to start afresh I would tread the same route.

And what I can say is that I have tried all my working life to be a professional. When under the pressure of time, I have never allowed myself the luxury or weakness of saying of a script, 'This will have to do.' That is death to a writer. I cut and revise, cut and revise mercilessly and before a piece of work leaves my desk it has to be the very best that I can do. The script, when produced or published, may not live up to my hopes or the expectations of the audience but that is not for lack of effort on my part.

With one or two exceptions I don't think I have ever written anything I am ashamed of and, on a few occasions, I have produced work like *Woman in a Dressing Gown*, *Buster*, *Hot Summer Night*, *Tommy Boy*, the trilogy of *Rosie Carr* novels, *The Buckingham Palace Connection*, *The Ballad of Queenie Swann*, *Sergeant Cork*, *It's Great to be Young*, *Rivals of the Racecourse*, the early *Dixon of Dock Green* scripts and *The Lions of Judah*, which can stand up with the best.

At the beginning of this book, I quoted Peter Ustinov. His assessment of my place in the pyramid of writers was not far off the mark. I am nearer to Edgar Wallace than to Graham Greene or Kingsley Amis. I took a medium-sized talent and by sheer persistence and industry honed it into something sharper and better.

I might echo the words of the late Vicki Baum, bestselling author of such novels as *Grand Hotel* and *Nanking Road*, when she wrote, 'I know what I'm worth: I am a first-class second-rate author.' Not a bad assessment, I think, when one considers the number of third-class fourth-rate authors whose works have been rewritten by industrious editors and hyped into blockbusters.

The sum of it all, I suppose, is that I have done my best and in doing so I have given some pleasure to millions of people and useful paid employment to thousands of actors and technicians; I have fought a corner for my fellow authors and for other causes; I have cared for and loved my family and been loved beyond my deserving by them and many friends.

No, no, no. All that may be true but it rings with complacency. Of course I have some regrets, damn it! I regret not having the intellectual background, the depth and breadth of knowledge which a better education might have given me. I dislike the conceit of the academic mafia and their closed high-table world while, at the same time, I envy their easy, confident approach to classical history, literature and the great philosophers. I regret that, for many years, an enduring fear of falling back into the poverty from whence I came drove me into some projects and ventures that dissipated valuable energy.

Above all, I regret that I lack the demon which might have given my work a sharper edge and driven me up the last two or three rungs of the ladder. Paradoxically, I have been too lucky in my life; the result is not that I lack anger but that I have too little of it and I think it shows in my work. There is, I'm afraid, no cure for that.

In the meantime, I will soldier on, spilling stories on to the page from this box of dreams I call my head.

Evening all.

Index

233